£18 95

Language and Literacy in
the Primary School

CONTEMPORARY ANALYSIS IN EDUCATION SERIES
General Editor: Philip Taylor

Contemporary Analysis in Education Series

Language and Literacy in the Primary School

Edited by
Margaret Meek and Colin Mills

 The Falmer Press

(A member of the Taylor & Francis Group)
London • New York • Philadelphia

UK   The Falmer Press, Falmer House, Barcombe, Lewes, East Sussex, BN8 5DL

USA   The Falmer Press, Taylor & Francis Inc., 242 Cherry Street, Philadelphia, PA 19106-1906

First published 1988

Library of Congress Cataloguing in Publication Data is available on request

ISBN 1-85000-352-1
ISBN 1-85000-357-2 (pbk.)

Jacket design by Len Williams

Typeset by Mathematical Composition Setters Ltd, Ivy Street, Salisbury

Printed in Great Britain by Taylor & Francis (Printers) Ltd, Basingstoke

Contents

Contents

General Editor's Preface

Language is the pathway to a full and productive life. Literacy gives access to the culture of the modern world. All children want to talk, most want to read and write. Many nations set a high value on a literate citizenry, not always for the best of reasons. Everywhere the rhetoric of primary education creates a high profile for both literacy and language. What is less certain is our understanding of how language makes for literacy and literacy informs language.

It is the singular success of *Language and Literacy in the Primary School* that the frontiers of our understanding are pushed back. More than this, the new insights come with the excitement of discovery and the passion of commitment. Something new and of singular interest comes with every contribution and little stands between the reader and the realities that are language and literacy. Margaret Meek and Colin Mills have orchestrated an important contribution to what has been, is and will remain the most important issue in primary education, language and literacy. They are to be congratulated as are all that made their work possible.

Philip Taylor
Birmingham 1987

Introduction: Agenda For Discussion

Margaret Meek

> We know far too little about learning from vicarious experi-
> ence, from interactions, from media, even from tutors.
> (Jerome Bruner)

This book is an exercise in collegiality, a coming together of teachers
as learners, to offer examples, episodes, texts, *specula* — little mirror
glimpses — of ways of reflecting on everyday encounters with
children in an educational context. We have not confined our
remarks to school, but when we are involved in things that happen in
classrooms, we are in those which, with increasing significance, we
still call 'primary'.

We have made this collection at a time when we are facing deep,
crucial questions about what school is for and what we believe
children should learn. We ask ourselves how we are to educate the
rising generation in a society which is different from the one we
knew when we left home to encounter the institutionalized instruction which lasted at least eleven years, and which now seems part of a
historical past. Our disjunction from our own education, a separation
which we share with all our contemporaries, makes us all the more
concerned about what might happen to our children if they do not
find school a congenial place to be.

We are bound to realize that there can never be a fixed body of
knowledge which we can easily and completely transmit to our
children. The best we can hope for, and it is a valid hope, is that they
will learn ways of learning, from observation and experience, from
reflection and ordering, from the experience of others and by means
of the mind's capacity for organized thought. We can be sure that, in
whatever our children come to know, an abiding feature will be
language, from the most natural ways in which people talk to each

1

other to the highly methodized ways by which technology stores whatever counts as information. We are also likely to assume that *literacy*, now in forms more manifold than our ancestors could ever have imagined, will continue to assume the importance which we have given it in our culture. (It is interesting to note, in passing, that although we have at least 600 years of written texts, we have made learning to read compulsory for only 120 of these).

The theme of the book is a unified whole because language, in all its aspects, keeps together children's doing, feeling and thinking. We see this in what they say to adults and to each other, in the stories they tell, and in their learning how to make the world a meaningful place to be. In these essays the children's presence is constant and compelling. We are reminded, over and over again, that what they think and say about what they know and understand is carried by the words they use. As adults we too can make meanings, other meanings, of what they say and do. But sometimes, when we hear children stretching and enhancing this ability, we may wonder if we make the most of its possibilities when we engage in the interventions we call teaching. In these pages, the emphasis shifts to the learners. Intervention is replaced by *interaction*.

A particular linking feature of the essays is the variety of ways in which the writers — from Canada and Australia as well as the British Isles — listen to children. In the first chapter we hear the utterances of a child less than a year old; in the last essay a professor of education explains how, on a significant occasion he did not listen carefully enough. A common attribute of the writers is a readiness to change and adapt both their thinking and their pedagogic practices in response to what children teach them. They know that change 'comes about only through the painful recognition of one's own vulnerability' (Paley, 1986). So they recognize that there is nothing final in what they have written; their texts are clearly ideas in transition.

For their editors this is where their importance lies. Every year research in the human sciences pushes back the point at which we find beginnings, ontogeneses, of language acts and interactions, the point at which we notice children's ways with conversation, and their early literate behaviour. Each new awareness by adults points up the social nature of all language learning, and the importance of literacy events in the lives of children before they go to school.

The emphasis on the social context which occurs throughout this book is an acknowledgment that school learning is only part of all learning. We stress the collaborative partnership between parents and teachers which is so necessary at the early stages of children's entry into this wider world of childhood, because, in schools, the problems which beset adults also involve children. We hear many different voices in a class or in a playground. Teachers may regard these as either a hindrance or a rich resource. Not all children can read when they come to school, although many can. Who decides what counts as reading in a class? How do girls fare? Will school simplify society's stereotypes, or take account of every child's encounters with differences in language, literacy and behaviour?

The new directions in thinking about these things which are signposted here are neither short-cuts to revised methodology (yet *another* way to teach reading), nor motorways bulldozed through ancient educational thickets, (the streamlined testing of spelling). Instead, the reader is invited to walk along well-trodden paths with new companions, so that different parts of a familiar landscape assume an enhanced significance. We explore the possibilities of partnership with parents beyond the sharing of the reading scheme. When children's purposes in reading and writing are foregrounded, the texts they produce and the books they choose do not always fit the expectations of adults. In these pages the 'autonomous learner', beavering away at his or her construction of a personal educational edifice, gives way to the collaborative pupil in a classroom where meanings are negotiated and shared. Children's understandings of imagery, metaphor, pictures, symbols and signs, what they learn from television and other media, are as important as their encounters with print and paper. Throughout everything we have brought together, language means everyone's language, so that at all times bilingualism is considered important.

We have presented classrooms as 'sites for cultural making' (Hardcastle, 1985), where, from their earliest days in school, children encounter the views of the world held by others, and where the universalized 'child' gives way to young people, distinctly themselves, entering a variety of social discourses.

This is no utopian vision, nor are these ideas self-sustaining. We make plain where teachers as researchers raid the understandings of experts and break through the boundaries of established academic disciplines in order to seek the enlightenment they need to make a coherent rationale for their practice. The bibliography is an important part of the total text. Our invitation to the reader is to take part in a dialogue with the writers and to join in the making of an educational discourse for the benefit of all teachers and all learners. If these ideas have the force we believe they do, then they will help to reshape educational practices in ways we have yet to explore.

Part 1: First Words

Three observer-listeners invite us to look with them at familiar situations where adults and children talk together. Here is James Britton's grandchild demanding her speech act rights and learning to take her turn in family conversation. Robert Withers establishes the children he knows as characters within the story of the class where they are to learn together. Colin Mills chooses particular episodes in early reading lessons to highlight the social nature of this learning. In each of these situations children are entering both their culture and their history. These are also particular instances of what are now current topics for research: the interactional nature of language and learning (Wells and Nicholls, 1985; Tizard and Hughes, 1984) and the social and cultural nature of classroom language (Burgess, 1984).

As they explore these utterances and exchanges with intimacy and detachment, the writers engage with *discourses*. As they proceed, another question emerges: what is educational discourse and can it be distinguished from other kinds? As readers we are invited to speculate about the relation of children's early language and learning to forms of analysis derived from established academic disciplines, and to ask: what is distinctive about *teachers*' understandings of classroom talk and its relation to language learning and development (Barnes, 1976; Medway, 1980).

1 A Way with Words

James Britton

Long before they go to school children establish reciprocity with other people in their earliest forms of language as they sort out the world and establish themselves in it. Here we see Lucy and her sister becoming both social beings and individuals.

Since the works of L. S. Vygotsky first appeared in English in 1962, James Britton has been the most consistent proponent of their relevance to the education of teachers. On the groundwork of Vygotsky's social theory of language, Britton offers us a challenge to 'de-pedagogicalize' school language learning so that teachers may be free from the colportage of educational lumber and enabled to 'set up a community that is a source of learning'. This is the direction we now take.

It seems appropriate that the tape I want first to refer to was made on Christmas Day. Lucy, whose performance is to be celebrated, is 6 months and 2 weeks old and her audience consists of her 6-year-old sister, her parents and grandparents. Lucy has been recorded on four or five previous occasions: she has been heard crying (she has good lungs and makes a powerful noise), and gurgling and making quiet signals of contentment. But it is notable that these latter sounds frequently slide into whimpering and thence, growing more distressed, into crying.

Today she addresses the company. Using one or two insistent and repeated intonation patterns and virtually a single speech–sound (in the *da* range), she holds the floor with amazing confidence and persistence. It would seem (though this can be no more than speculation) that it is the sound of speech around her that starts her off; occasionally that sound seems to renew her efforts. Adults respond to her from time to time, talk across her efforts a good deal,

7

sometimes listen in amazement and amusement. With few pauses she maintains her performance through it all, loudly and vigorously, for a full nine minutes. The overall impression — and listening to the tape powerfully renews it every time — is one of wonder that the intention to join in the conversation — or, if that is begging too many questions — the desire to do as she is done by — should exert so strong a pull. What, one must ask, is set in motion by this eager taking on of the functions of conversation, as it were in make-believe? Are the foundations laid here for later developments or do these early behaviours mean no more than the tadpole's tail means to the frog?

There is a gap of well over a year between this 'make-believe' and anything that one could call actual conversation. Lucy meanwhile continued to make noises — usually continuous, often rhythmical — that expressed a range of feelings — anxiety, contentment, anger, aggression, delight and disgust. But it was a long time before individual sounds began to emerge with what appeared to be consistent meanings for her; and, in the absence of the kind of systematic sampling and analysis that Halliday (1975) employed in listening to his son, it was only those uses that moved recognizably in the direction of conventional words that we were able to identify. Thus, for example, at 14 months something resembling the sound *tzat* began to be consistently used in a context of enquiry (*What's that?*).

At 22 months, her exchanges are still more or less limited to single word utterances but she has accumulated a considerable store of these and adds to them daily by repeating words she hears used in the context of her activities. Here are brief exchanges taken from the same occasion at that age. Lucy is with her mother, whose name is Alison, and they are at her granny's house (familiarly known as 'Danny'). A cup of tea has just been passed to Alison.

A. Thank you. That's just what I need!
L. Zank you. Zank you.
A. Mm, I said thank you!
L. Zank you!
D. [*laughing*] That's very nice.
L. Zank you, Waller.
D. French now — voila?
A. Thank you Waller — that's Mrs Waller.

A. [*to L.*] What's your name?

L. Kathy.

D. Katherine?

A. Is it really Kathy?

L. No.

A. What's your name really?

L. Sheila.

A. It's *not* Sheila! What's your real name?

L. Lucy.

A. Yes.

D. What's mummy's name—do you know that?

L. Yes. Chocolate!

A. Chocolate? I'm not called chocolate. What's my name? What's mummy's name?

L. Alison.

D. Do you want me to feed the birds, do you? I'll get the... — now you stand on that chair. [*They throw crumbs, etc. out on to the terrace.*] Here he comes, look! Gobbling up the apple peel!

L. T-zat?

D. That's a blackbird — he sings very nicely. And there's a teeny one, a hedge sparrow, nice little brown one. Oh and there's a starling — starlings come down like dive-bombers. That's a wise blackbird — he's taking a big piece of crust on to the flower-bed where nobody can see him.

L. Up!

D. Oh! he's pecking it all up. Peck, peck peck!

L. Peck, peck, peck!

D. Yes. Especially the pigeon. The clever ones take a big piece and go and hide in the bushes where it can't get taken away.

L. T-zat one?

D. Pigeon. There's a sparrow — a blackbird —

L. Hiding.

D. Hiding, yes, he just goes on eating and nobody comes to take away his piece. Pigeons —

L. No? Hiding.

D. Yes, a great big piece of brown bread. Pretty — they've got nice colours, haven't they, little white bits on their necks.

L. Hiding.

D. Hiding. Yes. He's hiding behind the steps, isn't he?

> *L.* Pishun.
> *D.* Can you say 'pigeon' — 'pigeon'?
> *L.* Pigeon — peck, peck, peck!

It is not until some ten months later that Lucy, at a little over $2\frac{1}{2}$, has mastered enough of the structures of speech to take up conventional conversational uses — the interchangeable *I* and *you* of dialogue. (Examples of transitional forms in young children's speech are familiar enough: '*You have some of dat over dere*' was one 2-year-old's way of asking for a piece of cake.) I refer to this in particular because according to one linguistic theory the use of this convention in speech is the only means of entry to a typically human view of the world — a *subjective* view in which we extrapolate from our own individual consciousness to the status and condition of other living creatures; this is to claim that taking on a language habit makes possible the development of a mode of thought essential to our humanity. As Emile Benveniste (1971) puts it, 'Language is possible only because each speaker sets himself up as a *subject* by referring to himself as *I* in his discourse. Because of this, *I* posits another person, the one who, being, as he is, completely exterior to 'me', becomes my echo to whom I say *you* and who says *you* to me. This polarity of persons is the fundamental condition in language.' He goes on to indicate that this relationship, being reciprocal and yet not symmetrical (since my first-hand experience is always primary to me) is a type of opposition that occurs only within language, and from our experience of it in dialogue we derive 'a principle whose consequences are to spread out in all directions.'

In pursuit of examples that illustrate this theme — the role of early language in mental development — I must move from Lucy to her elder sister, Laurie. In both the instances that follow, Laurie has co-opted me into her makebelieve, and my contributions to the dialogue are shown in brackets. In the first, Laurie is 3 years and 10 months old. The principle 'props' are two ancient teddy-bears, one of which has been designated a girl, the other a boy.

> Lets play mummies and daddies in the car! Yes!
> (No!)
> I want to play it!
> (I'll give you a swing in the chair)
> No! — I want to play this game!! Now, you sit at the front with the boy and I'll sit at the — I'll drive and you sit with the boy. Yep?

(Yes)

And you can have this blanket. You'll sit *here* and I'll sit *here*:
I'll drive — get into the car. Open! Open! You sit with the
boy. You put the blanket on him. The girl's got to sit here.

(Yes. O.K.)

Bring the Panda book.

(Mm?)

Bring the Panda book.

(Bring the Panda book — that's it, put it in)

You hold the book. Get the cushion — need — for her.

(Yes)

She needs a cushion. Open the door! Door's open!

(Door's open)

You — you get the pillow.

(Oh, that one — I see)

There — she can sit back with you. *I'll* wrap her up. Don't
drive —

(Are you driving?)

Not yet 'cos I haven't got her in the back with you. There!
And I've got to pull my socks up a bit. 'Tend I've got smart
shoes on. We're going to go to the park. [*Driving noise*] Is
your door shut? Shut! [*Driving noise*] (Now round to the left,
round there. ... Now round to the right — to the right!)

Open! Open! We're there!

(Have you got the brake on?)

I did. Let's get the arber(?) baby now. Arber baby. She's
dying!

(Oh no!)

Not really. She's only dying for a pee. [*Laughter*] Bring him,
bring him with the blanket here. Open!

(A lot to bring away, isn't there?)

Bye! I'll see you later.

(Bye, love — see you later — have a nice day. Take care!)

Yes, Bye. I just forgot to give you your goodbye kiss ... and
the baby.

Bye. See you later.

(See you later)

I'll see you — um — tonight.

(Yes, see you tonight. Don't be late: don't be late.)

No.

Laurie's opening instruction clearly sets this game in motion and it is she who determines the roles and the ensuing rules. Autonomy, in fact, is the name of the game in children's makebelieve play. Laurie usually chooses for herself the dominant role — mother, teacher, elder sister, etc. I think it comes over in the transcript, though more clearly when one can hear the tones of voice, that Laurie is *improvising* — working it out as she goes. This applies, I believe, to the modification she so readily made when I didn't want to accept the serious turn of events indicated by 'She's dying'! Vygotsky (1978) makes a comment which goes some way towards explaining the improvisatory nature of this kind of play: he suggests that in such play children behave in the light of *ideas* whereas in everyday life they have to respond to what they *perceive* in the world — a world over which they have very little control. 'Playing at mummies and daddies in the car' is an *idea* and pursuing that idea is a creative, exploratory, piece of improvisation. Vygotsky finally puts his seal of approval on makebelieve play by suggesting that it is inaccurate to call it, as we sometimes do, 'imagination in action'. It is nearer the mark, he suggests, to call imagination in adolescents or adults 'make-believe play without action'. That is to say, the only form of voluntary imaginative activity that young children are capable of takes the active form of make-believe play; but when that social behaviour has, at a later stage, been *internalized* it constitutes the mental ability we call imagination. By this view, a child assigning the roles and improvising the action, finding a way through its complications, at times responding to and accommodating the contributions of those who share in the game — such a child is in fact generating the life-long ability to create hypotheses, contemplate alternatives to reality, enter into and originate works of art — the power, in short, of imagination.

My second example of makebelieve play was recorded when Laurie was 4 years and 1 month old. Once again, my occasional comments are shown in brackets.

> Now it's time for little darlings to go to sleep.
> (Yes)
> You've got to go to sleep now. ... Your blanket ... pillow. Lie down! Now you're going to have a little — if you don't want to go to sleep — you *must* go to sleep 'cos — or you will be afraid of night 'cos the owls come at night. ... Yes, they go to-whoo! They don't frighten *you* — they don't eat you, only rats or mice — that's good, isn't it?
> (Yes)

Now I've got to sort your cover 'cos you messed it up last
night, didn't you?
(Yes, I wriggled about so much, didn't I?)
Yes, 'cos you're afraid of the *owl*, aren't you?
(Yes)
To-*night* I have to sleep in my own room ... which is
downstairs ... and Dad sleeps downstairs too and you only
sleep *up*stairs. And the baby sleeps [*pause*] downstairs too and
the big girls — and your two sisters sleep down too and you
only sleep up, don't you? So you have to be very quite. If you
hear — if you — *um* hear a *monster*, I'll come running up. I
hope — if you dream about one, just cry and come down and
say 'Oo-oo, Mummy, I had a bad dream.' Yes. ... Now
you're going to go to sleep, aren't you. Close your eyes.
[*Long pause*] ... Morn*ing*!

The hesitations, pauses and other signs of improvization are clearer
here: the details of the family *finely* documented are inventions —
on-the-spot inventions, I believe. But the truth of the matter
certainly lies in the fact that Laurie felt isolated in the bedroom she
occupied, at this time, alone. She seems to be rehearsing — so to
speak in reverse, speaking as mother, the comforter — the theme of
being brave enough to sleep upstairs when everyone else sleeps
downstairs!

   In activities of this kind — just as later in the exercise of the
imagination — children improvise on their conception of the real
world, organizing the objective aspects of their experience and
equally, on other occasions, they sort out *themselves*, organize the
subjective aspects of their experience. These powers of the mind have
been generated by language-using behaviours — behaviour powerfully illustrated in its earliest phases by the pre-speech vocalizations.
This idea is entirely consistent with Vygotsky's notion that human
consciousness is arrived at by the internalization of shared social
behaviour; shared activity is the necessary precursor of individual
processes of speaking, thinking, imagining. I wish we could take
more notice of this idea in school; in this way we might set out on a
kind of de-pedagogicalizing process of seeing learning as a function
of community, trusting in the way participating in social rule-
governed behaviour results in the development of implicit rule-
systems—by means that are inherent in the very way such rules are
socially derived. In this way we might take from teachers the burden

of being the middlemen in all learning and release them to set up a community that is a source of learning—a much more productive and a happier place than a mere captive audience for the teacher as instructor.

2   The Story of the Leaves:
The Lesson as Text

Robert Withers

Here is a familiar scene in an infant classroom; the children and their teacher are making leaf-prints. To the casual observer, the pupils seem to pull away from the task, to be easily distracted, to 'lack motivation'.

By moving out of the traditional language of educational psychology and other ways of analyzing talk in classrooms, Robert Withers considers the lesson as narrative text created by the pupils, the teacher and the researcher-narrator. We are encouraged to read classrooms as the social context of learning where children's lives, their intentions and motivations are intrinsic to all observed behaviour, and especially to each conversational utterance. Our main themes, cultural, social, linguistic and narrative, emerge in the school setting.

Experienced teachers are often dismissive of their initial teacher training and of the 'theory' which they were taught. I have found, however, that often enough such teachers retain the language of educational psychology and unconsciously use its structures in thinking about learning and teaching. They have been taught to conceptualize the teacher's task as that of trying to push or pull each individual child into activity of the required type, and then to structure that activity so as to keep it going. This will have been explained to them in a technical vocabulary, and so we teachers have learned to talk of 'providing a stimulus', 'reinforcement', 'meeting individual needs' and 'motivation'. The idea of motivation which lies behind this way of talking depends upon viewing the child as an individual organism exhibiting states and to which things happen. In the literature of motivation those states are sometimes said to include perplexity in the child and conceptual incongruity between the teacher's intentions and the child's understanding. Thinking in this way, seeing the teacher as someone who makes things happen to the child, may lead us to neglect the social nature of classroom activity.

When teachers talk of 'providing a strong enough stimulus' or of 'reinforcing the right kind of response', they give the abstractions of educational psychology a place in educational thinking. This way of talking can make us forgetful of the very things which we desire to bring about, such as the development of literacy, of artistic imagination, of historical interest, or mathematical awareness and a willingness to work cooperatively and collaboratively. In the search for a stimulus we neglect the uses of language, the functions of story, and that the child's activity takes place within a particular kind of social context. Analyses need to be grounded in descriptions of classroom episodes so that an appreciation of the social context can be retained.

Studies of classroom interaction and language might provide examples of the kind of study which is grounded in classroom activity. However, analyses of infant classroom processes too often treat what takes place as self-evident, or else they impose an external perspective upon the actions of teachers and of children. This study examines the language of motivation in infant classrooms and attempts to do so while providing a recognizable account of the events portrayed. This is not to say that the participants would choose the terms of the analysis for their own explanations of the episodes. The aim is to produce something which brings out the way in which teachers structure what they do within the conditions under which they have to work.

On this particular occasion discourse was recorded in a normal classroom lesson and a narrative approach employed to discuss it. The narrative structure is investigated as the researcher finds in the episode the features of a story. There is an introduction, development of character, tension, climax and resolution. Unlike the conversational exchange analysis prescribed by some researchers (see Stubbs, 1983), the technique employed assumes that the purposes of teachers should be recoverable from the analysis. In the story of the leaves we can see that the teachers and pupils are engaged in building up a text and, in doing so, they create the story of their lives.

The Story of the Leaves

Twenty-two coat pegs, coats, bags, tables, chairs, a butler sink, two tall cupboards and a teacher's desk are contained within the confines of a long, narrow room. The only area of free space has a carpet and cushions and is isolated from the rest of the room by book shelves. Small bodies jostle each other, cramped by chairs at the back and tables in front. In this active infant classroom, Mrs T. an experienced and kindly teacher, is working with three boys under the direction of the Head of Infant Section, Mrs Y. who is teaching the rest of the class. Mrs T. has invested time and effort during her lunchtime collecting leaves and setting up the table with a plastic covering, paints, paintbrushes, water, paper and cloths. She has told the boys that they will make leaf prints together, and that they will need to wear aprons. Pupil 1, who rarely smiles, shows himself to be a serious character obsessed with the bigness of leaves. Mrs T. responds to this 'epistemic curiosity' in an oblique fashion, talking as if his concern is with patterning the leaves on the paper, for that is *her* interest. She wishes to impose a structure on the story, directing the production of the text along particular paths. It is not clear where an investigation of bigness might lead. Nevertheless, Mrs T. does want to remind the boys of other stories, stories in which they are engaged. Frequently she asks them to identify the species of leaf with which they are working, and she will relate the use of the bumpy side of the leaves to the notion of 'veins'.

Episode 1

Teacher.	You're going to use that one. What have you got to remember? What have you got to remember?
Pupil 1.	This is the biggest.
Teacher.	Yes, and what else? Bumpy side. Do you think that's going to work, James? I think it looks very dry.
Pupil 1.	I've got another big one. It won't do it that big one on there.
Teacher.	Er, well see if it'll fit. Might go in there mightn't it — do you think? No, it just goes over-over the side. Would you like another piece then?
Pupil 1.	Yes, try another big piece.

Resuming after some minutes]

Teacher.	Now what letter?
Pupil 1.	Ner.
Teacher.	Ner. Well done. Good boy. Ben. Thank you.

17

Pupil 2 produces variations on the sound 'blue', but this perceptual curiosity, or sign of tension perhaps, is not allowed to distract Mrs T. from her current concerns. Suddenly he announces that he cannot do any more, but Mrs T. is quick to continue his part in the story activity as a character and as a joint author of the text by introducing the novel ideal of 'an easy leaf'. First she provides a solution to his difficulty of having hurt his wrist, and then binds him back into the story with words which demonstrate their intimacy of purpose in the plot: 'Let's find an easy leaf then, shall we?'

    Episode 2

Teacher.	You're going to do some painting. What colour are you going to use?
Pupil 1.	Pink. Blue I mean.
Pupil 2.	Blue, hu hu blue blue.
Teacher.	Blue, That's better. There you are. Cover all the veins over.
Pupil 1.	⌈That's the bumpy side.
Pupil 2.	⌊You got ( ).
Teacher.	That's the bumpy side, that's right. How are you doing James?
Pupil 2.	I can't do any more
Teacher.	You can't do any more? Why's that?
Pupil 2.	I got hurt [*holds wrist*].
Teacher.	Oh no. Come on (2). Let's find an easy leaf then shall we? What about. ... That one looked quite difficult. What about this one? Feel bumpy?
Pupil 2.	No. Yes.
Pupil 1.	I haven't got enough paint on mine.
Teacher.	It's better to let this ( ) a bit. Right in the middle. Press it down hard David. That's right, and then you get plenty of paint on. I shouldn't put too much on the brush because if it's too wet it'll go all messy won't it?

As Pupils 2 and 3, smiling frequently, do not want to join in and they develop their resistance to being characters in the story, Mrs T. increases her efforts to keep them within it. Their hands can be washed afterwards, she tells them, because 'They'll just get dirty again.' She offers them a satisfying conclusion to the story; they will show their pictures in assembly; and she offers them guidance with the words, 'Good. Good Boy.'

Episode 3

Teacher.	We could do it green as well because the green would show up nicely with the red — wouldn't it?
	Put it on the paper to do it. On there.
Pupil 1.	Start another bit.
Pupil 2.	Can't do it any more.
Teacher.	Why not? Come on — let's do some. We want to make a really nice picture because I think these are going to be used in Assembly one morning this week. Shall I help you do one? Shall we ... why not have em ... we'll have yellow shall we?

Quite normally these words are not intended as, nor seen as, reward. No change in activity or direction is offered because the children are to be part of this story and not of another. Mrs T. has invested too much in it and in its setting. The words of the children are reinterpreted ('Now? When you've finished school?') as Mrs T. keeps them within the limitations of the story which is allowed and which the school would accept.

Episode 4

[*2 minutes*]

Teacher.	Are you going to try this then David? Hold it still. Let's press it. Let's go all the way round like that. Don't move it. All along the line.
	⌈Press it hard.
Pupil 1.	⌊Done it.
Teacher.	Good. Put the brush back in the pot. Good boy. Turn it over. Press it down hard. What do you think of that one?
Pupil 2.	Not doing it.
Teacher.	It's alright.
Pupil 2.	I need to wash my hands [*showing them*].

Pupil 3.	Look at mine.
Teacher.	Go and wash your hands afterwards because they'll just get dirty again.
	Go and wash your hand afterwards, shall we? Let's wash them afterwards [*pulling Pupil 2 towards her*]
Pupil 3.	Look at mine.
Teacher.	Yes, look at mine.
Pupil 2.	⌈Look at mine.
Pupil 3.	⌊( ) got more ( ) on them.
Teacher.	Yes [*Pupils 2 and 3 show each other their hands*]
	Lift it up carefully. Ooh look! David, David! [*remonstrating and pulling him back to her*]
Teacher.	⌈Look at what Ben's just done.
Pupil 1.	│I have that big colour. I'll have that big one.
Pupil 2.	⌊( ) [*screwing up his face, making a thrusting movement with his lips and shaking his head from side to side*]
Teacher.	You like the big one? You're going to do it red as well?
	⌈Could I have this one?
Pupil 2.	⌊I don't want to do it⌈I don't ... I don't want to do
	│it any more
	⌊Yes you can have ...
Teacher.	Don't? Ooh, come on.
	[*Pupils 1 and 2 grin at each other*]
	[*1 minute*]
Teacher.	James ... James ... Why don't you choose another leaf?
	Are you going to choose? Why don't you choose a small one this time?
	There must be some here.

Despite all her efforts the two boys depart, rejecting authorship of the text, but Mrs T. does not panic or give them extra attention for she knows that she will be able to bring them back at some point by discussing with them what they have done.

Episode 5

Pupil 2.	In ( ). I'm going to Guy's house.
Teacher.	You're going to Guy's house?
Pupil 2.	Yes.

Teacher.	Who's that — Guy H?
Pupil 2.	No.
Teacher.	No?
Pupil 2.	Guy — Guy — Guy T.
Teacher.	Guy T? After school tonight? [*Pupil 2 nodding*] Are you?
Pupil 2.	No. Now.
Teacher.	Now, when you've finished school. That'll be fun won't it. And I expect when you walk to Guy's house you'll see leaves, won't you? Some of these leaves came from on the lane didn't they, this morning?
Pupil 1.	That's a leaf.
Pupil 2.	I've finished.
Teacher.	I think we had a little bit too much paint on there, don't you?
Pupil 2.	I've finished [*pulling sleeve of apron off*]
Teacher.	You've finished? Let me ( ) for a little while.
Pupil 2.	No.
Teacher.	Oh come on. Look what Ben's done. I don't know which one he used. Which one did you use, Ben? That one? Did you? I don't think so.
Pupil 1.	Another one.
Teacher.	I think you squished it too much.
	I've finished [*takes off apron*]
Teacher.	No. Come on — what're you going to do now?
Pupil 2.	Wash my hands.
Teacher.	Then what are you doing to do?
Pupil 2.	Nothing.
Teacher.	Nothing? Why? Don't you like this very much?
Pupil 2.	Do some drawing.
Teacher.	Tell you what ... um ... I don't think you want to wash your hands yet. I think we'll do a picture together — just you and me. Mm? Shall we? [*Shakes his head*]
Teacher.	No? Well shall we ... er ... watch Ben do his?
Pupil 2.	I got — I wanna wash my hands.
Teacher.	Don't wash your hands yet. Wash your hands at break time. Alright? [*placing hand on his arm gently*] Come on. Help Ben do his picture. Come on.
Pupil 3.	I've finished.

Teacher.	You come and help Ben then. Come on [*Pupil 2 begins to undo his apron string*] ⌈Come on!
Pupil 2.	⌊Play.
Teacher.	Oh no! You've got to. Come on. Come on because Ben's going to do his picture isn't he? Want to come and help? [*takes apron from Pupil 3 who moves rapidly away from her*] Come on [*holds out her hand — he holds his right above his head out of reach*].
	(P2 and P3 move away and the Teacher continues to work with P1. The transcript resumes after some minutes.)

When the Infant Head of Section approaches, their withdrawal is explained in teacherly terms: they lack concentration. They did not, then, rebel. Pupil 1 is the pupil who will succeed, who is hard working and has concentration. When, hands now clean, the other two return and seek permission to play they are immediately bound back into the story as the Infant Section Head asks Pupil 3 to explain his work. 'Tell me about this picture you've made', she says, and the story moves towards its conclusion.

Episode 6

Infant Section Head.	Hmm!
Teacher.	Yes, they've lost their concentration actually.
Infant Section Head.	Yes.
Teacher.	The other two.
Infant Section Head.	Yes. What interesting colours. Did you do this one Ben? [*Pupil 1 nods*]
Teacher.	No — that's Paul [*Pupil 1 shakes his head*] These are Ben's. That one's quite ... that one's the nice one.
Infant Section Head.	Yes. What are the colours Ben? ⌈What colour is this leaf?
Pupil 2.	[*reappears with clean hands*] Can I play with Sandra?

Pupil 1.	Yellow.
Infant Section Head.	What colour is this leaf?
Pupil 1.	Green.
Infant Section Head.	What colour is this leaf?
Pupil 1.	Red.
Infant Section Head.	Which is the biggest? (2) Very good.
Teacher.	That one's quite good. ⌈David hasn't got
	⎸ a lot
Infant Section Head.	⌊Yes …
Teacher.	of concentration
Infant Section Head.	No, no, no, no. He tries.
Teacher.	He tries yes — ⌈but …
	⌊Mrs Y, I …
Pupil 3.	[*reappears*]
Infant Section Head.	Yes, James, tell me about yours. Tell me about this picture you've made. You've made two. How did you do it?

Analysis of Classroom Episodes in Narrative Terms

Researchers sometimes try to argue that their particular form of analysis is indispensible to proper understanding, but there are many different ways of analyzing an episode, different ways of talking about the same set of events. If the familiar forms, terms and ways of talking about classroom events do not help us to understand what is happening, then we need to find more useful ways of talking. In the description given above it was useful to talk about the production of a text, of the development of character and of a story. We often, and perhaps in a fundamental way, make sense of what has happened by relating a narrative. Classroom episodes and classroom research might, then, be profitably understood in narrative terms.

Events are events in a story when they are seen as having a relationship one to another. The story of the leaves is the narrated event. The teachers and the pupils produce the text and the teacher tries to shape the discourse to produce a particular kind of text in which a single story is told. The pupils, however, are more than just characters since they are also co-authors of the text. A problem for the teacher is the degree of collaboration in authorship which she can establish.

Since events can have more than one description, they may be narrated in more than one way. Different stories can be told about the same set of events, or the same story can be told, though in different terms. The act of narration is basic to the understanding of classrooms. This is not to deny that other forms of research have a place, but it is to say that narratives are implied and underpin the work of researchers who relate their findings differently. The narrative approach lends itself to the detailed description of the classroom setting within which the activity takes place.

It seems that much classroom research and educational psychology are determinedly abstract, making no reference to the conditions within which teachers have to structure their activity. For this reason so much educational theorizing has seemed to have little resonance for teachers, and its usefulness to them has been reduced. In their search for generalizability, researchers have found themselves with little to say which has relevance to actual classrooms. The account produced here is particular, but its veracity should be recognizable to infant teachers.

In this account the researcher is the narrator. For the most part the narrative is focalized on the teacher and shifts to the Infant Section Head only at the end. The mood of the narrative assists in the recovery of the purposes of the teacher. That is, it allows discussion of the way in which she structures her consciousness of activity, her intentionality. Genette (1980) calls this 'openings onto the psychology of characters'. Other tellings might involve changes in focalization and voice, as well as in order and selection. Clearly, focalized through a pupil the narrative would be greatly changed in character. Accounts of schooling which are focalized through the children's subsequent autobiographical narrating are now coming to be recognized as a valuable source of understanding of classroom experience. Some researchers, wishing to exploit this form of narrative, now advocate that researchers should, in the interests of reflexivity, research themselves researching. This reflexivity would result in a narrative focalized on and through the researcher. Particularly important narration, in terms of mood and voice, is that of action research. Holt's *How Children Fail* provides an analysis in which he tells the stories which children tell about themselves (Holt, 1965). This metadiegetic narrative within narrative is important in the context of ethnographic research, and in the accounts which teachers give as action researchers.

All portrayals are particular and selective, and so the analysis offered here cannot claim to be exhaustive. What does emerge, however, the way in which infant teachers engage the pupils and the attendant problems of creating a single story, is explanatory of a good deal of school experience. Furthermore, the metadiegesis of the final part of the narrative reveals a common strategy of infant teachers. Pupils are frequently asked to produce a narrative about what they have been doing, and teachers tell each other about what the children have been doing. At the end of the story of the leaves, the focalizing centre is the Head of the Infant Section who reaffirms the story of the leaves and the children's part in it, thereby holding the story together.

Teacher Control

The story of the leaves clearly relates to questions of teacher control of pupils, that is, the power relationship. One of the contributions of exchange analysis has been to bring these issues to the fore by taking an external viewpoint which sees the teacher shaping the organization of discourse into a predictable pattern. It has been claimed that the teacher's use of pseudo-questions evidences great inequalities of power and status. The weakness of such analyses, however, is that they fail to account for the educational purposes of the teacher and are based upon recordings of small groups of secondary school children in specially contrived settings (see Stubbs, 1983). In this sense, therefore, they are simple, failing adequately to account for the range of functions in language use and in natural settings. Narrative theory would suggest that we should look for a range of functions, such as ideological, communicating and directing functions. Thus we might look at questions of power and control through the ideological functions of language, noting the modality of the verbs, the implicatures and the overwhelming sense of intimacy of purpose (in part created by those pseudo-questions).

This chapter has drawn on the work of Gerard Genette, and one theme can be summed up in his words: 'Every day we are the subjects of narrative, if not heroes of a novel' (Genette, 1980, p. 230).

3 Making Sense of Reading: Key Words or Grandma Swagg?

Colin Mills

Going into school with student teachers encouraged the next writer to explore the ways in which early literacy was socially learned, in classrooms. Following Rob Withers' lead, and using stories co-created and interpreted by children and teachers as evidence, he suggests, first, that any discourse about reading needs to be uncovered to reveal its roots. Then he probes some of the interpretative processes in everyday social action that connect with the kinds of understandings children bring to their early independent readings of books. Implicit in this writer's story is that 'real' texts, 'requiring children to make sense, explore possible worlds', are central to the process.

Looking Afresh

In my work as a trainer of teachers I often take students into classrooms, where they observe and talk to young children learning to read, and to their teachers helping them to do that. I like to think that these observations help them to know and to understand some of the ways in which teachers and children live and work together in classrooms, creating and sustaining the activities, situations, episodes and routines that make up literacy lessons. Back in college they will read books, go to lectures and take part in seminars that will put them in touch with current theories and ideas about the development of literacy. But during the time in school I ask them to tell me about the things they have seen. What they say is often novel and insightful. They ask searching questions about the books in the classroom, and ways in which teachers organize their time, the diverse modes in which different children enter into, and participate in, the social activities that enfold reading and writing.

As their tutor I am often confronted with the fact that, although I have spent my working life in and out of such classrooms, there are things that I do not see, or take for granted, as a result of my over-familiarity. For the students there is enough that is recognizable in the classroom scenes they look at to enable them to make sense of them. It is not so long since they were young children: they often show surprise at seeing the same books with which they think they learned to read. Yet what heightens the novelty of the processes they see is that they are thinking and orienting themselves into a new role, that of a teacher. They seem to read the 'culture' that is an infant school classroom and to begin defining their understandings with an acuteness of purpose. Learning a culture, learning a role, is what the students share with the children.

Looking afresh, with the students, at what I thought I knew well has led me to some ideas to be extended and developed in this chapter. First, our theories about reading have not made room for discursive issues that always pervade the practice. Examining the ways in which talk about reading goes on, not in dry textbook terms but in situated action in classrooms, enables us to see current issues and directions more clearly. Second, in our framing of theories about reading, specific contexts and processes, the felt life of classrooms, have been given scant and inadequate attention. Looking at children and teachers taking part in, and talking about, events that constitute 'reading lessons' suggests fresh concepts that illuminate our talk and our thinking.

Social Practice and Discourse

Whereas the study of classroom processes has drawn increasingly and fruitfully upon ethnographic traditions (Pollard, 1984) and literacy has been conceptualized as 'sets of social practices' (Heath, 1983; Street, 1984), these two sets of insights have rarely been drawn upon to look at activities in the primary school classroom. For three years I worked alongside two teachers in a small 5–11 village primary school. They were making changes in their practice, moving from a reliance upon structured reading schemes and formal testing to the use of 'real' books, and encouraging the close involvement of parents. In doing this, they were taking part in a general shift in thinking and in practice described by Moon in this book (see chapter 11).

During the time I worked with them I discussed the changes

they were making, the ways in which their thinking about what constituted 'reading' was shifting. One of the teachers, a women of 27 with five years' teaching experience, has a special responsibility for the infant department of the school, where all forty to fifty 4–7-year-olds are taught together, in one very large area, with two teachers:

> When I was training in College, reading came over as a very structured business. I remember hearing about 'primary skills', 'intermediate skills', 'higher order skills'. We did a course in Children's Lit., but that seemed to be separate. There was never much talk of pleasure! Then, when I came here, we used *Ladybird*. I remember being so bored by it, and seeing the children being bored. Many of the parents took the children through it all before school. It became a very competitive business.
>
> I went to a talk by Cliff Moon, and I heard about the 'real books' approach, so I persuaded the other teacher who was then in the school to give it a try. I feel so much more honest now, because I know that the children really get turned on to reading, and they're often starting to read with books they know from home. I need to work harder at knowing the stages they are at, but I think this approach, this method, is just as structured. We've taped favourite books that the children can take home — and I know that they all enjoy reading, and now know how to make choices. (Miss E.)

The other teacher in the class is Mrs R. a woman of 35 recently returned to teaching full-time after a break looking after two young children. The younger of the two children is in the class Mrs R. shares with Miss E.

During the early months in which I was working in the school they put on a parents' evening to explain their changes in practice to the parents. What gave rise to this was what Miss E. described to me as 'rumblings' at the school gate and amongst the parents who came into school as voluntary helpers. I heard some of these conversations and spoke to some of the parents. Were the children new to school 'progressing' as well as they could be in their reading? How did the teachers know at what 'stage' each child was in her/his reading? A parent had come into school one morning and questioned Miss E. as her child had taken home a book from a classroom collection that the parent considered 'too hard'. The head of the school said to me one day in the staff room: 'You see the parents — teachers, solicitors, social workers — want to know why the kids aren't reading Ladybird books, and going home with words in a tin.'

At the meeting Miss E. gave a carefully prepared, thoughtful and assertive account of the ways in which she had changed her practice. An advisory teacher from the Local Education Authority spoke about recent thinking in early literacy, drawing upon the work of such theorists and teachers as the Goodmans, Frank Smith, Cliff Moon and Liz Waterland. Throughout the evening there was time for the parents to look at the books their children were reading, to take part in practical work, and to ask questions. During one of the large-group discussion sessions one of the fathers, an interested and articulate man who was a member of the school's governing body, said that he was concerned about his son's reading. He had been in school a term, had brought books home and read to his parents and older brother. He was showing 'interest', but he did not appear to know 'the key words'.

By looking at what Miss E. and the father at the parents' evening say when they describe what they are seeing and doing, we can discern how their views of the processes of reading are determined, often constrained, by the language, metaphors, *discourse* in current use. When the father refers to his little boy not having 'the key words', he is using a definition from a commercially produced reading scheme, now many years old. When teachers and parents talk of structure, stages and progression, they are drawing from a mode of thinking, a discourse, about reading which is rooted in a behaviourist psychology. Schematized categories are used to gloss the descriptions of reading competence which they can see in the children they spend their days with. This extract is taken from a diary which Miss E. kept, and discussed with me, during the time I was in the classroom:

> I try to get over to the parents that I want the children reading books, not just words! I try to get over to them, and to the children, that there is progress in their reading — not just measured in the hardness of the words. I know where each child is in their reading. For instance, Tammy came up to me the other day and said: 'Do you know any more books about little girls who go and hide away?' She'd read *Sally's Secret* and *Tilly's House*, so that was what she obviously wanted in her reading. I know these are stages in independence. I encourage them to read in groups, then, maybe, in

twos. Then on their own. I know that by having lots of books available, I'm giving them choice. (Miss E.)

Miss E. has an emergent view of what the reading process can be like, based upon her observation of and reflection upon her own classroom practice. She is beginning to conceptualize it as a social process, connected in subtle ways with children's affective lives. She is seeing progress in her own terms: as children moving confidently from book to book, achieving more complex discourse understandings. In her diary, her discussions with parents and with other teachers, she is trying to articulate these insights. Yet she derives much of the language she uses from a view of reading which foregrounds sentence decoding and hierarchical skills. She is attempting to justify her methods ('this approach') in terms of her new-found view of the process. She is trying to bend a discursive style which originates in a notion of 'normality' and 'growth' to describe what she values as diversity and individualism in her classroom. She tries to talk in terms of individual 'stages', yet she has a view of reading as a social process, learned with others. It could be that her training as a teacher has provided her with a discourse that is not matching with the practice she is seeing, encouraging, describing and trying to communicate.

Much of our current understanding of the determining power of discourses, and the ways in which they serve to organize and order what it is possible to think, derives from the French philosopher, Foucault (1972). Recently educators have adapted his concepts to examine classroom processes, social practices and the ways in which ideas, attitudes, values and 'stances' towards knowledge are learned in school. Walkerdine's work on primary school mathematics seeks to show how young children enter pedagogic discourse through social practice (1982). Burgess (1984a and 1984b), focusing upon literature and humanities teaching in secondary school classrooms, conceptualizes classroom life as ways in which pupils are constituted as participants in different kinds of practice through discourse. This mode of looking at classroom discourse is fruitful in a searching out of the ways in which literacy is 'socially constructed' in classrooms, rooted as it is in Vygotsky's view of higher mental functions as 'socially formed and culturally transmitted' (1978, p. 126).

Stories

Some stories from my observations in Miss E.'s classroom reveal some of the social practices, the complex real processes, that are *constitutive* of modes of looking, talking and thinking that are central to literacy. They are stories which seek to keep the narrative flow, the sense of what happened. In trying to explore, in a vague and hazy way at first, the connections between social practice and literacy, the ways in which children were becoming readers within the context of a bustling and lively classroom, I looked and listened carefully to all aspects of life in the classroom. Routines, conversations, early number work, PE lessons were observed and participated in, as well as storytelling sessions, times when children were reading with one another, and with their teachers.

The Story of the Hymn Books

One day, quite early on in my time in the classroom, the children were gathered around Miss E., who was getting them ready to go home at the end of the day. I had switched off my tape recorder and put away my notebook. At that time there were forty-five children, aged from 'rising 5' to 7 years, the whole of the school's infant department. Nine of the children had been in school for just three weeks. They had started at the beginning of the spring term, when I had begun my work. I was tending to focus my attention upon them for some part of each day, watching for the ways in which they were being socialized into reading and writing. I had already grown quite accustomed to these routines at the end of the day. It was often the time at which the many activities of the day were discussed, mulled over: stories written, models made, paintings done, books read. I tended to use the time, not as a vigilant observer, but as a chance to read my field notes, wind back by tape recorder, and go through any ideas I wanted to talk through with Miss E. or Mrs R. after the children had left. This day my attention was brought to the session in a sharp and particular way when Miss E. produced a large brown cardboard box, and held it up in front of the assembled children.

1	*Miss E.*	In this box, there's something we've been waiting for for a long, long time: can anyone guess?

There then followed a series of exchanges in which the children, mostly the older ones in the class, gave the names of animals.

2	*Robert.*	A bear, Miss E.

| 3 | *Martin.* | No ... er ... a giraffe [*laughter from older children*] |
| 4 | *Lucy* | A hamster .... |

Throughout these exchanges, Miss E. showed mock-surprise and exasperation. At one point, she said:

| 5 | *Miss E.* | I think you're thinking of *One Hunter*, aren't you? |

This referred to a picture book recently read with the older children, Pat Hutchins' *One Hunter*, where varied animals are hidden in a jungle setting, well camouflaged. Then:

| 6 | *David.* | Maybe it's Robert's hamster. |

Recently Robert's mother had brought a pet hamster into school. The children had observed it, played with it, drawn it. A class book had then been planned and written together, *Harry the Hamster Goes to School*.

7	*Miss E.*	No, good boy for remembering. Harry was in a box like this, wasn't he? But if it was Robert's hamster, I think we'd hear a noise like sssss ... beginning with ssss. What's a word, beginning with sss?
8	*Melanie.*	Scratching ....
9	*Miss E.*	Yes, good girl, scratching. (Miss E. looks in mock-surprise, holding the box up to her ear). I don't think I can hear that noise, can I?

I noticed throughout these exchanges that the nine new children in the class sat throughout, looking and listening to the responses and actions of the older children.

One little boy, in particular, caught my eye: Dilwyn (5.1), a small, rather reserved boy whom I had been observing a lot over the weeks since we had both been new to the classroom. In earlier episodes I had seen him looking over at the book corner where the older children read books together, and talked openly and freely about the books there. The morning of the day that the 'box' had arrived had been something of a milestone in that I had watched Dilwyn look over at the corner with interest. One of the other 'new' children, Amy (5.2), had ventured over for the first time (Miss E. later told me) to join her sister, Anna (7.2), one of the older children in the class. Dilwyn slowly followed after Amy, and, after looking at some picture books, sat in between Amy and Anna who read aloud to both younger children.

In a long episode a few days earlier I had made notes of how Dilwyn had watched carefully and learned to participate in the process of asking one of the teachers, or one of the parent helpers in the classroom, for a word that he wanted to spell. Now this 'box' episode could be providing Dilwyn with a model of the guessing, play with words, linking of reading experience to real-life experiences, that constituted 'being a pupil' in Miss E's class (Willes, 1983). After another series of exchanges, in which various uses for the box were proposed, talked about, Miss E. opened the box and pulled out some polystyrene blocks that were used as packing:

10	*Miss E.*	[*looking at blocks*] Aren't we lucky? But I still can't see what's inside. ... [*pause*] Oh no. ...
11	⎡*Robert*	I can't stand this. ...
12	⎣*David*	
13	*Miss E.*	[*laughing*] No, I don't think I can either.

The refrain 'Oh no, I can't stand this' is one that I had often heard during my first days in the classroom, sometimes from Miss E., sometimes from some of the older children. At times, such as in this exchange, it was a joint cry! Finding out where it came from was one of the 'rites of passage' I had to go through to be a member of the class. It was a repeated chant in a story shared by Miss E. with the class many times, Jill Murphy's picture book, *Whatever Next!*

Sustaining the air of mystery, secrecy, suspense and surprise, Miss E. pulled out of the box a blue BBC hymn book:

14	*Lisa.*	Ah ... the hymn books. [*General movement and jostling to see the book Miss E. holds.*]
15	*Miss E.*	Yes, that's right, Lisa, the hymn books. Now, the newcomers won't know about these will they?
16	*Various voices.*	No. ...
17	*Miss E.*	Would one of you big children like to explain [*Hands raised, jostling*]

18	*Miss E.*	Yes, Stephen, yes. ...
19	*Stephen.*	Miss E. ... er ... you sent for these, we sent for these before.
20	*Alex.*	We use them, sing from them on the radio.
21	*Miss E.*	Yes, these are the song books that we sometimes sing with, from. Not just on the radio, Kelly, Dilwyn, but in assembly sometimes — when we all go in the Hall with Mr J. and the juniors. Now, some of these big children said they'd like to buy one. Who can remember saying they wanted one?
22	*Sophie.*	Ordering one. ...
23	*Miss E.*	Yes, Sophie, ordering one. That's a good word, Sophie. Some of you ordered one. Who can remember, I wonder?

Social action was accompanying the words we listened to. At the stage at which we left it, some of the children confidently put up their hands. Some wavered, raising and lowering their hands. Of the group of nine young children, the 'newcomers', nobody raised their hand at this point. Dilwyn looked rather puzzled by the whole business. Amy, the little girl who earlier in the day had followed her elder sister, Anna, over to the book corner, turned round and whispered something to her elder sibling. She then turned round to face Miss E., looking much more confident. Anna was one of the children who held up her hand with certainty. Amy then whispered to the girl who was sitting next to her, who happened to be Mrs R's daughter, Katie (5.0). Katie then looked around to the set of lockers at the side of the room, to where her mother tended to sit if Miss E. was talking to the whole class. Her mother wasn't there — I was, with my notebook and tape recorder. Mrs R. was in an adjoining small resource room, preparing some children's art work for display.

Miss E. then went through a slow process of counting the books out of the box, encouraging the children to join with her. The counting took on the form of a ritual chant. There were twenty-four books in all, and she again counted the hands of the children who said that they had definitely wanted one. The total number of children who said they wanted one was eighteen, although there were some waverers and floating voters! Significantly, at this stage Amy put up her hand. Miss E. continued:

24	*Miss E.*	I'm afraid I've got some very bad news, children.
25	*Michael.*	You can't have one! [*shouting*]
26	*Miss E.*	Erm ... Michael. You don't always have to say something silly. [*Lightening tone, smiling*] I wouldn't play a trick like that, would I, Stephen.
27	*Stephen.*	Yes, Miss E. [*Laughter from class, and mock indignation from Miss E.*]
28	*Miss E.*	No, the news is that I'm afraid they've gone up from 50p to 75p. [*Some bustle, and confusion*]
29	*Miss E.*	I mean, when we ordered the books, quite a long time ago. ...
30	*Darren.*	A long, *long* time ago.
31	*Miss E.*	Yes it was a long, long time ago. Well, I told you they were 50p. Well now they've come, I'm afraid the price has gone up to 75p. Now, who doesn't want one?

At this stage there was considerable confusion and bustle amongst the children, and I focused again upon the younger children, the newcomers, who tended to sit together, near the front of a large arc which formed when all the children sat around the area of the classroom reserved for this kind of communal gathering. Of the nine new children, four put up their hands, with a quiet certainty, when asked, 'Now who doesn't want one?' One, a boy, Kevin (5.4) looked very confused and a little anxious. Four who were grouped together — Mrs R's daughter, Kelly, Amy, Anna's younger sister, Catherine (4.8) and Dilwyn — looked at each other, behind them at the older children, at Miss E. Dilwyn, once or twice, looked at me at the side of the room. Katie looked once over to the resource room, where she'd guessed her mother would be. Miss E. continued:

| 32 | *Miss E.* | If you want one, and Mummy says you can have one, can you bring in. ... |
| 33 | *Gareth.* | Seventy-five pennies. ... |

| 34 | *Miss E.* | Yes, good boy. Bring in seventy five *pence*. You don't have to have one, though. |

I sensed at this stage that Miss E. was getting rather agitated, unusually so for her. It was getting near to home time (3.15) and I guessed that she thought many of the children, especially the younger ones, were unsure as to what she wanted to communicate in the message home. Mrs R. entered the main classroom at this stage. Miss E. turned and voiced her concern to her colleague:

35	*Miss E.* [*to Mrs R.*]:	I don't want them all going and demanding the money.
36	*Mrs R.*	No. ...
37	*Miss E.*	Now you mustn't go out today and say ... [*silence*] say ... what. ...
38	*Stephen.*	Mummy, mummy, can I have a hymn book. ...
39	*Miss E.*	Well, yes ... but I don't want you to say. ...

[*short silence*]

40	*Robin.*	Can I have a hymn book?
41	*Miss E.*	No, oh dear. When you go out of school, after school today. When you run out of the gate, what doesn't Miss E. want you to say. ...
42	*Ellie.*	Mummy, mummy I *must* have a hymn book.
43	*Miss E.*	That's right, you lovely girl. When you go out, Miss E. doesn't want you to say, 'Mummy, Mummy, I *must* have a hymn book.' Do you little ones understand that? [*Miss E. focuses upon young 'newcomers', and there is general nodding and agreement.*]
44	*Miss E.*	When you go out, and when you're telling your mummies about the hymn books, Miss E. doesn't want you to say 'I ... I ...'
45	*Katie.*	I must have a hymn book
46	Michael.	Her Mummy's here! [*Giggling from children*]

47	Mrs R.	Yes, I'm here, Michael.
48	Miss E.	Yes, Michael, Katie's Mummy is here. But lots of mummies aren't here — and I just didn't want your mummies to think that you've ... Dilwyn
49	Dilwyn [speaking for the first time].	Got to have a hymn book.
50	Miss E.	Good boy. But if you want one. ...
51	Dilwyn.	I can ... I can ... bring some money.
52	Amy.	75p.
53	Dilwyn.	Tomorrow. ...

Reading the Story: Seeking Meanings

On first listening, and upon subsequent examination of field notes made during the early weeks in Miss E's classroom, such events meant little to me. I was rather exclusively concentrating on 'literacy related events': reading, writing and social activities related to them. I was, after all, in this classroom, one I knew of as a place where children learned to read successfully, to explore what I hazily posited as 'the social context of literacy'. The episode of the hymn books only began to make sense and to shape into an idea that became significant to me, when read alongside other such episodes, narratives lifted from the daily patterns that all teachers will readily recognize.

For a long time I viewed such an episode as one concerned with control and with the communication of information — and there is a sense in which Miss E.'s talk here is shaping the children's talk into acceptable patterns. She is socializing them into such aspects of classroom life as turn-taking, appropriateness and explicitness. She singles out, gently but in a no-nonsense fashion, the 'clown' in this episode, Michael, an older boy (7.1) who was often singled out for similar comment. But beyond the surface linguistic structure of the episode there are meanings, patterns being developed and sustained, and some of these are central to literacy.

One important feature of the episode is that the text as a whole, the set of exchanges between teacher and children, is in fact a narrative, a slowly unfolded 'story' of the hymn books' arrival in the classroom. It is not linear, but it is constructed by the participants in its telling. Miss E. perhaps plays a major role. But it is *created*, made, in the classroom as they talk together. There is nothing surprising in the fact that Miss E.'s and the children's classroom discourse can be read as a 'story'. The story or narrative form has long been acknowledged as 'a primary act of mind' (Hardy, 1977). Providing the scaffolding for children so that experience and social action can be intermeshed through talk is the prime way in which children are helped to become 'meaning makers' (Wells, 1987, p. 195).

The particular status I want to claim for such classroom talk relates to the personal learning I experienced during my early days' observation in the classroom, and the ways in which I came to listen to and value such interaction. What the teachers seemed to be doing for a great deal of the time was shaping the children's experiences into narratives. Out of school experiences were patterned, celebrated and evaluated — as stories to be shared. 'News time' and 'sharing time' were useful sites for the analysis of the ways in which teachers and children (and often children and children) collaboratively constructed narratives out of daily experience and social action. These stories enfolded pathos, drama, expectation, climax and were often woven together by experiences, commentaries upon those experiences, local and tacit knowledge and the relationships, developed and emergent, between Miss E., Mrs R, and children and their parents.

The local and tacit knowledge (Hundeide, 1985), required to understand such stories is important. The 'newcomers' needed the provenance of the hymn books explained to them. Often, during my early days of observation in the classroom, I did not have the cultural knowledge and the awareness of children's lives to interpret many of the stories I heard. Here is an extract from one of the early 'news' sessions I observed. James (6.2), one of a group of four or five boys who always tend to sit and work together, has had a birthday party over the weekend:

1	*Mrs R.*	Yes, I saw you going to the party, James.
2	*James.*	Where, Miss?
3	*Mrs R.*	Ah ... you guess where I saw you going.
4	*Andrew.*	Macdonalds, Miss.
5	*Lewis.*	That's where we had the party.
6	*Mrs R.*	And I bet I know who else was there! ... Erm ... let me think, was Lewis there, James?
7	*James.*	Yes, I bet you can't guess who else.

A long exchange follows, where James and Mrs R. construct the guest list, and talk about how much food was eaten.

8   *Mrs R.*   Oh dear, I wonder what happened to my invitation?

Boys giggle. Others collude with Mrs R. in her mock-indignation.

9   *James.*   No girls came, Miss. [*Explosion of laughter*]

In this episode, as in many others observed and recorded, there is a sense in which the generally-known is shared and celebrated. Mrs R. *knows* that the group of friends would all be at the party. They all have their birthdays around the same time, and each weekend seemed to bring a party at Macdonalds, or Viking Burgers. They differed only in that each party had a different person in the middle receiving the presents of Action Men or He Man figures. The unspoken joke at the heart of the episode, appreciated by the older children and becoming understood by the younger, was that the children knew that Mrs R. knew who would be at the party. Secrets are shared, but not spoken. Similarly, the joke in the tail of the episode, predicated upon Mrs R's 'missing invitation', is rooted in the local and tacit knowledge that by that age, in this class, parties tend to be single-sex events. And one wouldn't normally invite a teacher anyway.

In communicating the essence of that story I am, like the children, relying not just on the linguistic surface structures, but on the cultural knowledge, and the interpretation of gesture, intonation, facial expression, laughter and silence that all tellers and understanders of stories draw upon. These kinds of interpretative devices are the connections between everyday social practice and elaborate literary forms (Potter, *et al.*, 1984).

Stories also shape the everyday flux of social experience within a classroom. Experiences shared, and activities engaged in, would be collaboratively recorded in narrative form. *Harry the Hamster Goes to School* was an example of something lived, then written about, then read and talked about. The new children, in particular, would have daily experience patterned in a way that helped them both to order and to recall their learning of concepts. 'You remember yesterday when we all shared out the sweets and talked about equal shares. Well today, let's try and do that with some numbers' (Mrs R.). Novel experiences and activities would often be set in the form of a story about what will be, the better to predict and prepare for the unknown:

> *Miss E.* Now, we're going to get changed in a minute, and walk very quietly ... are you all listening ... very quietly to the Hall. After we've listened to a radio programme called Movement, we'll tiptoe back to the classroom. Remember when we went to the Hall yesterday. Come on then.

The story of the hymn books and their arrival and allocation is unfolded with a sense of secrecy, of suspense: 'In the box, there's something we've been waiting for ... can anyone guess?' There is also the conveyed promise that the secrets are to be discovered and explored, collaboratively. There is something private, special, unknown that could be discovered together. The teachers often prefaced discussions, periods of collaborative talk, storyreading sessions with such invitations realized through this stance. The functions of the teacher's language is important here. Michael Halliday's is still the most complete statement of functions (1975) and his identification of the imaginative function which, in Bruner's words, is 'the means whereby we create possible worlds and go beyond the immediately referential', is a useful tool for analyzing the kinds of talk that Miss E. uses in such an invitation. The children are encouraged to seek new meanings; the stance towards such meaning is a hermeneutic one.

In exchanges 2 to 4 of the episode, where the children posit the various animals that could be in the box, they draw upon understandings and possibilities derived both from real experience and from stories they have read. Lucy's reference (4) to Harry the Hamster connects another 'story', based on real experience, to this one being constructed. David takes this link up (6), and it is extended by Miss E. (7–9). Miss E. links a recently read picture story (5) with the one they are telling now. So, life-text and text-life moves are being given social credibility. Notice how Miss E. colludes with the stories they are telling, even the fantastic ones.

When Miss E. is uncertain as to how to communicate to the younger children the quite complicated notion 'not *having* to buy a hymn book', a story involving appropriate behaviour and action, her instinct is to present the idea in the form of a story, a projected one about what *could* happen when you leave school today. This story again involves conversational implicature, what does not need to be said as it is local knowledge, (Michael's comment upon Katie's Mum being there) and is collaborative. Miss E. wants to involve the younger children in the telling. They read the gestures and the expressions of their older classmates. They are learning that to understand stories which wrap social action, they must draw upon systematic forms of sense-making, codes of interpretation and interpretative processes.

This episode shows that through such classroom discourse, private meanings and personal experience are made public and shared. In Miss E's acceptance of the children's ideas (2–4; 7–9) there is a publicizing of the notion that such speculation, such bridging of real-life and story experience is a normal feature of social practice.

Studies which have sought to explore the 'social context' of literacy in classrooms have tended to focus upon time spent on particular activities, the efficacy of certain teaching methods, or upon teachers' assessments. Where an ethnographic stance has been taken, the tendency has been to look at classroom organization, or group-ings of pupils. The work of Brice Heath (1983) uncovers some of the more intricate ways in which literacy learning is interwoven with the texture of relationships, social patterns and the ways of taking meanings from the community. That work, and the studies of literacy theorists such as Street (1984), provide us with tools and concepts to analyze classroom events in a way that foregrounds the socially constituted aspects of reading and writing. In this book Dombey (see Chapter 5) shows how the storytelling session is a key site in which meanings are stored, interpretations collaboratively constructed. The teacher conducts and draws together the diverse voices and readings of the children.

Much of my time in the classroom was spent observing 'story' sessions, and I will now select two different kinds of event to illustrate the modes of looking and interpretation I want to encour-age. The first event is a piece of collaborative reading. There was a vast range of books in Miss E's classroom: wordless books, picture books, good modern retellings of classic stories, 'bridging' books with less reliance upon pictures, more upon texts. Children looked at books whenever they wanted to, meeting in the book area, sharing and talking about their reading.

'Can I look?': Learning to Read as a Social Process

The episode I want to look at again involves Dilwyn and Amy, whom we met earlier. They were 5.4 and 5.5 respectively, no longer 'newcomers'. The other child involved was Steven, a lively and ebullient boy of 6.10. This episode took place towards the end of a busy Tuesday morning. The notes from my 'field' book were as follows:

11.36. Notice S. in the reading corner alone and note title of book, *Not Now Bernard*, by David McKee, one I have heard both Miss E. and Mrs R. read to the class, though not lately. S. is reading silently, yet 'voicing' the text. Smiling and obviously enjoying the book — sprawled on one of the huge cushions in book area. Children are milling all around him, but he seems oblivious.

11.40. S. is joined by D., who perches on the side of the cushion with him. S. goes back to beginning, and I hear him say in a loud voice, as if now sharing the reading with D. 'Not now Bernard' ...

11.43. Two boys looking at book, S. reading to D. Go over and put the tape unobtrusively near to them.

11.46. Two boys joined by A., who first stands in front of them, then sits herself on the floor facing the two boys.

11.50. Three still intent on book, taking turns: much switching of roles voices.

This is the bare 'action' of an episode taking eighteen minutes and involving three children. The transcript of my *Not Now Bernard* tapes spreads over many pages. The following short extract is from near the beginning, when Steven started reading to Dilwyn and they were joined by Amy:

Printed Text	*Children's speech*
	S. I'm gonna read this again.
	D. Can I look?
	S. Yeah.

Hello Dad, said Bernard.	S. Hello Dad, said Bernard. He's the boy [*points*] in the book. [*looking at picture*] S. Eike! He's hit his finger. D. Who's he? His Daddy?
Not now, Bernard, said his *father.*	S. Not now, said Dad.

The younger child invites himself into the reading. S. begins to read, pausing after the first page, to look at the picture on page 2, where Bernard's father, disturbed by the child, hits his finger. S. explains to D. that Bernard is the boy 'in the book'. He also recounts to D. what is happening, pointing at the picture, and directing the younger child's attention to it. S. accepts, and answers D's question: 'Who's he?' by reference to the text, changing 'his father' in the text to 'his Daddy'.

Printed Text	*Children's speech*
	S. [*banging floor*] Ouch, my finger. D. Ow. S. [*turning page*] This is his Mum.
Hello Mum, said Bernard.	S. Hello Mum. D. [*points at words*] said Bernard.
Not now Bernard, said his *Mother.*	S. Not now Bernard, said his D. mother.
[background noise]	
	A. said his Mother.

From the tape it seems that Steven bangs the floor or the cushion with his hand and says, 'Ouch, my finger!' Dilwyn's 'Ow' seems to be a play-acting 'Ow', rather than an authentic one — a dramatization of the story. Steven again explains on turning the page: 'This is his Mum.' Notice how Dilwyn joins in the reading with Steven on 'said Bernard'. They chant, song-like, and much more loudly, the second refrain, 'Not now, Bernard, said his mother.' Towards the end of the extract Amy joins in. She is an extrovert child, more confident than Dilwyn.

Printed text	*Children's speech*
There's a monster in the garden and it's going to eat me.	S. There's a monster and it's going to eat me.
	A. In the garden.
	S. We know that.
Not now Bernard, said his mother.	A. There isn't really
	D. Eh?
	A. It's not really a monster, I've had this with my ... with my ... with Mrs R.
	S. Don't spoil it.
	D. [*pointing*] Not now. ... Not now Bernard.
	A.
	S. Said his mother.
	D. Said his mother
	A. It's not
	S. It is [*rapidly turning pages*] Look! [*pointing to monster*]
	D. Ouch!
The monster hit Bernard's father.	S. See! There's the monster. He bites his Dad.
	A. And be broke all his toys and read his comics.
	D. Turn it back.
	S. Where?
	D. 'There's a monster in the garden' page.

Amy begins to take on the reading from the older Steven here. The reader must take it on trust from me that both Amy and Steven tell the story in the same chant-like way, catching the rising and falling, the tune of the text that I had heard from Miss E. and Mrs R. many times. Steven omits 'in the garden' and Amy adds it. 'We know that', says Steven, perhaps indicating that that is an explicit statement of their shared knowledge. Amy says that there is not really a monster, seeming to base that on previous readings. She *may* have a sophisticated reading of the story that she is sharing. The joke at the centre of the book is that Bernard's parents do not recognize the monster as such, even after he has eaten Bernard! Steven rapidly turns the pages of the book to prove that, on a literal level at least, there *is* a monster.

Amy projects to a later episode, where the monster will break all Bernard's toys and reads his comics. Dilwyn wants to go back to the stage in the story they were at before the 'monster' discussion. He remembers the point they were at, and seems to want to take control of the reading, to find out what happens next.

What we see here is a piece of collaborative interpretation. Dilwyn, the younger child, has the opportunity to invite himself into a story-telling with an older boy. The older boy is using modes of interpretation and understanding employed by the teachers (the rising and falling of voices and dramatization). The boys, together, make sense of both text and pictures. Dilwyn, listening to Amy and Steven, learns that there may be multiple readings of the text (is the monster real, or not?). All this happens within a supportive context: the children pace the reading, and take control of the operation.

There are similarities with the way in which the story of the hymn books was unfolded earlier in Dilwyn's school career. There, a text had to be co-created by teacher and children. Sense had to be made of a situation, a story had to be constructed, meanings had to be shared and sometimes argued over. In both situations children draw upon modes of understanding, pragmatic competences and codes of interpretation. When Dilwyn reads *Not Now Bernard* with two more confident and experienced children, he is able to hear the traffic of interpretation that goes on in deriving meaning from a text. The operation is a joint one, learned socially by the older boy in story-reading sessions, and in other such child–child encounters. The discourse that we need to describe and communicate such processes may be different from the traditional ways in which we have talked about reading.

'She Doesn't Look Like a Burglar': Reading as Interpretative Process

Lastly, and briefly, I move on in time to a year or so later. Dilwyn, the younger child in the above two examples, is now 6.6. He has read scores of books, and heard hundreds of stories read aloud in story sessions. I spent a lot of time reading with Dilwyn, one of the 'newcomers', when I was new to the class. During the time at which the next episode was recorded I was tending to spend time each week with Dilwyn and some of his peers reading and talking. He is now inches taller and more confident and worldly-wise. At the time he was very much enjoying the books of Allan and Janet Ahlberg, a husband and wife author-artist team. This extract comes from his reading of *Cops and Robbers*, one of the first books he read independently. For clarity I have not included the *actual* text, but Dilwyn's reading of it, which varies slightly here and there. I have transcribed our conversation and my commentary, the format I adopted during these individual sessions.

Reading	Commentary	Speech
	D. begins by looking at first page of book which shows busy police station in cartoon-type pictures. Bustling activity and humourous looking characters.	
		D. Look at this. This looks funny.
		CM. Yes
		D. Look at the dog. I wonder. ... Cops and Robbers. Where are the ...?
		CM. Shall we read?
Here are the cops of London town, Hard working, brave and true.		
They drink their tea.	Looks at picture.	D. Who's drinking tea? He's making tea. Let's look.
Stay up till three.		D. Does that mean three in the night.
		CM. I expect so
		D. They work at all night. We saw on a programme about a ... a police station place. They opened all the night.
		CM. Wonder why?
		D. 'Cos robbers work at night ... people lose things and smash things up. I've got a police car [*noise of car*].
Stay ... stay up till three And take good care of you.	goes back to text.	

We go on, taking time. Dilwyn tends to move between pictures, text and comments and questions about the story. We reach the page where all the robbers are introduced. Janet Ahlberg's lovely pictures

47

are framed, like 'mugshots', showing Grabber Dan, Snatcher Jack, etc.

Reading	*Commentary*	*Speech*
	When we reach this page, D. spends a long time poring over the pictures.	
		D. Grabber Dan ... Snatch ... Snatcher Jack ... Billy the Boy [*laugher*]. What a funny name. Peg Leg House ... no Ho. ... What's that name?
		CM. Horace.
		D. Peg Leg Horace. I wonder what that means. Do you know?
		CM. Perhaps it means he's only got one leg.
		D. Fingers M. ...
		CM. Maurice, Fingers Maurice.
		D. Fingers Maurice. ... [*pause*] I know why he's called Fingers.
		CM. Why?
		D. 'Cos he steals.
		CM. How do you know?
		D. Don't know. Grandma Swagg [*laughs*] Grandma Swagg. She doesn't look like a burglar
		CM. Doesn't she?
		D. No, she looks like a lovely old Grannie. [*mock gentility voice*] Doesn't she?
	goes on to next page.	CM. Yes, she does.

The extract had lots of pauses and extraneous giggles. Dilwyn looked at the pictures, at the words, and at me to 'gauge' my reading and understanding. He was bringing those same interpretative processes that he was beginning to employ when he read the book with the older children, that he was using when he listened to the story of the hymn books.

Dilwyn uses devices in his interpretation of messages, representations, pictures and symbols. When he perceives that Grandma

Swagg is not just a kind old grannie but a robber, he is understanding a joke that is at the centre of the book: things are not what they seem. It is hard to interpret and enjoy that story if you don't comprehend that early on. They look respectable, some of them — but they are robbers. How has he learned to do that? Partly, but not wholly perhaps, from the talk around stories and books that has gone on in Miss E.'s class. Remember the guessing game about the contents of the box of hymn books — could there really be animals in there? Understanding what is not said is the root of the humour of many popular picture books for young children. As in conversation, secrets are shared not spoken.

At the beginning of the episode he pours over the pictures, something his teachers have often done when reading a new text. I remember a whole half-hour discussion led by Miss E. looking at the 'map' of the story at the front of another of the Ahlberg's books, *Each, Peach, Pear, Plum*. He asks me for confirmation in his interpretations; he uses his common sense and his cultural knowledge. I do not want to make large claims for this piece of text. I am more concerned to encourage others to look closely at what has been too long overlooked in our collection of 'evidence' about reading. When children read their first independent texts, they not only bring linguistic resources, they bring social and cultural understandings. They bring understandings of other texts, codes of interpretation learned from their 'reading' of popular culture. They bring the 'stances' of wonder, interpretation and evaluation that they have learned from their teachers and from other co-readers (Isn't that funny? I wonder what?). They use also those shared processes of sense-making which they have learned socially.

Readers, Texts and Contexts

Many literary critics have recognized the interlocking of literary and everyday forms of understanding. Studies of literacy and literature which have taken social action into account have built up a particularly strong case for literary conventions as related to broader social processes. Indeed, I am borrowing from varied unacknowledged sources in journeying to a tentative proposal. That is, that we account for those interpretative, social processes in our *discourse* about reading. My major debt is to Vygotsky, significantly both a psychologist and a literary critic. In *Mind and Society* (1978) he worked towards a comprehensive account that would make possible rich description of the origins of higher mental processes. He urged, first, 'specification of the context in which the behaviour developed' (p. 6) and 'speculative reflection on cultural forms of behaviour ... tracing the qualitative changes [in behaviour] occurring in the course of development' (p. 7).

When children are learning to become readers, they are transforming sign-using activity. External activities are being reconstructed and beginning to occur internally. Dilwyn is beginning to do, independently, with the help of a skilled author and artist, the things he has learned to do with his classmates (look at what's shown for clues about what might be) and with his teachers (construct stories from looking and interpreting what he sees). In Vygotsky's terms an interpersonal process is becoming an intrapersonal one. We still need 'a reasoned theory of how the negotiation of meaning as socially arrived at is to be interpreted as a pedagogical axiom' (Bruner, 1986, p. 124). This chapter indicates some of the ways in which reading is 'socially arrived at' through social processes, and social practice, within classroom life.

How can we encourage the next generation of teachers, who started *my* story, to look at these social processes? What kinds of questions could they ask? They could begin by examining the discourse teachers, parents and children use to talk about reading. Where does it come from? Is is describing or constraining what's being seen or done? Dilwyn was making complex and subtle interpretations about Grandma Swagg; his classmate's father is concerned with key words. How might these two be reconciled? We could ask students to discern whether or not social relations in the classroom are conducive to the exploration that reading entails. Are children given the time and space to make sense of reading and to make their own interpretations? Reading requires children to make sense, explore possible worlds, invent, sort out what is not said. Real, lively texts connect all that with the polyphonic and diverse social interaction that goes on in lively infant school classrooms ('Oh no, I can't stand it!'). It is the living mix of varied voices that links literacy, literature, and talk with social practice. Reading changes for each generation of learners and teachers. Approaches change, aspirations change. Our way of looking at it and talking about it needs to change to take into account new readers, new texts and the contexts in which they will all interact with one another.

Part 2: Learning to be Literate

Literacy, in the sense of children learning to read and write, is an important strand in the complex of parents' anxiety when they leave their children at the gate of a primary school. Parents know from their own life experience that success in school learning is linked to performance and accomplishment, to 'making a good start' in classroom tasks related to written language. They want their children to be good at reading and writing for reasons that are powerful, if often inchoate. Sometimes they feel inexplicably oppressed by what they think is their ignorance of current teaching practices. They assume that, if their children do not come quickly to terms with what counts as reading and writing, they may fail to become successful school learners.

Recent scholarly attention paid to literacy by historians, psychologists, anthropologists, ethnographers, linguists and teachers confirms the lay person's belief that learning to read and write is a critical step in social belonging. These studies also widen our view of the processes and functions of literacy and our understanding of how literacy is differentially learned. We are now sure that, far from being either neutral or autonomous, reading and writing are sets of social practices embedded in contexts of social interaction (Graff, 1979; Halliday, 1975; Levine, 1986; Street, 1984; Cook-Gumpertz, 1986; Heath, 1983; Meek, 1982). Thus, what happens in classrooms to enforce schooled literacy is only one aspect of the literacy events which together make up any definition of what literacy is in a particular setting at any point in time.

Children's learning to be literate begins, as does their learning to talk, as a form of domestic interaction with language, this time with written language. They see their elders responding to written communication as part of their everyday lives. Many parents leave their children to find their own way about in the world of printed messages without being conscious of how children sort out TV advertisements, food wrappers, names on streets and buildings, signs on advertisement hoardings. They are confident that the children will take from the culture the necessary information to support and advance what they need to know about these things. They leave reading *lessons* to the teacher in school. Other parents intervene in particular ways, by reading stories to their children, by making objects, or by explaining the meaning and functions of various kinds of print and typography. In doing these things they unlock all the social forces which make children 'play for real' when they look at books and hear stories read.

The evidence suggests that, when they are read to, children encounter language in a form which is quite different from anything they hear at any other time in conversation. It is continuous discourse, a kind of monologue, to which both the adult reader and child listener extend a particular kind of attention (Halliday, 1978; Dombey, 1985), and from which the listener learns a number of reading lessons without being, in the more obvious sense, taught. A child who can recite nursery rhymes and then find them in a book discovers reading as a particular kind of intertext.

There are many kinds of emergent literacies, and it is to these we turn in the next three essays, all of which expand the idea that literacy is learned early as 'ways of taking from the culture' (Heath, 1983). Here are demonstrations of how children discover language itself, what they can make words do. Carol Fox reveals how children weave together stories from books and stories from their own lives. Henrietta Dombey opens up the interactions in a nursery classroom so that we see how meanings are socially created in that context when a story is read aloud to a class. Gillian Beardsley demonstrates how children behave towards each other as they use their early literacy events to share practical understanding in their play. We become aware of how children are literate in recognizable ways before they go to school, and that much will depend on how these competences are regarded at the next stage when formal reading and writing lessons begin.

These essays also make it clear that early reading and writing are located within systems of values: of subjectivity of individual children, of the importance of play, of the nature of narrative and the importance of books. Running through the shared themes of the writers is a set of theoretical concerns about how these literate activities are viewed by the children, their teachers and their parents who are all, at this time, moving into new partnerships.

4 'Poppies Will Make Them Grant'

Carol Fox

Continuing and extending James Britton's account of make-believe play, in this chapter Carol Fox explores the lengthy narrations which children compose before they go to school. She adds to the existing accounts of language development the creative principle of metaphor. Before they know that words are expected to be referential, children use them to create 'the flash between two signifiers'; to maintain the link between understanding and feeling, and to celebrate their new power in bringing themselves as narrators, and thus language itself, into being. The indication is that this power must be neither ignored nor allowed to desiccate in school for want of understanding of its nature.

For several years I have been analyzing the narrative competences of five young children aged 3½–6. Although all the children's narratives were tape recorded, the conditions for story-telling were otherwise as natural as they could be. The children only told stories when they felt like it, and usually only their mothers or fathers were present during story-telling. No restrictions were placed on the stories to be told, nor on the time and situation of the telling.

The children were selected for the study on the basis of their willingness to tell stories and their rich previous experience of hearing stories read and told to them. My purpose was to discover what influence written stories had had on their own spontaneous narrative productions. The story data comprise very large samples of child language, over 43,000 words in total, and these include fifty-one stories, taken from all five children, of between 300 and 1750 words. My research into the field of child language study has convinced me that it can only be in narration that young children produce such extended, sustained utterances.

Elsewhere (Fox, 1983 and 1984) I have reported briefly that the literary competences revealed in the children's stories are very extensive. While it has been possible to demonstrate that the children 'talk like books' in their story-telling and that their conception of what stories are is rooted in what has been read to productions within the mainstream theories of either language or narrative development.

The position can be stated briskly. Early child language is analyzed either at the level of the sentence or below, or, if it is treated as discourse, it is face-to-face dialogue which is examined. We are familiar now with the tendency of psycholinguists to see language chiefly as syntactic structure, omitting from their descriptive and explanatory accounts of language intentionality, affect, the social situation of the utterance and the society or culture which is constituted by, and constitutes in turn, the linguistic interactions of everyday life. Narratives rarely appear in the data of psycholinguistic studies. Even Ruth Weir (1962), whose data are her son's extended pre-sleep monologues, who, ahead of her time, used a *functional* framework for analyzing those monologues, and who fully acknowledged the satisfactions and pleasure of Anthony's play with words, even she would have us believe that an infant talks to himself in the dark in order to practise phonological patterns and syntactic rules. When narratives appear in Halliday's (1975) socially-based, functional account of language development, Halliday's interest lies in the text-forming components of his son's stories, the beginnings of systems of cohesion and information structure (p. 112). Yet stories are much more than series of sentences strung together by cohesive devices.

Children's stories have fared little better with those who have actually made narrative a central concern. Many studies search, like the psycholinguists, for structuring rules, for the syntax of stories, or story grammars. Some experiments in story recall/comprehension use specially devised narratives, as though the meaning a story has for a particular child had nothing to do with the way the child might re-tell or re-call the story (Stein and Glenn, 1979; Whatey, 1981). Only Labov (1972) stresses that the point of a story is *the way it is told*, and that therefore whatever gives a story its colour, its life, its particular stance or point of view, is the most vital element of the story's structure, the element which wards off the response — 'So what?'.

Another tradition of child narrative analysis is psychoanalytical in orientation (Pitcher and Prelinger 1963; Ames, 1966). Here there is great emphasis on the affective 'deep structure' of the stories children tell, on the power of narrative to express symbolically the repressed conflicts of infancy. But here all is reduced to theme and content, and language itself receives no attention. The narratologists tend to see stories entirely as form with little meaning, while the psychoanalysts see them as all meaning but with little significant form. A short extract from a story in my study may illustrate the impossibility of a theory of narrative which separates form and content:

> but then he went out in the middle of
> the night
> and there was this sound going—dooo-dee
> doo-dee [*child sings*]
> he looked all around
> nobody was there in a small street where
> it had lots of holes
> he looked down one of them
> he looked down the other
> they were all alike
> but he looked down the next one
> and what was there?
> just a surprise thing
> his Daddy was there (Josh, 5.0)

Neither the story-grammar approach nor the psychoanalytical approach is likely to do justice to this passage, for it is not the hero's action nor the meaning of that action which make this section of the story powerful; it is the fact that the child as narrator has chosen to tell these events in a certain way, manipulating the listener into a state of tension which is relieved at the eleventh hour (or rather, the eleventh clause); it is this which makes the passage so much more than 'Hero discovers father in hole in the road'! If narrative enables children to make meanings in language in a particularly rich, extended, complex and powerful way, as I believe it does, then we need to develop much more inclusive theories of language learning. I want to suggest that whatever lies at the heart of story-telling lies at the heart of language itself, so that narrative is no longer out on a limb in mainstream studies of language development.

We might start with the child as a speaking subject. The

Chomskyan notion of competence (1957 and 1965) has often been criticized because it locates language inside the infant's mind, and because the language it locates there is an 'idealized', perfect sort of structure which belongs, as Hymes remarked, more to the Garden of Eden than to this imperfect world (1971, p. 39). Communicative competences were much broader, and included rules for language use, units of linguistic structure which were not sentences but discourses, and relationships between speakers positioned in society in different ways. Hymes complained that Chomsky's emphasis on what was innate in humans and universal in grammar was 'but half a dialectic'; the social situation, or the context, constituted the other half, (*ibid*, pp. 55–6). The notion of competences, whether syntactic or communicative, has persisted, and for good reasons. It seems irrefutable that children do have knowledge of the rules of grammar, do have knowledge of the rules for language use, and do have knowledge of the rules for conducting various modes of discourse which include telling stories. Moreover children are not aware of this knowledge, are unable to make it explicit, and yet it is systematic, rule-bound and capable of formal description. In this sense competences for language belong to the unconscious, but what kind of unconscious is it? The idea that it consists of a blueprint for making structuring rules which are co-variant with an infinity of external contexts is rather mechanical in the face of the tremendous emotional force of the stories children invent. Consider the following story told by Justine (5.0):

> But then a bird went and eated them all up, and he ate all the people up 'cos it was a monster. Do you know what? He ate all the houses up too, the concrete, and all the books and all the curtains, and all the glass and all the tinsel and all — and — and — and all the teachers, and all the school children, and he ate their school. He ate islands and water, sea and starfish, and fish like that, and everything, even the whole world.

Linguists would probably judge most of Justine's sentences here as 'simple' and narratologists would say the same of her story structure; in either case a 'building blocks' analysis would not only fail to do the story justice, it would be almost irrelevant. As for the context, we have to ask where it is; is the context the situation of a 5-year-old telling her father a story, or is the context inside the story she tells? Given that the first kind of context generates *a* story rather than this particular one (which is one of several told on the same occasion), we have to look at the (possible) meanings of the story Justine tells. I would suggest that whatever her story means is not only constituted by her knowledge of grammar or narrative structure, nor by the addition of the social situation of its telling even if we include in that her past experience, the stories she has heard and her knowledge of things in the world. I would suggest that Justine's feelings, almost certainly unconscious ones, are also constitutive of her story. It is this whole affective domain which has been omitted from child language study, and from the majority of studies of narrative competence. Only Labov (1972), in eliciting stories which were about life-threatening situations from the black adolescents in his study, places affect at the heart of narrative structure.

It is in studies of play that affect is given a central place. Vygotsky tells us that 'The central attribute of play is a rule that has become a desire' (1978, p. 99), and he warns against the 'pedantic intellectualization' of play which omits affect and volition as its governing factors. Though he was writing within a Marxist framework Vygotsky's account of play has Freudian overtones, for symbolic play is seen as a means of wish-fulfilment, and the child's voluntary submission to rules of his own making as the means to achieving maximum pleasure. Affect is also central to Piaget's account of symbolic play, and though he takes issue with Freud in several major respects, he locates all symbolic thought, including play, in the unconscious in its inception, refusing to separate the affective and the intellectual even in the most logical and scientific modes of thinking: '… even when intelligence is at its most lucid the inner mechanism of assimilation is outside awareness, which first grasps only results and then by a recurrent and even incomplete reflection works back from the outside to a centre which it never reaches' (1951, p. 208). Imaginative stories are forms of verbal symbolic play, and for Piaget both their affective and intellectual aspects emerge from unconscious processes.

So far the theories touched upon here do not arise from studies of child language. When we do look at those studies it is striking how often play and affects are implicated in them without receiving any special attention either from psycholinguists, or in interactional studies from sociolinguists. For example, there are the studies of Baby-Talk (BT), or Motherese, the linguistic register which mothers use in adaptation to their infants. Brown (1977, p. 6) tells us that BT is not only adaptive to the limitations of the baby's comprehension and production of language, but it also has the function of expressing affection; and Ferguson (1977, p. 232) includes emotion as a major element of BT. Yet studies of BT say nothing about this whatsoever. A survey or work on BT by Snow (1977), Rogers (1976), Garnica (1977), De Villiers and De Villiers (1978), among others, reveals only linguistic structure; the child and the mother, and the situation within and between them as speaking subjects, are omitted from the picture.

Where, then, can we find a more fully developed theory of language development? I would like to propose that an all-inclusive framework might be provided by the notion of metaphor as a fundamental mental process. Recent work by Walkerdine, Urwin and their colleagues (1984, 1985), has taken us some distance towards developing such a theory. In the following section I shall outline the theoretical insights on which they have drawn, and then suggest some further studies which strengthen the case for metaphor. In this section I shall argue that metaphor lies at the heart of language itself, and I shall conclude by testing against this notion the narratives which are the data of my study.

First, we need to consider interpretations of Freud which have been able to take account of modern structural linguistics. Ricoeur (1970) and Lacan (1977) suggest that the unconscious part of the human mind is 'structured like a language', a view which is compatible with Chomsky's notion that to study linguistic structure is to study the mind. Lacan argues that the only medium available to the psychoanalyst for interpretation is the patient's speech (p. 40), and that therefore Freudian theory is essentially linguistic. This can best be illustrated through Lacan's re-reading of Freud's great work *The Interpretation of Dreams* (1900). The methodology of dream analysis starts with the dreamer's verbal report of what has been remembered of the dream. By a process of stripping off layers of signification associatively linked to the language which initiates the analysis, an interpretation of the whole dream with a logical, meaningful structure emerges. Thus the dream is a 'text' written as it were by the dreamer to be interpreted or reconstructed by the analyst (p. 57). Freud himself refers to dreams in linguistic terminology (1900, pp. 425, 430, 450), and he compares dreams to sentences which lack the necessary conjunctions to make them coherent, or to sentences which are only substantive and lack a grammar (p. 442). He points out that language plays a role in the content of dreams, for by its very nature language is able to disguise meaning, as in puns, jokes, slips of the tongue, etc., and is therefore eminently suited for the purpose of dreams, which is to escape the censorship normally imposed by the conscious, wakeful mind on unconscious desires. The interpretation of dreams is a matter of moving from meaning to meaning in an analysis, not of their content, but of the language which speaks it.

The concept of language uncovered by Lacan and Ricoeur in Freud's work is as a system shot through with ambiguity, a system open to multiple interpretations, a system which can give no direct account of subjective experience. This view of language is clearly demonstrable in jokes, dreams and poetry, but is it true of language itself in its everyday uses? Does language have such a tenuous relation to reality?

Lacan, using the linguistics of Saussure (1959) and Jakobson (1960), proposes that linguistic structure itself is constituted by just such a movement from meaning to meaning as Freud's methodology for dream analysis discovered in the unconscious. Lacan unlocks the secure bond between a word (signifier in Saussurean terms) and its referent (the signified) by pointing out that meanings can only be articulated by recourse to other words, which in turn need more words to articulate them, and so on. Words are not securely related to their referents at all, but take their meanings from the *differences* between themselves and other words; words are marks of separation. Thus we are locked into language, a chain of signifiers, which can never really grasp what it refers to. For Lacan this sliding movement of the signified under the meanings of the words we utter is an unconscious process. Following Jakobson, whose main interest was in linguistic functions, Lacan suggests that meaning is structured in language along two major, intersecting dimensions: the horizontal, where words combine with one another according to grammatical rules (best represented by the linearity of writing), and the vertical, where words are selected from the set of possible meanings. Jakobson calls the horizontal dimension the metonymic, and the vertical, because it works by processes of association of some kind or other, the metaphoric. Linguists have traditionally paid most attention to the horizontal, combinatorial axis, particularly to syntactic and phonological structures, but it is the metaphoric axis which is revealed in dreams and in poetry, and which makes possible the double, hidden and disguised meanings which are present, through the sliding of the signified, in all speech.

So far this very brief account of Lacan's reading of Freud, Saussure and Jakobson has tended to stress the linguistic in the mind/language duo. On its own it does not take us very far in the search for an affective basis for language acquisition. But Lacan, a psychoanalyst, is less concerned with language than with the processes by which subjects construct themselves and the part played by language in that subjectivity. He proposes that language acquisition causes several kinds of 'splitting' in the infant: the split between subject and object (or internal and external), the split between conscious and unconscious, between presence and absence, and between the instinctual drives of the body and the repression of those drives which is necessary for existence in a social world. It is *only* as speaking subjects that we are able to construct ourselves and our realities, a notion which, cast in non-psychoanalytic terms, will be familiar to readers of Cassirer (1944), Langer (1942) and Gregory (1974).

Lacan gives us a very useful metaphor for this 'moment' of splitting — the mirror-image. In the early months of life the infant has no subjectivity, no sense of a self in relation to an external world, no sense of the boundaries between its own and its mother's body. It is when it catches sight of itself in a mirror that the child conceives of itself as a unified whole, that it perceives itself as an object which is signifiable (a prerequisite for language), that it can begin to move away from the domination of the body's drives to the perception of an outside which is separate from itself, and, since the mirror-image follows its every move, that it can achieve an illusory sense of mastery over itself. Lacan states that the ego which is formed at this stage is an 'Ideal-I', one which is fully autonomous, not yet determined by its relation to society, an ego which is turned 'in a fictional direction' (p. 2), which to some extent remains with us throughout life. The child can only separate itself as a subject from external reality when it finds itself a position in signifying relations, i.e., language. Such a separation is built into linguistic structure, as we have seen, by the nature of the sign in which the signified, permanently elusive, is ever shifting under the signifier. Lacan's metaphor for the signifier, the word, which establishes the rules, taboos and definitions imposed by social life, is the Law of the Father. What must be relinquished in taking on the Father's Law — the gender identities, primarily, and the rules which govern behaviour and speech — is the initial dependence on the mother to satisfy the body's needs. The price of the entry into language is the repression of those needs and desires, hence the constitution of the unconscious where they remain hidden.

Lacan's theory puts the affective into language acquisition by placing psychosexual development at its very heart; it is the narcissism of the mirror-stage, followed by the conflict of relationships and gender identities involved in the Oedipus complex, which cause or necessitate (rather then motivate) language learning. However, it may be objected that it is narrow, phallo-centric and deterministic to place so much importance on the Oedipus complex and its resolution (Urwin, 1985, p. 278–9). Urwin and her colleagues argue that while Lacan's notion of mutual desires between mothers and infants need not be excluded as having a major role in development, our interpretation of what is involved in the mirror-stage and language learning could be broader than his. She proposes that a very productive modification to Lacan's theory is to replace the emphasis he gives to language (as system) with an emphasis instead on discursive relations: 'here we are focusing on the ways in which language is implicated in the production of particular regimes of truth, associated with the regulation of specific social practices — such as the practices of the home, the family, the school, the hospital, the world of science, and so on.' (p. 280). For me this is a very pertinent modification of Lacan, for I am concerned with a particular linguistic discourse, that of story-telling. If we look at the entry into language as the entry into sets of discourses, we avoid the 'step-by-step' or 'building blocks' approach to language that is so inadequate to tell us anything about children's narrative competences.

Urwin makes another important modification to Lacan, this time to his account of the mirror-stage. She suggests that the functions of the mirror are 'in part served by the significant adults in the child's life' (p. 286). She sees the formats and routines, the rituals and games between mothers and babies, the exaggerated pitch and tone of Baby-Talk, the facial grimaces and bodily gestures and the conversation which is addressed to babies, as adaptions to the child which 'mirror' her subjectivity for her. She further suggests that the birth of the child may reactivate the mirror-stage in the parent, bringing back into play in interaction with the baby the imaginary relations which Lacan asserted were never really lost as the child learned to speak (p. 293).

Urwin's modification of Lacan at last makes sense of several aspects of pre-linguistic and linguistic development. The mother is no longer playing Peek-a-Boo, or using Baby-Talk, or holding proto-conversations with her baby in order to model for the child the rules of grammar or of turn-taking in conversation. She is mirroring (rather than modelling) the child's subjectivity in an imaginary relation, or, to use Lacan's term, 'a fictional direction', by means of which the child will experience the difference between self and other, between conscious and unconscious, between desire and language, and so be able to take up a position in a world in which

things are signifiable. This formulation not only has the great
advantage that it combines affectivity, social relations and language
in the constitution of the subject, but it also places imaginary
relations — *play* — as the crucial factor in development. In the
concluding part of this chapter I shall attempt to show that young
children's stories are metaphorical mirrors which are able to reflect
several aspects of their inner experiences simultaneously. But first, let
us return to the notion of metaphor as a primary mental process.

Several recent studies suggest that the process of learning
language may be more dependent on the human tendency to make
one word stand for another word, one meaning do double duty for
another meaning, than the word 'metaphor' may at first imply. This
is because we are apt to think of metaphor as the icing on the
linguistic cake rather than as the cake itself. Aristotle took this view,
reserving metaphor as a device for poets, not to be admitted to
ordinary, clear, literal uses of language (*Poetics*, Ch. 22, p. 59). But
we have seen that by describing the poetic *function* of language
(rather than poetry), Jakobson's selective axis of language structure,
whereby speakers choose words on the basis of association of some
kind — similarity, dissimilarity, synonymy, etc. — claims that *all*
language has a metaphoric component. As in Lacan (and in Freud)
doubt is cast on the notion that there *is* a clear literal language which
unambiguously stands in a direct relation to what it refers to. This
idea is familiar from Langer's *Philosophy in a New Key* (1942). Langer
claims that metaphor is the 'vital principle' of language, the 'law of its
life' (p. 141). She claims that what may now be considered a literal
term is in fact a metaphor which has become 'dead' from overuse;
once its original analogous quality has gone we are inclined to see the
term as directly denotative. She suggests that it is the metaphoric
principle of language which has led to the capacity of language to
generalize, abstract and formalize ideas, by a process of stripping
away the original analogous associations so that the concept alone
emerges in the word. This view fits the movement children make in
their language development from the immediate and expressive
towards the more 'disembedded' and abstract uses of language, in the
transition from speech to writing for example (Olsen, 1977). It runs
counter to the psycholiguistic view that they start with a highly
abstract and formal grammar.

Howard Gardner and his associates (1975 and 1978) and Rumelhart (1979) have done some work on young children's use of
metaphor. In one experiment Gardner *et al* discovered that young
children produced a higher number of metaphors than any other age

group, that their metaphors were produced spontaneously without time for deductive reasoning and that their metaphors were often unconventional or even inappropriate. This latter characteristic he attributes to young children's lack of knowledge of the conventions of language use. A limitation of this study is that the concept of metaphor is the Aristotelian one, the rhetorical figure. In their later paper, however, Gardner *et al* extend the notion of metaphor to include verbal symbolic play, and see story-telling as the most promising field for the study of children's metaphoric production, since stories usually include not so much a string of facts but several layers of meaning. Gardner suggests that stories should be studied, not for their plot moves, but for their non-literal qualities. There is an interesting shift between the two Gardner papers, from metaphor as ornamental figure to metaphor as a process situated inside a discourse.

Rumelhart (1979) takes a more radical view. He suggests that initially children have no way of distinguishing between literal and figurative uses of language because *all* language is non-conventional for them at first. He calls for a new account of semantics, one which acknowledges that literal and figurative language interpretation in the beginning depends on knowledge which is much greater than the definitions of the terms involved (p. 83). He derives this conclusion from his work on story grammars. Stories, he says, are not understood by a 'bottom-up' compounding of the separate parts of the story, but in a 'top-down' fashion; to understand a story we bring to it a story schema which is constructed from our knowledge of how stories work. The same is true of learning new words. When the young child talks about 'opening the door' and 'opening the light', there can be no distinction for the child between metaphoric and literal usage since the child does not know the conventions for assigning words to particular domains. This does not mean that everything starts for the child as literal. How could it, since literal uses are decided by convention s/he has not yet learned? Rather, it implies that everything at the beginning is non-literal. Rumelhart's argument is similar to Langer's, that we start with what is metaphorical and end up with what we believe to be referential or literal. Indeed education demands that for many of its discourses this must be so, a point made very forcibly by Walkerdine (1982).

Walkerdine also argues that young children are unaware of the literal/non-literal distinction. She argues that children do not graft words onto familiar objects in a direct relation of signifier to signified. Instead they use processes of signification which are metaphoric. In role-play they try on positions in a variety of discourses (school, hospital, parents and so on) in which they have never taken part in real life. The discourse and all its practices are not negotiated among the children in their play, nor do they need to announce the game and its rules to one another. They take up these new discourse roles spontaneously, just as the children in Gardner's study produce metaphors, and the children in my own study tell stories. Walkerdine suggests that children are able to do this because the opening move of the game acts as the metaphor both for the child's own position in the new discourse and for those of the other participants. In this way different discourse modes are called to mind instantaneously, through the metaphoric, associative principle. Drawing on Jakobson and Lacan, Walkerdine proposes that linguists should give more attention to the axis of selection in language and less to its combinatorial rules.

Space does not permit me to describe the other avenues along which we might travel in an exploration of language and story as metaphor. However, we should look at Miller Mair's reformulation of Kelly's theory of personal constructs in terms of metaphoric processes (1976). We should also look at Bartlett's work, *Remembering*, particularly if narrative is at the centre of our focus on metaphor, for Bartlett's theory that memory is essentially reconstructive and creative, that its basis is affective and that such a theory of memory 'brings remembering into line with imagining' (1932, p. 214), is completely compatible with the view of language explored here. A further area of interest is sociolinguistic or ethnographic; we need to look at the many studies of the forms of verbal duelling, competitive story-telling, ritual insults, rapping and the like, in which linguistic competences which are poetic and figurative are displayed as the symbols of adolescent rites of passage.

Returning to children's stories, both those they hear and those they tell, as metaphors for their lives, a helpful way to bring together the themes of this chapter is to watch Freud watching a child at play (Freud, 1920). Freud observed an 18-month-old boy in the very early stages of language production, a child who never cried when his mother had to leave him. The child had one obsessional game which was to throw away from himself small objects, while at the same time uttering a long, drawn-out 'o-o-o-o!', accompanied by an expression of interest and satisfaction. Freud understood the 'o-o-o' sound as the German word 'Fort' — 'Gone', so the child was playing 'gone' with all his toys. One day Freud saw the child playing 'gone' with a cotton-reel tied to a piece of string. The child would throw the reel very skillfully over the side of his cot, uttering the 'o-o-o' sound, and then pull the reel back into the cot uttering the word 'Da' — 'There'. Freud observed that both the Fort and the Da parts of the game afforded the child great pleasure (p. 284). For Freud the Fort-Da game is the representation of the child's achievement in coping with his mother's absence without protest. However, the child's pleasure was not confined to the symbolic return of the mother, the Da part of the game, since he was seen to play the Fort part far more often and to obtain great pleasure from repeating the unpleasurable part of the experience. Freud's conclusion is that the source of the child's pleasure in his play is the sense of *mastery* it gives him: 'At the outset he was in a *passive* situation — he was over-powered by the experience; but, by repeating it, unpleasurable though it was, as a game, he took on an *active* part' (p. 285). The pleasure of the game lies not only in the child's imaginary mastery over his mother's disappearance, it also represents his revenge on her, his rejection of her; in this way, Freud suggests, play is pleasurable because in it the child can take on the imaginary position of the powerful adult. For Lacan the child in the Fort/Da game achieves his imaginary mastery *linguistically*, by repeating the contrasting phonemes 'Fort' and 'Da'. In this sense linguistic structure itself offers the child mastery, language itself is the mirror which can reflect all the child's meanings in metaphors (Lacan, 1977, p. 103).

Freud's interpretation of the Fort/Da game stresses that in play the pleasure principle, as a double form of mastery, is the driving force; Lacan's account of the Fort/Da game stresses that it is through the *language* of the game that the child is able to achieve his imaginary mastery; and Urwin's reading places the emphasis on the way the child can position herself not in language per se, but in discourses which reverse the power relationships in the child's life (Urwin, 1985, p. 286). All these forms of mastery are offered to children in the discourses of imaginative stories, but how are stories the mirrors of experiences for children?

Story is a reflection of the child's conflicting feelings about her place in the world, as one who is dependent on adults and as one who is in control. For the story quoted at the beginning of this piece Josh (almost certainly unconsciously) drew on two stories he had heard read many times, which had been repeated for him much as the 18-month-old boy repeated the Fort/Da game. They were Sendak's *Where the Wild Things Are*, and Allan Ahlberg's *Burglar Bill*, both powerful stories about these very issues of children's dependence and control. I am not competent to analyze stories in terms of Freudian psychosexual theory, but I don't think that is necessary for us to see the ways in which good stories work as metaphors for children's feelings. Josh's story actually reverses the content of *Burglar Bill*, as if his telling were the mirror-image of the original; the baby finds a father rather than the father (Burglar Bill) finding a baby; the big brown box with little holes becomes a street full of holes, and open space; and the father/burglar becomes a father/policeman. This is not supposition on my part, for Josh uses some of the language of *Burglar Bill* in his narration.

Story is also a demonstration that the key to this reflection of ourselves and our inner lives lies in language; the mirror-world created by the child is a world of words. Not only are syntactic mastery and phonological mastery crucial for the creation of this world (the combinational axis of language), but the metaphoric dimension of language, in which the terms used are significant in the sense of having several layers of meaning, is also crucial. This is why children will not tolerate alterations to the reading of their favourite stories, and why every word matters. Further in stories children are able to create Lacan's 'Ideal-I'. Indeed several 'Ideal-I's' are created, as the child is the narrator of a text which speaks to him, not only as the author of the story, but as all its characters. The heroes and heroines of the great majority of the stories in my data are easily recognizable as fictionalized versions of the story-teller. The opportunity offered to the child for mastery is supreme; the child controls what is told, the order it is told in, who (what kind of narrator) is to tell it, the characters who act and speak it and the response of the listener — look back at Josh's use of 'delaying' clauses in the passage quoted earlier, and at Justine's step-by-step inclusion of larger and larger elements which are consumed by the monster in her story. As author and story-teller the child is all-powerful in the discourse; the two 5-year-olds in my study would tolerate no interjections from adults into their narratives.

The discourses of story-telling pre-exist the child. The culture provides mirrors or metaphors which the child learns to use. It provides ancient symbols — the witch, the giant, the forest, the step-mother — and modern ones — the policeman, the teacher and a host of TV and cartoon characters. It provides rules, rules for structuring stories and rules for delivering them. But stories also offer the child the opportunity to escape the Father's Law by manipulating the rules subversively. I am indebted to Margaret Meek for the insight that children's stories are often replete with excess. It isn't just that children take the opportunity to break the bounds of propriety in what they say, but that they delight in *linguistic* excess. It is what they can make the *words* do in their stories which gives them so much pleasure, not what they make the people do.

When I read the transcripts of the two 5-year-olds in my study, I am aware of a whole array of complex mental operations taking place simultaneously in their story-telling. There are all the different kinds of audience the children are internalizing, there are the many ways in which they are fictionalizing themselves and others, there are the ways in which they interweave stories from books with the stories of their own lives, and then there are the distinctive forms of the language they use, which sound quite unlike anything they would utter in face-to-face conversation. Even at the level of syntax there are unusually complex sentences with multiple embedded clauses. Yet all of this is summoned up on the spur of the moment, with no more than seconds for reflection and no time at all for any kind of rehearsal. A view of language as metaphoric process, and of linguistic interaction as discourses which mirror for us ourselves and our positions in the world, discourses which are called to mind on the instant in the way that, as Lacan says, 'the creative spark of the metaphor ... flashes between two signifiers' (p. 157), this view of language and language use accommodates imaginative stories fully.

For Josh and Sundari the pleasure lies in the many forms of mastery afforded by the space made available to them in narrative. The way they tell their stories is as important as what they say, as they sometimes show when they celebrate their skill in fine words and phrases whose conventional use they do not yet command. Some examples will illustrate this final point, that it is the narrative discourse itself, its sound, the narrative 'voice', which mirrors for the child the metaphors which are stories. It is the tune of the language which counts.

'And then they were lost indeed, till they saw the prettiest house they had never seen' (Josh)

'as you know what also means' (Sundari)

'Once upon a time the Incredible Hulk was walking down by midnight' (Josh)

'Her name was a weary name called Donna and his name was a lovely name called Gregory' (Sundari)

'What was his dismay when he got up there? There was gnashing of teeth' (Josh)

'A little Bo-Peep story was a long time ago told by a little girl' (Sundari)

'And now he looked through his kaleidoscope. What did he see but the English riding away in his boat? (Josh)

'She was so sad she told a nearly crying story, a nearly, nearly, nearly crying story' (Sundari)

'"Poppies will make them grant" said the witch of the East' (Josh)

5 Partners in the Telling

Henrietta Dombey

The received wisdom about early literacy is that those who are read to by attentive adults in the mainstream culture have undoubted advantages when they are faced with the literacy of school. The complex nature of these reading encounters has been made plain elsewhere by Henrietta Dombey who has shown how 'children take on simultaneously new ways of organising discourse, new meanings, new words, and new syntactic forms' (Dombey, 1983, 1986). Here she extends her argument to children being read to in the non-mainstream social context of a nursery school class. Significantly, the teacher's understanding of the importance of books for children and the particular nature of her pedagogy bring about results in this situation comparable with those of more obviously favoured children.

Story-reading is a feature of most primary schools. Its rituals seem to be universal, but there are important differences within this common operation. Here we see how the text of the lesson, as examined by Withers (p. 15) and Mills (p. 32), includes the social coherence of meaning created by the teacher and the children from the lessons of the text.

'I've got tiger stripes too!' shouts Shaun across the nursery classroom, pointing to his jumper. Shaun is just 4 and although physically small is keen to take on all comers in an amiably pugnacious way. He dances from foot to foot, making play with his fists, but as his smile suggests, it is only play. He has been captivated by Polly Cameron's *The Cat Who Thought He Was a Tiger* and his remark, tossed to me across the classroom, suggests that the story has in some way crystallized his image of himself and also suggested new possibilities. He might even settle for some of the restrictions of childhood, just as the cat (actually a stripey kitten) settles for sleeping indoors and feeding from a saucer.

Books have come to hold considerable meaning for Shaun: he no longer thinks of story-time as a tedious interruption of his physical activities. Instead it has become an opportunity to explore new worlds that differ in their laws and possibilities from the world of his first-hand experience, but that nonetheless enable him to understand his own life more richly.

Unlike some of his classmates, Shaun is not always well behaved at story time. Sometimes he does not seem to be listening closely, appearing to be more concerned with tickling Gary or showing off his lorry. But he is very responsive, interjecting 'ohs' and 'ahs' and volunteering appropriate predictions at key points. He also remembers the stories he hears, not merely as a sequence of events, but as the interplay of the emotions and intentions of the characters. Sometimes he shows that he can reconstruct some of the language of the telling. As he turns the pages of a book, his eyes and his fingers reveal that although he is still very hazy on the letters of the alphabet, he has learnt many of the conventions of print.

In short Shaun has learnt some very important lessons about reading. In this chapter I explore some of the features of his experience in a nursery classroom that seem to have contributed to such learning, in particular, his experience of hearing stories read aloud.

The beneficial effect of hearing stories read aloud on children's early reading is now widely recognized, if rather scantily analyzed. For decades it has been earnestly but rather vaguely recommended as a valuable experience, but within the last ten years more precise arguments have been made. Holdaway has shown us that the nightly ritual of a bed-time story can help the child not only to develop an interest in the contents of the books, but also to take possession of their language (Holdaway, 1975). Heath has shown us that the meaning of these stories develops as child and parent make life-to-text and text-to-life moves, illuminating the story with experiences from the child's own life, and enriching the child's first-hand experience with references to events of characters in books (Heath, 1982). Meek has helped us see learning to read as an essentially literary experience, one which is initially made available to the child most richly and most accessibly through such story-reading (Meek, 1982). I have argued that this literary experience is a highly complex multi-level one, in which the child takes on simultaneously new ways of organizing discourse, new meanings, new words and new syntactic forms (Dombey, 1983).

Can we provide this sort of experience in school? Not all

children come to school with a rich experience of hearing stories read at home. Can we give something similar in the nursery class to those children like Shaun whose homes do not include any significant amount of sharing stories from books? Existing studies are not very encouraging. In 1977 Lomax found that in the Scottish nursery classes she studied, children with no extensive experience of stories at home were precisely the ones who tended to choose other activities in preference to listening to stories (Lomax, 1977). Judging 'gains' on the rather narrow and superficial measure of vocabulary increase, she found that when they could be persuaded to listen, children hearing stories in 'controlled conditions' appeared not to have made any significant advances (Lomax, 1979).

Taking a rather more optimistic view, I chose to study Shaun's class because his teacher, Mrs G., is enthusiastic and knowledgeable, about both children's books and about children learning to read. Earlier visits to her class had suggested that she succeeds in communicating her enthusiasm (and also something of her skill) to nearly all the 3- and 4-year-olds who spend the morning or afternoon with her. I was interested to examine more closely what it is that she communicates and how she achieves her success. I reasoned that a careful study of such an apparently successful class might enable us to help more nursery and reception children towards a rich and rewarding initiation into literacy.

This nursery class is not an easy proposition. It is attached to a first school on a depressed housing estate on the fringe of a southern coastal town. The nursery children are principally those nominated by the Social Services Department as having a particular need of some social and educational experience outside the home. Because of a high incidence of unemployment and single-parent families, and a shortage of physical amenities, the estate is designated a Social Priority Area. The children are brought to school by harassed mothers, apparently apathetic fathers or lost-looking elder siblings who have left school but are without work of any sort. There is a bleak and empty quality about the estate that makes the school both a vital meeting place and also the object of regular attacks of vandalism.

As well as Mrs G. the teacher, the nursery class is staffed by Mrs P., a nursery nurse of considerable experience, and a shifting population of mothers, teenagers on work experience schemes, and secondary school pupils learning about the care of young children. It is an orderly place, with a pattern and rhythm that the children appear to appreciate for its predictability. A high level of planning, generous adult help and a separate 'resource area' for noisy activities permit many different things to go on simultaneously, from setting out the dolls' house to cake baking, lego play and sharing story books. The low incidence of disorder, conflict and frustration make this appear like many other well run nurseries. But the experience these children are given of books seems to be rather special. Many nurseries are sparsely equipped with books, in marked contrast to the generous provision of play material. But here the main room has a rich stock of books, mainly picture books, arranged on display stands or in movable boxes at browsing height. The books play a large part in the life of the classroom. During the various free play sessions the children look at them singly or in groups, with or without an adult. This kind of activity increased dramatically from the beginning of the school year and by May visitors were besieged with requests for stories.

Story-reading is also woven into games. Today four children are on a bus driven by a fifth and all except the driver, are 'reading'. Sometimes one or two of the girls sit on Mrs G.'s easy chair, taking on the role of the story-reader as they instruct any children nearby to 'sit on your bottoms' in the ritual story-starting formula of this classroom. For it is Mrs G.'s story times that provide the heart of these children's experience with books.

Usually at about ten o'clock, the 'morning' children tidy away their jigsaws, take off their painting aprons, wipe up the water slopped on the floor and gradually assemble in a wriggling mass on the carpet by Mrs G.'s easy chair. It takes some time to settle them, but Mrs G. generally achieves this by inviting speculation about what kind of story might lie inside the book in her hands, or, if it is an old favourite, by sharing memories of earlier readings. Today, a warm May morning, Mrs G, is holding up a book new to the children, Leo Lionni's *Fish Is Fish*.

The Situation

The situation of this story-reading and others like it is protected. Mrs G. does not set herself in competition with the attractions of the plasticine or the water tray. Distractions are cut to a minimum and although Jeffrey, new to the class and only just 3, is tolerated as he rolls around the edge of the group, Mrs G. tries to ensure that a helper sits with anyone who might distract others, so Mrs P. is sitting with Karen. For Mrs G. wishes to take their minds away from their immediate physical surroundings and help them enter a world constructed through language and pictures alone. She is asking the children to spend the next ten minutes or so with her, in each other's mental company, in a world created by their interactions with the book she is holding in her hands.

Mrs G. recognizes that this is no easy matter for these wriggling, distractible 3 and 4-years-olds who, if Wells' findings are reliable, know language chiefly as a communicative system heavily dependent on its physical context and on the meanings and experiences that are shared between participants who know each other well (Wells, 1981). These children have probably used language principally to converse with members of their immediate families about what is happening around them. Now Mrs G. is asking the children in front of her to make sense of language that stands independent of its physical context and to do so as members of a group whose interests, experiences and ideas about the world vary markedly.

The book in her hands has not been taken from the shelf at random. Often Mrs G. reads old favourites at the request of the children, but today the choice is hers — a book new to all the children and known only slightly to Mrs G. The fishtank by the door with its population of tadpoles and minnows has excited plenty of comment from the children who have stood in little conversational knots in front of it, their eyes and fingers following the movement of the fish and the tadpoles darting between the waving weeds. But subject matter is not Mrs G.'s only criterion. The book has also been chosen for its bizarre and inviting pictures, but above all for its powerful story involving strong emotions in real dangers and including the threat of death.

This then is the situation. It is largely under Mrs G.'s control. She has decided that it is story-time, has decreed that other activities shall cease, has assembled the children and communicated to the adults that she is not to be interrupted. In all these respects it conforms to a pattern well-established in this classroom. Today she has even chosen the title. But what is happening inside the situation? What does the story-telling consist of? For a coherent account of this we need to look at the discourse structure of the language produced, not the patterning of individual utterances, but of the way these fit together and form larger wholes. Close examination of a short extract should reveal something of this patterning. I have chosen this particular extract because of its typicality of the whole story-reading in terms of the patterning I intend to discuss.

The Discourse Structure

In her reading Mrs G. has just got to the point where the fish, propelled by the frog's account of the marvels he saw when he ventured out of the pond, has just jumped onto the bank. I have set out the words of teacher and children on the left-hand side of the page and those of the printed text (together with a brief account of the pictures) on the right-hand side. The unspoken utterances are numbered for ease of reference and the braces indicate simultaneous speech.

Extract from reading of Fish is Fish

	1	T. {He landed in the dry warm	He landed in the dry warm
	2	Ka.{ Don't he?	grass and there he lay
		T. grass{and there he{gasped	gasping for air, unable to
	3	Ka. {Dry {	breathe or to move. 'Help',
	4	{****	he groaned feebly. [*Picture*
		T. and groaned 'cos a fish	*of minnow lying on his back*
		Ka. *********)	*on bank beside pond*]
		T. can't live outside of water for	[*pages 23 and 24*]
		very long.	
	5	He began to die.	
	6	He started to shout 'Help!'	
A	7	Sh. But the frog might push him back.	
	8	T. D'you think he might?	
B	9	Let's find out and see.	
	10	There{he is look!	
C	11	Pa. {Oh!	
	12	T. Lying on his back!	
D	13	Pa. He's showing he's, he's tail	
	14	T. Luckily the frog who'd been	Luckily the frog, who had
		hunting butterflies nearby, saw	been hunting butterflies
		him	nearby, saw him and with
E	15	Pa. No. not near{him	all his strength pushed him
	16	T. {And{had	back into the pond. [*Picture*
	17	An. {And Shaun	*of frog pushing minnow back*
F		was right	*into pond*]
	18	T. You. Shaun was right	[*Pages 25 and 26*]
	19	And with all his strength, you	
		know how when you're feel-	
		ing very strong, with all his	
		strength, he pushed the fish	
		back into the pond.	

G 20   That was a good friend
                       ⎧wasn't it?
    ⎡21 *Sh.* ⎨And he never died, did he?
  H ⎢
    ⎣22 *T.* I don't know.
J   23   Let's turn over the page and
                   find out.
      24   He never died.

Still stunned the fish floated about for an instant. Then he breathed deeply, letting the cool water run through his gills. Now he felt weightless again and with an ever-so-slight motion of his tail he could move to and fro, up and down, as before.
[*page 27*].

As the extract above shows, Mrs G. is not simply delivering a narrative by reciting the words of the text in her hands. Her telling is very different from the presentations on *Play School* or the sound tapes of children's stories available in classrooms, bookshops and libraries. Her telling is essentially an interactive matter. The children are not merely recipients of the telling, but partners in the telling, even though they cannot yet read and have not seen the book before.

This extract has a fragmented appearance typical of the whole story-reading. The narration is broken up by conversation, which is not neatly separate from the narration for there is no orderly pattern of turn-talking, either within the conversation or between it and the narration. Karen cuts across the narration with echoic fragments to which she seems to expect no response. Other contributions seem attempts to snatch a conversational initiative without waiting for a pause, in a way that does violence to the speaker of the moment, usually Mrs G. Anita interrupts her at 17 as does Shaun at 20; at 16 Mrs G. herself interrupts Patrick's legitimately turn-talking contribution. But underneath this apparent disorder there is a certain consistency about Mrs G.'s utterances that gives a shape and a pattern to the whole. To discover what this is I propose to look at the interpersonal patterning, at who is initiating and who is responding, and then at the ideational patterning, at the commodity that is passing between the participants, what it is they are talking about.

Leaving Karen's echoic fragments on one side, I have grouped the conversational utterances into nine exchanges, marked A to J on the transcript. Most of these seem incomplete and therefore ill-formed. In five of the nine exchanges initiations stand alone: they are not followed by overt verbal responses. However, of these five, two are requests by Mrs G. for some investigative attention and thus do not appear to need any verbal response and cannot therefore be judged ill-formed. This leaves three exchanges in which an initiatory utterance does not receive the verbal acknowledgement generally considered necessary. It is worth noting that none of these abortive initiatives is an interruption: two are utterances inserted by Patrick in an apparently appropriate pause and one is Mrs G.'s own question at 20. Furthermore it appears that interruptions, far from being discouraged, are actively encouraged by Mrs G., who responds fully to the interrupting initiatives of Gary and Shaun. Thus the initial impression of disorder seems substantiated in five of these nine exchanges. In these exchanges Mrs. G. seems to be following more often than leading. She initiates only four of the nine, of which one receives a minimal verbal response, two call for no verbal response and one is ignored. She may be the narrator, the one who delivers the text, but in the conversational interaction in which the narration is embedded the children are making the running. They take the greater number of initiatives and seldom accept the subservient, delimited role of responder. Mrs G. is more generous: of the five initiating moves made by children only two are ignored.

This is very different from the classic pattern of teacher initiation child response and teacher feedback, found by Sinclair and Coulthard to typify the exchanges of the junior classroom they studied and by other investigators to typify classroom interaction between teachers and children even at the nursery level (Sinclair and Coulthard, 1975; Heath, 1978).

The role Mrs G. is adopting is very different from the role of a priest conducting responses with a congregation, or a leading counsel interrogating the prisoner in the dock. Despite the formal framework, the ordered situation she has created, she does not insist on the formality of carefully regulated turn-taking, let alone arrogate to herself alone the right to make the opening move in a new exchange. The distribution of initiation and response is more like that between pre-school child and parent at home, where both Wells and Tizard and Hughes have found that children tend to make more opening moves than their parents (Wells and French, 1980; Tizard and Hughes, 1984).

Of course this is not a conversation between one child and an adult, but an adult and four children, the currently vocal section of the group of twenty or so, most of whom remain silent for the duration of the story. These four children, however, all act as if they have conversational rights associated more with home than with school. That this is not simply a matter of slow socialization is suggested by the fact that they have all been in this class for some seven months and also by the very different findings of other nursery studies. But the strongest indication that these children are not transgressing the laws of the classroom is to be found in Mrs G.'s responses.

It cannot be said that Mrs G. is preoccupied with eliciting and rewarding well-formed, turn-talking utterances. Patrick's two contributions, both inserted at pauses in her narration, are explicit utterances, formulated in Standard English, one a syntactically complete sentence, whereas Anita's and one of Shaun's are interruptions, one including a Non-Standard use of 'never'. Yet Anita and Shaun are rewarded by responses to these 'ill formed' contributions whereas Patrick receives no such reward for his law-abiding utterances. So, unlike many teachers as reported in the findings of many investigators, Mrs G. does not appear to be at all concerned with formal niceties. Does this mean that this is merely a disorderly jumble of narration and conversation? To answer this we need to turn to the ideational patterning, to the content of these informal exchanges.

Karen is, of course, wrapped up in her own world. Throughout this story-reading she has taken elements from the pictures and the words of Mrs G.'s narrative and carried these off, magpie-like, to use as starting points for a display of her own private preoccupations — talk about her home, a counting chant and animal noises, all of which Mrs G. studiously ignores as she does her interruptions in this extract.

In both his substantial contributions Patrick is concerned to extend or correct a physical detail in Mrs G.'s reading of the story. He comments that the fish is lying on his back and later tries to correct Mrs G. when she refers in her narration to the frog as 'nearby'. Elsewhere in the reading he is very insistent about biological details, asking where the tadpole's hands are and offering generalizations about tadpoles, frogs, fish and snakes. None of these contributions reveals any concern about what happens in the story. Patrick stays firmly with his own concerns, interpreting objects or events from the story as having a general significance rather than the particular significance conferred by the story. He treats the reading principally as an opportunity to exchange biological information. In her failure to respond to his initiatory moves, Mrs G. implicitly declares that such contributions have no validity in this situation.

But what Shaun and Anita have to say is very different. Shaun's strikingly appropriate first contribution at 7, 'But the frog might push him back', is a tentatively expressed prediction of what is to happen at this, the turning point of the story: it is the culmination of his close and constructive attention to all that has been narrated up to this point. Shaun is making a complete whole of what he hears and going well beyond the information he has been given. Mrs G.'s response does more than merely tolerate this contribution. In redefining the rest of the reading as a process of finding out whether Shaun is right, she endorses what he has said as centrally relevant.

When Anita interrupts her narration at 17 with the confident assertion that Shaun was right, her topic is the act of prediction itself, and again Mrs G. validates the contribution by her response. Shaun's interruption at 21 is another powerful and centrally important prediction and is accorded the highest status by Mrs G. as she reduces the complex and subtly ornate description of the printed text to the stark formulation of Shaun's own words, 'He never died.'

Mrs G.'s criteria of what makes a contribution acceptable clearly have less to do with form than with function. It is meaning she is concerned with, not the niceties of turn-talking. In her responses she legitimizes precisely those contributions that help her forward the narrative. She accepts only contributions that concern the kernel events, those central to the narrative structure. The peripheral events, the satellites of Barthes' model, are left to wither ignored (Barthes, 1975). This is not to say that she has an unalterable notion of the narrative under construction. Despite her privileged position of holding the book in her hands and being the only one who can read, she is prepared to allow different readings. After Shaun's first intervention, her initiative at 20 shows that the story has become for her a tale of friendship, a nursery version of The Good Samaritan where the act of friendship matters more than its practical outcome. None of the children responds to this initiative despite the request for assent in the tag question at the end. For them perhaps as for Shaun what matters is the culminating event, the rescue of the central character from danger. In her adoption of the words of Shaun's interrupting prediction she sanctions the acceptability of this alternative reading.

The Educational Value of This Kind of Discourse

Investigators have suggested that children not from the dominant culture become comparatively unsuccessful participants or even bemused bystanders in the discourse of the primary classroom (Gumperz, 1981; Michaels, 1981; Heath, 1982). It seems that teacher–controlled classroom discourse concerns topics, practices and discourse forms more familiar to children from the dominant culture. Children from other cultures fail to operate successfully not only because of the unfamiliarity of the rules of acceptability, but because these remain largely implicit (Michaels, 1981). Teachers may give partial explanations such as 'Share some one thing that's very important' or 'Speak slowly and in correct sentences', but the children may not know what the teacher means by such central explanatory terms as 'important' or 'sentence', and so are no wiser.

However, Mrs G. prefaces every story-reading with an invitation to the children to join her in finding out what happens and it is in terms of this finding out that their contributions are judged for their relevance. Despite occasional lapses, it seems that with the exception of Karen and Patrick these children have learnt this rule, or rather have agreed to observe it, perhaps because it gives coherence, significance and satisfaction to story-time. Mrs G.'s rule is not a piece of apparently arbitrary etiquette, nor is it a mechanism for holding the children in a subordinate position; it concerns the creation of order in children's minds rather than a more easily observable order in behaviour. It grows out of a recognition that if the story and its telling are right, the action of narrative construction can be one that involves the deepest interests and concerns of young children and can result in a profound sense of satisfaction in the restoration of order, justice and safety to the fictional world.

This is not, of course, the only way stories are read to a nursery class. When Mrs G. is absent the substitute teacher does not elicit the same constructive attention. She seems intent not on developing a narrative collaboratively, but on delivering an unalterable text, followed up by an interrogation in which she attempts to elicit 'factual' information, setting herself up as judge of the correctness of the children's answers. Teacher initiation, pupil response and teacher feedback form the pattern of the day. For the children story-time becomes the occasion not for active construction, not for giving a shape to what they hear, but instead for mechanically registering details and responding to direction. Since all the events are flattened by being given equal significance, the emotional colouring of the whole is lost. The substitute teacher strives to ensure that the children have grasped the correct sequence of events, but they wriggle and poke each other as any overt attempt by them to construct a narrative is rebuffed gently but firmly and the story is reduced to a recitation of 'the facts'.

For Mrs G. the narrative is not a fixed sequence of 'facts' but a story of danger and friendship. The essential work of constructing or 'reading' the narrative is one that inevitably involves active engagement. By her words and her actions she models for the children how a reader sets about this business. She presents not a carefully rehearsed recitation of the text followed by an interrogation of the children, but an interrogation of the text, conducted out loud with invitations to the children to join her in this enterprise. She is doing out loud and with others something of what we all do silently and by ourselves when we read a novel or short story. Elsewhere in this reading she makes the text-to-life and life-to-text moves of which Heath writes. But here she is focusing on displaying to the children how to give coherence and significance to a text, and inviting them to join her as active participants.

It seems that Mrs G.'s goal is to focus on meaning conceived in a complex way as the meaning of the whole narrative and to hand over a large measure of control over that meaning to the children in front of her. Within the tightly structured situation she has set up she takes a comparatively self-effacing role, acting as responder to all the initiatives she considers relevant and even allowing the children's initiatives to intrude on and modify the words of the printed text. She may be the judge of acceptability in terms of her publicly stated rule of relevance, but she is not the arbiter of correctness. She does not label Shaun's predictions as right or wrong, but points the children towards the text that is to come as the source of the key information, thus enabling them to make such judgments for themselves.

As far as Shaun is concerned, the success of this endeavour is surely indicated by the aptness of his contributions. While he has yet to develop a confident familiarity with the syntax and lexis of the written word in general and of such narratives in particular, he has mastered some very important narrative conventions. Later that morning he reveals that he is under no illusions about the likelihood of any of the frogs giving material assistance to a minnow stranded on the rock in the classroom fishtank. But he knows that in a fictional world when Character B has been introduced as Character A's friend, he is very likely to step forward to help Character A out of danger, and that such an action will be successful. When Mrs G. asks him at the end of the story how he has come by such knowledge Shaun answers confidently, 'I just knew.'

His two predictions are expressed in very different ways. The first is tentative, a possibility not a certainty, formulated in the present tense that we use when we talk of what is possible and imminent. It is the voice of a spectator who feels an excited uncertainty about the outcome of events. The second prediction, however, is a statement of certainty in which Shaun adopts the sure voice of Genette's classical subsequent narration (Genette, 1980).

Anita is eagerly involved in notching up Shaun's successes, but the rest of the children are relatively quiet today. However, their quietness and apparent intentness on discovering the outcome suggest that they too are involved in an active process of meaning-making and that Shaun is doing out loud what many are doing to some degree internally. Their silence does not necessarily imply passivity. Mrs G.'s stories provide the source for rich dramatic games and the inspiration and model for talking their way through books on their own. Later in the day there are games on the climbing frame that involve children helping each other to safety, and at the end of the morning two of these silent children, Esella and John, help one puppet 'read' the story to another, telling a tale of crossness, sadness, fear and happiness.

Mrs G.'s story-time is surrounded by formality, created out of her shaping intentions. But inside this formality the only rule that governs is the rule of relevance and this is both conceived as something more complex and powerful than the recitation of the facts and also communicated clearly and repeatedly to the children. The children are not bound by the formality of turn-taking, nor confined to the role of response-givers. It is precisely the informality lying inside the formality of this situation that enables them to take the initiative and thus to take possession of the story.

6 'No, I'm the Draw Master'

Gillian Beardsley

Gillian Beardsley uses insights drawn from discourse analysis, sociolinguistics and cultural studies to redefine some of the early understandings of literacy that young children have as they enter school. Choosing extended and collaborative play as a site for analysis, she shows how mutuality of purpose is developed as the children share their understandings of reading and writing, and of what they think that these processes intend. The chapter indicates the ways in which patient observation can help to unravel the tacit knowledge we used naively to gloss as 'pre-reading skills'.

The setting is a post office. I am standing in the queue together with other customers including a number of parents with young children. At the side the post office video is playing for our benefit. Message after message coming across in waves of words and visual presentations, from buying stamps to holiday information and advertisements for insurance. The children playing at the foot of the TV pedestal are occasionally looking at the screen, asking questions of parents and grandparents and noticing stamps, letters, booklets and money changing hands. They see actions and literacy events taking place on the edge of other activities and, even though not directly attending to them, are absorbing some of their current literacies.

Recently much attention has been given to the literacy experiences of pre-school children. Alongside this a view of literacy has developed encompassing a world where print and symbols of print are constantly changing in relation to their social functions. The instructional symbols for operating washing machines, videos, microwaves, bank cashpoints and computer terminals have become as much a part of the systems of meaning around us as clothes labels, free offers and presentations of different life styles as depicted by the media. Literacy is no longer seen as a unitary ability, but as a series of competences involving not only reading and writing but also the interpretation of new formats which arise from and are an integral part of our everyday lives.

Here in the post office children are learning to be literate in their encounters with the social nature of literacy as it exists in the world outside school. To the onlooker it is a familiar and unremarkable scene. Yet as a teacher and teacher trainer I wonder what else it can tell us about how children understand and interpret their culture and the different presentations of literacy which occur within it. Are there also messages here which may be more significant than we realize and which need to be a part of our knowledge of early literacy learning?.

One of the values of the ethnographic work of Heath (1983) has been in showing that reading is a way of taking from the culture, and that there are variations in 'ways of taking' both generally and specifically from different social contexts. The post office, the home, the playgroup and the school all provide settings in which literacy events may occur, but because our view of literacy is changing the ways in which we interpret it are having to change too. It is only when we explore some of these familiar situations in different ways that we can begin to appreciate the new directions in what is taking place and in how we explain them.

If we look at settings where children behave as if they could nearly read and write, we can watch what they do with what they clearly know about reading and writing. Then we should be able to see what they think reading and writing are and are for. So far what has not emerged is information on the precise nature of the children's understandings. We therefore need to examine the social, semiotic and cultural practices in the situation where early literacy is to be seen. Then we can begin to describe the distinctive nature of these literacy practices and their relationships to the social practices from which they are derived.

It is highly likely that many pre-school children acquire literacies for which there is no immediate purpose; for example, knowledge of the sequence of advertisements or associating symbols with land-marks on the way to see Granny. These things may become part of their behaviour in other situations as they play and take on the experiences with which they have become familiar. Looking at such episodes of their play could help us to foreground understandings which have not previously been given prominence.

Literacy is changing, but play is a constant factor in which children signal competence, knowledge, ease, familiarity or all of these, and incorporate elements of the cultural context from which they draw their concerns as they interact with one another and exchange ideas. From amongst the many play activities children engage in, fictive play perhaps most effectively reflects their awareness of episodes in their lives. An example of such play can be considered in its totality and enable us to be situationally analytic in interpreting the conscious and unconscious demonstrations of cognitions and affects within it. As Bretherton points out. 'The fictive world of play is more fruitfully studied in a multi-modal phenomenon with different symbol systems serving complementary not necessarily parallel functions' (1984 p. xii). In the following transcript, using insights from the social context, the discourse and the culture, I shall try to uncover the things which may help us to see what constitutes children's perceptions of literacy. These are not immediately apparent, and they have not previously counted as evidence, but a closer examination of them may give us greater knowledge of young children's literacy understandings. By looking at an example of some length, we can begin to appreciate particular characteristics of these understandings and the nuances of meaning within them, as well as the significance of what is taking place.

The Setting

Three boys, Christopher, Adam and Alex, attended the same playgroup, and had been used to playing together for about a year. They frequently engaged in imaginative play with a variety of large and small toys, and according to playgroup policy this was rarely circumscribed or directed.

The playgroup was held in a large church hall next to the school where the children were to enter the reception class the following term. Three weeks before the transcript was taken, the boys' parents had attended a meeting at this school and had been given information on its general aims, suggestions concerning their children's transition into the reception class and details of the reading and writing schemes in operation. The 'Letterland' scheme was used to introduce children to individual letters through the use of pictograms. This material, produced by Lyn Wendon (1978), is part of a phonic approach to reading. It uses pictorial representations to depict individual letters. Wendon draws the Hairy Hatman to represent 'H', while 'W' is represented by the Wicked Waterwitch. The cards on which these pictograms are drawn were shown and explained to the parents, who were also given pictogram sheets to practise recognition of the letters and to talk about them with their children.

During the play sessions I observed, the boys were encouraged to use three puppets and to show them how to participate in whatever activity they were engaged in. Felt tipped pens, pencils, paper and envelopes were always available in case the children wanted to use them, and this varied according to the ways in which their play developed. On this occasion we were in a small room off the main hall. Various trains, coaches and tracks were put out for them, as well as timetables, tickets, writing materials and the tape recorder. I sat at the side of the room in order to observe what took place, an arrangement the children were used to and accepted.

In this particular episode the children came into the room and Alex immediately went to the pens and paper and began writing his name and other letters, e.g., 'A a p p q t t'. Early in the transcript he also tried some numbers copied from the train timetables with the help of Adam, but as the train theme developed he continued to write letters on different pieces of paper, some of which were put in envelopes and others were folded and given to the puppets. This continued throughout the session. Adam and Christopher were also interested in the timetables, but as an adjunct to their play, and once into the theme they were more engaged in developing the sounds and actions. The discourse thus emerged from opportunities for play in a familiar social environment, and from the children's interactions as they organized and shaped their theme.

Alex, Adam and Christopher, Aged 4 Years

1	C.	I'm going on the rail travel, I'm going by rail travel, rail travel.	C. sets up some tracks with his
2	Ad.	What are these called?	puppet. Ad. and Al. are using pens and writing on the paper train time-tables.
3	Al.	Books, for the train.	
4	Ad.	You can't do this one, you can't do this one. Do you want me to show you?	

5	*Al.*	Er	Adam shows Alex
6	*Ad.*	You watch this.	how to write
			numbers from the
			timetable.
7	*Al.*	I got it — down — up.	
8	*Ad.*	That's a number.	
9	*Al.*	Yes.	
10	*Ad.*	That's a number I've done that.	
11	*Al.*	I've done a 3 — 1, 2, 3. I can do it number 3.	
12	*C.*	I'm going to build a diesel railway — that one there.	
13	*Ad.*	I'll be the station master. I'll give these to the people to tell them where we going. Here you are for your train.	Timetables. To his puppet.
14	*Al.*	Get in the train. Christopher, Christopher get in the train, get in the train.	
15	*C.*	Get in the train.	
16	*Ad.*	Get in the train now before we go out. You can draw a picture if you want	To Alex.
17	*Al.*	Yes that's ...	
18	*Ad.*	We will be off in a couple of minutes when I just phone the station to tell them we are coming at 50 miles an hour. Hang on ...	Phones and looks surprised.
19	*Al.*	The line's broke I can see ... the line's broke of the telephone you can't phone him.	
20	*Ad.*	I can phone.	
21	*Al.*	It's broke the lead/puffer.	
22	*C.*	The workmen are coming. Do you know why the workmen are coming? Because the stationmaster can't phone up the station cause the wires are down — they're broken.	Aside to observer.
23	*Al.*	I told you the wires are broken — master. Won't be no use.	

24	*Ad.*	Nobody yet at the station. We're off now so you had better sit in there. We're off quick — you in that train as well.	To Alex.
25	*Al.*	No I'm the draw master. I draw these things to tell them where we going.	
26	*Ad.*	Do you?	
27	*Al.*	I do after our next, after we've been visited.	
28	*C.*	Whistle!	Adam makes the
29	*Al.*	Yes I know.	train noises for starting and going through the journey.
30	*Ad.*	This one's going fast. You know this ... you know that train, well you're on this train that one goes fast, you on this train now [*whistles*].	
31	*Al.*	Rice Crispie train.	
32	*Ad.*	We're there.	
33	*Al.*	Right ho Master. You can go now. Don't forget you time book.	To Christopher.
34	*C.*	No.	
35	*Al.*	That tells you when we're leaving.	
36	*C.*	Alright.	
37	*Al.*	Your train book.	
38	*Ad.*	While you go shopping, while you go shopping I'll grab some dinner. Go on then go shopping just pretend.	
39	*C.*	We go on this train.	Moving to other side of the room.
40	Al.	I'm, I going to stop here I am.	
41	*Al.*	You have to go home and I have to have my dinner, in the train. You go in your house. You go in your house and have your dinner. We stay on the train and have our dinner don't we?	To Christopher.

42 *Al.* Yes. There nice there the train things you know Sooty and Sweep and Sue has these.   Looking at time-tables.

43 *Ad.* Where are your letters please?

44 *Al.* I've made one of my books — give me it back after — right.

45 *Ad.* He got one.

46 *Al.* They're for passengers not you driver.

47 *Ad.* I know I'm giving these to ....

48 *Al.* It tells you where you want to go

49 *Ad.* I give you that in case you can't remember where you are going. It's got lots of things in it for you.   To observer.

50 *C.* [*Sings*] Rail travel, rail travel, rail travel, rail travel.

51 *Ad.* There I'll give that to the other Master.

52 *Al.* Thanks driver they're to give to people.

53 *Ad.* I've got those sort.

54 *Al.* That's what I've just done that is.

55 *Ad.* Do you want to do some more for me?

56 *Al.* Yes I'm doing one. I hope we go to Letterland!

57 *Ad.* After that other Masters got some ....

58 *Al.* Have you got Letterland Adam?

59 *Ad.* What?

60 *Al.* Have you got Letterland cause I have.

61 *Ad.* Eh?

62 *Al.* I got more than you.

63 *Ad.* What?

64 *Al.* I got more than you.

65 *Ad.* What?

66 *Al.* You heard, Letterland.

67 *C.* Yes Letterland.

68 *Al.* I've got more Letterland cause my Dad got me some.

69 *Ad.* There's Worcester there, and   To observer.
write some numbers there and it
will say where you want to go.

This example of children playing can reveal insights on how they read the literacy messages they have encountered. What they are demonstrating is literacy as it has been presented to them within the daily contexts in which they find themselves. For Adam, and Christopher this has arisen both from their shared knowledge of the many cultural manifestations of a particular train story and from the ways in which their parents have interpreted literacy for them.

Christopher's singing through parts of the example served to remind all the children of the external aspects of their play and their previous train experiences. The TV literacies which bring alive *Thomas the Tank Engine* create a culture which they all share. Recently a group of my first-year students used the *Thomas* stories with children in infant classes. In collecting material and talking with the children they became fascinated by the whole culture of *Thomas* in the form of clothes, toys, continental quilts, pyjamas, tablecloths, placemats, mugs, pens and notebooks, as well as the tape book packages and the TV series. It soon became clear that *Thomas the Tank Engine* was not just a character in a book but a whole way of life. It was not just a book that was introducing Christopher to literacy, but a mesh of understandings drawn from popular culture!

To fully appreciate the ways in which the children were using this aspect of their culture we can draw upon theories from both sociolinguistics and discourse analysis to reveal the underlying meanings within the structures and organization of their activities. Malinowski's (1935) notions of the 'context of situation' and the 'context of culture' taken up by Halliday (1978), are valuable in identifying elements which interrelate to form the setting and to determine the development of the discourse. Halliday's (1978) use of the construct of 'situation type' in sociolinguistic theory provides us with a framework through which to examine the characteristics not only of the nature of the social action through which the children are exchanging their meanings, but also of the relationships and forms of language determining their choices and decisions. It is the situation which helps to determine the 'text' or 'instances of linguistic interaction', but this can only be developed in relation to its social context or the meanings around it. The context thus provides the link between situation and text, 'though a systematic relationship between the social environment on the one hand and the functional organisation of the language on the other' (Halliday, 1978).

Context

An episode of this length enables us to appreciate the characteristics of the play situation and the elements of the culture which are embedded in the context of the train theme. In arguing for the culturally relative aspects of play, Sutton–Smith (1984) confirms it to be a 'framed event', but suggests that 'in play the metacommunicative function always retains primacy.' It can be distinguished by a combination of cues that make it clear that the participants recognize the situation they are in to be one of play.

In his opening metaphor (1) and again in (12) Christopher signals a focus for the children's activities by introducing a possible topic. Adam (13) and Alex (14) take up the message and show their acceptance of the idea, but at the same time change its nature through introducing roles and establishing the specific train personnel of passengers and stationmaster, thus framing the play as a recognizable train game. This framing is a particularly important element in the transcript because it enables the children to explore their own interests within a known theme.

Early in their play they abandoned the thematic objects for a more imaginative activity where only the puppets as participants, the telephone, timetables and writing materials were used. Rather than a context shared because of the objects available to them, these children were drawing upon representations which were part of their common culture. The concept of 'script' used by Nelson and Seidman (1984) helps to explain the ways in which such shared representations are organized within children's play activities. Scripts were 'composed of a sequence of acts organised around goals and specifying actor roles props and scenes', and were based upon experimental knowledge. Nelson *et al* (1984) found that once the script was suggested it served as a background framework in which the participants were able to play their roles and develop the theme. Within such a shared script the need to clarify meanings is reduced.

Once into their play script after (12), Christopher, Alex and Adam were able to maintain their exchange of meanings throughout the episode. However, this did not preclude some important clarifications by Alex (19, 21), Christopher (22) and Adam (11, 30, 41). These explanations appeared to have a definite purpose in developing the play along prescribed lines and in clarifying content rather than their place within it, again suggesting some previous experience they wished to pursue.

Walkerdine's (1982) argument that the context is the critical feature of the signification and an essential part of the language and thinking taking place was particularly apparent in the way in which, once the discursive context had been established, the children were operating and taking positions within it using the roles of that domain. Alex (23) calls Adam 'Master' a shortened form of station-master and throughout the episode the children refer to one another not only by name but also by the roles they have chosen for themselves. Alex established his role clearly (25) and gave his writing activities a purpose within the framing of the play, but this was confirmed for him by Adam (43, 51) when he gives a definite function to the papers Alex has produced.

The ability to change role without announcing it explicitly and have this recognized by other participants was also demonstrated by the children. Adam (26–32) moved from stationmaster to driver by using train noises and announcing 'we're there', which was picked up by Alex who then referred to him as 'driver' (46). The context was in no way external but was regulating the signifying features within it. Only Adam steps out of this and takes on an attitude of play when he tries to persuade the others to adopt his ideas (38), but this shows not only his awareness of the imaginary aspect of the situation but also his need to develop the sequence in his own way.

The context of the train game was at no time external for Alex, who, although keen to write, was always involved as a participant in the script. Just as the language, thinking and context were inseparable parts of the signification for him, so were his interpersonal and ideational understandings as he drew out the area he was most interested in (56). He uses the discourse to frame and explore his new knowledge and his insertion of the topic of 'Letterland' is in keeping with his awareness of the perimeters of it within the game. This supports Nelson *et al.* (1984) in their conclusions that shared script knowledge not only encourages coherent play but also enables children to make transformations from it.

The registers, vocalizations and tones used by the boys provided further cues to their involvement and knowledge of the script they had established for themselves. Both the train noises and tones of voice to suit the characters were used by Christopher (15, 60) and Adam (8, 24). Clearly children as young as this are still learning the principles of negotiation with their peers (McTear, 1985). The ability to initiate, respond and take account of preceding talk, as well as question and reason, are part of the skills required for the construction of conversational exchanges. Throughout this episode there was a high level of competence in turn-taking which, although an expected development in young children's conversations, was nevertheless sustained with almost no closed examples. As in general play sequences amongst young children the turn-taking tended to be fairly rapid, but there were also some extended utterances which served to summarize (Christopher, 22) and extend the content (Adam, 24, 30, 41), as we shall see in a closer examination of the discourse strategies they used.

Discourse

Any consideration of children's conversations must take account not only of individual utterances but also of their shaping within the coherence and overall structure of the episode. To sustain dialogue children need to be able to develop their exchanges into connected discourse. The boys achieved this through the use of cohesive devices, conversational turn-taking and repairs.

The children made use of cohesive devices to maintain their semantic meanings across utterances and to carry on their interpretations of the script. Alex's (25) use of pronouns to refer back to the timetables and puppets was reflected in 'these things tell them where we are going.' Adam (30) acknowledges the existence of the two trains by referring to the one he is driving, 'you're on this train, that one goes fast.' Some use was also made of ellipsis (16, 17, 47) to maintain the flow of the talk as in Adam's case (16), when he also used it to follow up his own script theme. Having acknowledged Alex's place within it, 'You can draw a picture if you want ....' he hurries on, leaving out the prepositional element in his concern to complete his utterance (18).

A more sophisticated use of cohesion, causality, was used only once, but was employed most strikingly by Christopher (22) in perhaps one of the longest utterances of the episode. His remark is unlike other parts of the dialogue because he stepped outside it and became the narrator. He was using what Labov (1972) describes as an 'abstract' or utterance which provides a summary or encapsulation of the dialogue. It is this strategy and his observation (28) of Adam's train noise that begin to confirm his more objective interpretation of the play in terms of his own version of a narrative.

The contribution made by both Christopher (22) and Adam (41) also suggested a knowledge of themes explored in previous train experiences. As Walkerdine (1982) points out, the historical and social dimensions must be included to understand fully the discourse taking place. Viewing it as part of a series of similar discourses helps us to appreciate its position for the children within their activities.

The episode is sustained particularly well through the children's competence in turn-taking and their ability to make conversations joint productions. Adam and Alex used both appreciation and questioning not only to maintain their dialogue but also to make sure the other speakers were following (51–56). A further feature in the turn-taking is the timing which enables the participants to respond appropriately. Alex and Christopher (33–37) gave a polished timed series of exchanges where Christopher, clear in his role as passenger, adopted a distance voice as if he was walking away, and again interpreted it according to his experiential background. This is what Vygotsky (1978) would interpret as memory–in–action rather than as a novel imaginary situation.

One of the most crucial points in the situation for Alex was the change in theme which occurred during the Letterland sequence (56–68). Requests for clarification can act as conversational repair mechanisms when the first speaker has an opportunity to carry out the repair. Although the non-specific requests used by Adam are perhaps the simplest of the request strategies (McTear, 1985), Alex's ability to respond by grammatically extending his repair over several utterances was competent. At the same time Alex maintained the semantic sense of it for himself and showed his affective concern with the topic rather than a real attempt to make his utterance more comprehensible for Adam. He was expecting shared knowledge, and although his second question (60) was made slowly with careful articulation, he began to lose patience and almost shouted his response (66). Only Christopher's intervention gave him the motivation he needed to finish the sequence.

Although the children's ability to sustain dialogue through the episode can be explained in terms of the discourse strategies they had at their disposal, it becomes clear that this emerged within the coherence of their script knowledge. We now turn to the kinds of experiences which had enabled them to select this particular semantic content and develop their game.

Culture

Throughout this transcript the children were engaged in a process of semantic choice which enabled them to re-enact their social and cultural understandings. Thus we have a dynamic situation in which they were not only playing imaginatively, but were interpreting aspects of the literacies they had already encountered. We perhaps underestimate the effects of representations such as television and tape and book packs in relating print and spoken narratives in the young child's repertoire. Hearing the voice of the story-teller while reading the *Thomas* culture through television animations and words and pictures in the book is a powerful way of making those associations. It is part of 'a continuous stream of images almost all of which are deeply familiar in structure and form' (Fiske and Hartley, 1978). It becomes no accident that Alex can interject: 'The line's broken I can see', and 'It's broke the lead/puffer', and Christopher can comment on the action and bring in the workmen. Later Adam says, 'I'll grab some dinner', all suggestions reminiscent of the particular narratives they have heard. They also seem to have a very clear picture of these previous encounters which enables them to introduce and take up ideas with confidence. In Adam's case in a later part of this play sequence he makes use of the actual text when he refers to 'That fat chap' as from the fat director in several of the *Thomas* stories. The children were therefore using those common aspects of their culture, admittedly not shared by all children, but available within the social environment, and were reworking their experiences of the literacies they had met.

Through this reading of a series of narratives with which they were all familiar they were able to adopt different forms of behaviour with confidence. Using the telephone and writing timetables were carried out with certain expectations of what might follow and became an integral part of their understandings, as did the sequencing of the episode in the form of a story narrative. We have to acknowledge the many possibilities the culture can offer in enabling young children to acquire literacy competences. As Carol Fox's (1986) work has confirmed, children by the end of their fifth year have internalized 'some surprisingly sophisticated modes of telling which are derived straight from children's literature.' I would suggest that they are also internalizing behaviour which is drawn directly from these many different presentations of their culture and are able to produce it in a highly competent way.

However, within this example Alex was demonstrating another

aspect of the literacy culture around him. He was involved in behaviour directly associated with print and part of the literacy of his future school. An important distinction is made by Harste and Burke (1984) between literacy which is experienced as a language encounter by an onlooker, and a language encounter in which the child is directly involved. Alex in his attempt to use his direct encounter with 'Letterland' is wanting to demonstrate and try out his new knowledge. The experience of meeting the Letterland characters in a focused situation within his own, where it was given some importance, made it a central concern for him. This introduces a further direction in our thinking, the view of parents and the way in which this is expressed as they encourage their children to become literate.

In the space of three weeks Alex, Adam and Christopher had encountered literacy messages in a more focused way through the use of precise characters to represent the letters in 'Letterland'. In different ways their parents were placing emphasis upon it as they were upon reading picture books, but because 'Letterland' provided a distinctive set of skills it enabled them to introduce a more direct form of activity, and one specifically related to their children's future literacy learning in school. We now need to see what effect this had on the kinds of activities which Alex in particular was concerned with in his play.

Alex

I have argued that the three boys were engaged in play of a kind which could only arise because of the specific social practices which influenced the semantic and grammatical choices they made within it. Nevertheless, for Alex a great deal was happening both cognitively and affectively which might be described in other ways. He was involved in an activity which was for him serious and absorbing and at no point did he detract from it. Initially he appeared to be wrestling with a problem, that of writing numbers and letters and of making the distinction between them (7–11). The fact that he was in a state of cognitive dissonance over this was evidenced by his relief in copying the numbers correctly and his need to continue to try writing the letters he had learnt at home (11). He was thus engaged in an active discovery of the letters he could remember and write down and was being what Clay (1983) would term a 'constructive learner' in the development of his own competence.

Through his writing Alex was learning an important part of the symbol system within his culture. Gardner (1984) postulates the development of competence in the use of different symbol systems as occurring through a series of psychological processes of 'waves' of symbolization. Initially the child gains knowledge of numerous symbolic representations but by around the age of 4 there is a marked change when he becomes capable of 'notational symbolization', and is prepared to invent simple notations to aid his tasks using known channels of symbolization as a means of sorting out information in a precise way. Gardner stresses: 'the child is engaged in earnest in obtaining the symbol skills of his culture, and in a sense the fun is over' (p. 310). Alex in his concentration on the formation and writing of his letters was not only involved in mastery but was trying to make sense of his experiences in terms of his own theories of the world. The culture had begun to intrude upon his unconscious acquisition of the representations around him by providing a focused channel of symbolization through which to operate.

Through the framework of his play Alex was able to practise the things he would become competent in later on and in this 'zone of proximal development' (Vygotsky, 1978) could pretend that what he produced was a correct representation of the timetables. What also emerged from the transcript was Alex's concentration and single-mindedness for his activity. While Adam and Christopher took on different roles as the script developed, Alex at no point stepped out of the character he had established for himself. His concentration undoubtedly enabled him to make some important progressions in his levels of understanding of the symbolic representations. He was not only engaged in transcribing numbers and letters but was learning to make distinctions between them. At the same time Gardner's third wave of 'quantitative mapping' was in evidence in his attempts to get the elements of the writing precisely correct. As Ferreiro and Teberosky (1983) found in their studies of pre-school children's knowledge of writing, a logic was applied to what they were doing. The restriction in the stock of known letters and the avoidance of using the same letter more than twice were evident in the letters Alex produced and to which Adam referred (43).

Once Alex had experimented with the properties of his letters he was able to engage in variations in the way in which he used his activity. He knew the functions of print and was able to demonstrate and emphasize this (33, 35). There was a sequence in his writing development which was explored and developed through his play and culminated in the introduction of 'Letterland', bringing out the real event in his life which had motivated his activity. Even then he disguised it by relating it within the structure of the play, giving it a legal form (56) before attempting to confirm its relevance with the other children. His play demonstrations involved both mental exploration and make-believe, which Bretherton (1984) suggests are 'different facets of the same representational functions.'

Looking at this episode helps us to appreciate the cultural characteristics which are entwined in the play of these young children. Their understandings incorporate all the different presentations of literacy as they meet them, and clearly reflect their ability to read the messages within their social contexts. As teachers our understandings of how children learn to read and write are already undergoing change, but if we want to acknowledge the things children already know about literacy we need to be able to view it in different circumstances and appreciate the specific competences and behaviours which are being played out. This requires careful analysis of the situations in which these behaviours occur and of the ways in which children use their encounters in both actions and discourse.

We also need to be aware of the kinds of messages which parents and teachers are giving to children about what literacy is and is about. Although we are able to look at what they do in different ways and appreciate the many nuances of meanings, there are still areas which are unknown and questions to be raised. How will these children use their knowledge of current literacies to explain their world when they enter formal schooling? What use will be made of these pragmatic literacies, and how will Alex use his hard-won knowledge as he comes to terms with the literacy demands which are made upon him?

The concentration and enthusiasm these children displayed in their play is an important element in their later motivation and one infant teachers are keen to develop and maintain. It would seem important that, in appreciating the knowledge pre-school children coming to school have gained during their first five years, we should look at their behaviour not only in terms of focused expectations of literacy skills. By observing children when they play we have a rare opportunity to appreciate both their outward demonstrations of the literacy encounters in their lives and the processes through which they strive for expression and mastery.

Part 3: Girls and Boys

As soon as they recognize themselves in the presence of others, children know that there are girls and boys. Despite moves by their elders to modify the differences — themselves a manifestation of changes in understanding — prevalent cultural practices, and language itself, confirm gender roles, especially within families. By asking questions about themselves, children begin to reinforce and make oppositional their gender-related awareness of humankind. During the last decade the examination by Unwin, Walkerdine and others of the individualism of child-centred education has added impetus to a perceived need to include gender as an important element in the study of the socialization of children as they grow to school age.

Gender roles are foregrounded in the next three essays. The children, Ben, Sarah, Jessie and Lucy, in what they do, say, sing, write and play, carry important topical discussions about the individual and the social as they explore what it is to be male and female. Ben's maps, Sarah's writing and the girls' playground domain are places of deep play and rich metaphor, to be linked with Carol Fox's analysis.

Myra Barrs sees in Ben's synpraxic speech and in the diagrams of his warlord games the early stages of notational symbolism which his later schooled literacy will replace with writing. Ben has also discovered a form of dramatic narrative and story-telling dialogue, half communicative, half inner speech which reflects his growing awareness of himself. His 'semiotic universe is an interpretive universe constructed by means of concrete social practices' (Stewart, 1984), as was that of the young Brontës.

Like Ben's mapping play, Sarah's early writing reminds us that miniatures are not small in significance. In learning to be a writer she places herself in the world where explorations of the interstices of the self can be undertaken, and allegories of power and desire created in the conventions of fairy stories. David Hutchinson's analysis shows that the enlightenment offered by Carolyn Steedman in *The Tidy House* (Steedman, 1985) can be tracked to an earlier stage. Sarah herself displays what teachers must recognize as expertise in a young writer's entry into a variety of written discourses and genres. These are lessons learned from early reading, but rarely, if ever, taught.

The society of girls which Elizabeth Grugeon discovered when she visited her daughter's school has long historical roots. This oral literature is familiar in the work of Iona and Peter Opie whose scholarship and primacy in this area is now shown to be more selective, censorious even, than was first realized. What Stewart calls 'travesties' and 'perversions' in rhymes and games are neither random nor nonsensical (Stewart, 1978). Instead, the genres with which the participants in the singing game are familiar are redefined here. Institutionalized into the society of school where rules are paramount, these girls, already aware that certain uses of language and a number of social practices privilege their brothers, join in common gestures that 'spiral away from any point of privileged signification or direction'. When they learn to read, this nonsense will, alas, decrease, and they will have to learn other ways of challenging the appearance of social stability. Meanwhile, their creative freedom is generally taken for granted when, in fact, its social cohesion and gender specificity challenge more individualistic notions of children's development at school.

7 Maps of Play

Myra Barrs

From her account of 5-year-old Ben's fantasy play Myra Barrs brings to light his moves towards maleness and mastery. In the almost obsessive continuity of his mapping games we see him as the warlord, commanding the narrative and the dialogue, manipulating his puppets and his adult accomplice. In the 'motivations and tensions' of his talk (Unwin, 1985) we discover how Ben augments the social formation of his male self with the characters in television dramas. His representational maps anticipate his later drawing and writing.

Here we enter into a developing understanding of how the discourse of the self is related to social practices. As Ben makes himself the subject of his narrative he contemplates the (traditional) power it gives him. He structures his power and his dominance like a language.

Towards the end of his brilliant, suggestive chapter on 'The Prehistory of Written Language' in *Mind in Society*, Vygotsky (1978) remarks that, in learning to write, 'the child must learn that one can draw not only objects, but also speech.' Throughout the book Vygotsky is concerned to investigate the whole area of symbolic development, and to show that a child's increasing power to use symbol systems is important, general intellectual development.

Abstract linguistic forms of intelligence are assigned so much importance in our culture that there is always a danger of adopting too narrow a focus in relation to children's developing intellectual powers. Howard Gardner's *Frames of Mind* (1984), which is an extended attempt to categorize the different forms that intelligence can take (or the range of different 'intelligences') offers an important corrective to this tendency. By highlighting other kinds of intelligence, such as 'spatial intelligence' and 'bodily kinaesthetic intelligence', Gardner outlines the breadth of human potential that is available for development under favourable circumstances. But he also suggests the ways in which these discrete intelligences can support and enhance each other.

For instance, in his chapter on 'The Socialisation of Human Intelligences through Symbols', Gardner speculates that some symbolic progression may be 'streamlike', occurring only within the particular intellectual domain that it relates to, whilst another aspect could be described as 'wavelike', spreading into and influencing other symbolic/intellectual domains. The work of such thinkers as Gardner and Vygotsky suggests that it would be valuable to adopt a broader perspective in relation to early literacy than is generally taken, and to look at literacy development in relation to symbolic development in other areas, for instance, in dramatic play or in drawing. It is possible that gains in one area may be reflected in other areas. It is also possible that, since literacy involves the use of a 'second order' or 'notational' symbolism, there may be observable links between children's growing control of different notational systems.

In what follows I want to tell a story which traces the links between dramatic play, drawing and mapping, and literacy development in one episode from the life of Ben, a 5-year-old boy. The events took place when a group of friends, including Ben and his mother, were on holiday together for ten days. Ben was the only child in the party. From the outset it was apparent that he was spending a great deal of his waking life in dramatic play. In the course of the week this play, initially private, was shared with some of the adults in the group, and with one in particular. The way in which this came about, and the resultant diagrams or 'maps' of the play, seemed to indicate important advances in Ben's grasp of the value of notational symbolism, and to prefigure the obvious progress in literacy that he made in the course of the week.

My other theme concerns the content of Ben's play. The importance within it of characters and narratives that Ben knew from television (especially from the *He-Man and Masters of the Universe* series) was reminiscent of much of the informal play in primary schools, particularly among groups of boys. This kind of play raises questions about the relationship between media narratives of this kind and children's own fantasy lives, and presents striking differences between boys' and girls' fantasy activities. It seems likely that narratives which are such powerful influences on dramatic play will also affect the development of children's sense of story, their narrative expectations and eventually their own written narratives — in other words their *literary* development.

At the beginning of the holiday Ben was immersed for some hours of each day in private fantasy play. This play was highly dramatic and centred on three dolls or figures from the *Masters of the Universe* television series: He-Man, Triclops and Buzzoff. The fantasy plays were enacted through these characters and were often highly physical, with the figures being made to fly through space, fall from great heights and engage in aerial combat. Initially these three dolls constituted the entire cast of the fantasy plays, but in the course of ten days' holiday, and several trips to the shops, new toys were bought which became incorporated into the dramas. This resulted in an extraordinarily mixed cast for the plays since the toys Ben bought were:

A set of dinosaurs (including Tyrannosaurus, Diplodocus and Stegosaurus)
A pirate in a ship, with a treasure chest
Two television cameramen
Two 'Smurfs' — a painter and a baby
Pinocchio

All of these figures were small — about 8 cms — and seemed to have been chosen so that all were roughly to scale and could therefore take part in the ongoing play.

The play was accompanied by commentary and dialogue. This was abundant, and the dialogue in particular was highly inflected, often spoken in a tone of great excitement. But all the talk was pitched so that it was just inaudible to any adults who were around, and consequently there was never any possibility of recording this stream of language. Occasionally, if adults were talking, the volume of Ben's language would be turned up, so to speak. But the moment there was a gap in the adults' conversation, his voice would subside again, so that it was impossible to catch. One thing that was clear was that Ben was playing all the parts in every drama, with different voices for the different parts. The other audible element was the musical 'soundtrack' that Ben used to fill in virtually all the gaps in the dialogue, and that generally consisted of extracts from the *Star Wars* music. All that could really be gathered about the nature of the plays was that they involved a great deal of fighting, shooting and general zapping, that they revolved around contests between goodies and baddies, and that there was often a 'quest' element in the narrative. Like the *Masters of the Universe* series, the stories combined elements of legend and saga with elements of high technology (lasers were often used for zapping), and they were decidedly macho in character — no female characters seemed to appear at all.

What was the source of the intense appeal that this kind of play, and the narrative genre apparently being explored in it, had for Ben? It was apparent to anyone observing him that he had at this stage a real need for this kind of deep play, and that he was unhappy when he was unable to engage in it. It was also evident that this play could only take place through some kind of intermediary figures, such as the doll-puppets. This fact was made clear when, on a day's trip into a nearby town, Ben, who had forgotten to bring any of his figures, was miserable and unable to play by himself alongside the adults as he usually did. The moment he acquired three new small figures from a toyshop, however, the game started again as ferociously as ever, despite the fact that the 'characters' were now two Smurfs and a Pinocchio doll.

His appetite for this play was apparently inexhaustible, and he seemed to need no participation from anyone else. One day, however, he made an unexpected invitation to Michael, a young man in his twenties who was staying in the house. He drew a small diagram, or map, on a scrap of paper, and gave it to Michael. The map was then used as the basis of an imaginary adventure game in which Michael was the main participant, an actor in a drama directed by Ben. The shape of the map was basically that of an inverted triangle, and the 'start' position was in the top left-hand corner of the triangle, where Ben had drawn a 'Michael' figure, a little man with a prominent laser gun.

This was the first game and was a very simple prototype in which both Ben and Michael developed a means of communication and, so to speak, of notation. The map was a joint product, the original shape being laid down by Ben and the map then being handed to Michael, who drew in the adventures that Ben invented. Subsequent maps were more cooperatively produced, but each time Ben laid down the initial plan of the game, and each plan had the same basic shape of an inverted triangle, though done on very much larger sheets of paper and having a much more elaborate collection of hazards.

Perhaps seven or eight games were played in the next three hours, and a map was made in the course of each game. Michael's role was always the same. He was a passive creature who was there to follow Ben's instructions and to enact his imaginings, but he was also the brave hero of all the dramas. He was thus the human equivalent of Ben's *He-Man* dolls, a puppet in Ben's fantasy play.

Ben's game plan for
unplayed game

105

But the involvement of another person in his dramatic play meant that Ben's language had to come to the surface and become audible to the adults around him. The nature of the language was obviously different in some ways from the language of his solitary play; it took the form of instructions to Michael, and there was little dialogue or commentary. Like the solitary play language, however, it was continuous, excited, and highly inflected.

By recording the conversation and studying the 'maps' with Michael once the game was over, I was able to understand more about the nature of Ben's play and the kind of fantasy world it was set in. Here, for instance, is Ben talking to Michael as he draws the plan for a game later to be entitled 'Stinging Fire'. His tone is encouraging and explanatory as he reassures Michael about the adventure he is going to embark on.

> *Ben.* There's this really bad mountain and you shouldn't go in it ... you know why? ... it's called Weak Mountain. It's got one, two, three, four, five, six, seven ledges [*drawing*] for guards to look and listen. But you only have to touch them they fall down.
>
> *Michael.* Oh, I don't need my laser.
>
> *Ben.* You have to get past these two weak guards ... it's really easy. ... You haven't got your sword. God gave your sword away to another man. He gave you a spear. You're sitting on a chair [*drawing*]. ... You're in a spaceship, actually, and you've got two guns on top.

This kind of calm and orderly explanation gave way to wild excitement and shouted and confusing instructions in the heat of the game itself, when Michael was attempting to carry out his assignment:

> *Ben.* That's Weak Mountain, you get really weak. Guards! They're dead. ... Fire with your gun! Quick! Don't go that way!
>
> *Michael.* Well where *do* I go?
>
> *Ben.* That way! [*explosion noises*] Get your sword out — guards are coming! They're coming up on the platform! This guard has got more heads [*drawing fast*]. ... That's how many heads the guard's got! Fire! Quick! One of the heads fell off! Fire! The

> snake's head fell off! Fire! The skeleton's head fell
> off! Fire! The dragon's head fell off! Fire! The
> magician's head fell off! ... Blow that spaceship up!

Michael. But that's my spaceship!

Ben. A robot's dead now which was in it.

Most games had the same basic shape although they contained many variations. All involved Michael in a quest into enemy territory in search of a treasure chest of some kind, and of a key (usually located in a different hiding place). Apart from multi-headed guards, the hazards to be encountered included vicious slugs, snakes with spikes, catapults, grass traps, stinging monsters, force fields, dungeons and weapons of all kinds, including a great variety of lasers. In the accompanying illustration, for instance, which is Ben's plan for an unplayed game, the key to the treasure chest can be seen to be buried under a mountain, while the treasure chest itself is under an acid lake, protected by a monster. Both are shielded by barriers, which will have to be broken through by the use of a laser gun. Additionally, there's an 'ice place' where you get frozen, to go through before you come to the acid lake.

It was clear that many of the elements in Ben's fantasy games came from *Star Wars* (which he knew very well) and from other sources like the *Masters of the Universe* television programmes that he was so passionately involved with. Every drama, however, was different; Ben seemed to have an inexhaustible fund of hazards to be combined into new narratives. To adults who had no previous acquaintance with this kind of territory, his mastery of this particular genre seemed astounding. On the afternoon when these games took place, Ben directed Michael through a series of seven or eight different dramas in rapid succession, over nearly three hours. The energy and intensity that he brought to this play was extraordinary, and exhausting for Michael as an adult participant. Yet this level of energy was normal in Ben's fantasy dramas, and he commonly spent at least twice as long as this daily in his solitary play during that holiday.

Ben's expertise in this particular genre made Michael more dependent on him for instructions than another child would have been. It also heightened Michael's resemblance to the doll-puppets who were usually the figures that enacted Ben's fantasies. All of Ben's fantasy play seemed to need to be enacted in this way, through puppets that could be controlled and manipulated. It was as if this play were a half-way house between full enactment and fictions that were completely free-standing. It was reminiscent of Winnicott's description of all art-play being located in a 'third area' between self and other. The dolls are transitional objects.

But Michael, of course, was not expected by Ben to act out the stories in the way the doll-puppets did. Instead the protagonist in the dramas was a miniaturised cartoon of Michael. Enactment was achieved by the creation of the game-plans.

Each of these began as a map of the territory and then because the actual site of the drama. In this respect they bore an obvious resemblance to children's board games.

One of the reasons Ben appeared to enjoy Michael's involvement in his play so much was that in this world Michael, an adult, was completely under Ben's thumb. He may also have enjoyed demonstrating his complete control over his adopted/invented world. Ben seemed to relish particularly the times when Michael was confused by the twists and turns of the plot; Michael's bemusement heightened Ben's confident sense of control.

If Ben's ability to create and control fictions through this kind of play was, as many people would agree, an important part of his growth as a reader and a writer, his obvious mastery of a particular genre seems no less crucial to his early literary development. The passionate attention that he had given to the *Masters of the Universe* stories meant that he now had a very thorough sense of how such a story should go. His awareness of a structure in the apparently diverse plots of his games with Michael may be evidenced in the strong common shape in all the game plans that he drew.

Ben was using as his source for fantasy play, not any of the fictions he was encountering at school, nor any of the 'good' children's stories that were read to him constantly in his very book-centred home, but a highly commercial and heavily marketed television series, with very different values from those of the children's books generally presented to him. These stories had the strongest appeal for him, as they have for many small boys, and the nature of that appeal should be explored further.

The *Masters of the Universe* series, as the title suggests, is a basically imperialist fantasy series of cartoon films, which all have a saga-quest format. He-Man, the main character, is a classic Wagnerian-type super-hero, a blonde Aryan type, with the enormously overdeveloped musculature of a body-builder. All the other male characters are also musclemen, fighters on the look-out for a battle. The characters coded as goodies line up against the baddies, directed by the evil master-mind, Skeletor, and slug it out with them in each episode. The exaggerated machismo of the series is one of its most striking features. Women, when they appear at all, are curvaceous blonde beauties in bikinis and boots or raven-haired temptresses.

Like *Star Wars* the films combine the appeal of magic with that of high technology; as often in science fiction, machinery is presented as magical. One of the strengths of the series' concept is its readiness to draw together elements of fantasy from a great variety of sources, from ancient myths to science fiction comics, and to serve them all up in one big stew. The characters speak a kind of uncomfortable high style common in science fiction comics, which occasionally descends into banality, but which is certainly not ordinary language. From a commercial point of view the series is a big operation. Most of the characters are available as plastic toys, and so are some of the vehicles. Castle Greyskull, the abode of the Sorceress can also be bought. These items have an international market: the films can be seen on children's television throughout Europe, and the toys and books that accompany them, and that are perhaps the real money-making part of the business, are sold world-wide.

Ben's commitment to these fictions is tolerated, but not encouraged, in his home. They are certainly tasteless productions, far removed from the quiet sensitivity of much of modern 'children's literature'; what they offer is much cruder, simpler and more stereotyped. Yet in many respects the territory they occupy is the same as that inhabited by other stories of legendary heroes: these heroic soap operas have visible ties with the worlds of Greek, Roman and Arthurian legend, and of the northern sagas, on all of which their makers may indeed have drawn.

These stories obviously provide something of importance in Ben's fictional diet. Whatever their faults, they are at least not trivial — they are big stories with big subjects like danger, evil, fear and death. There is nothing small-scale, domestic or interiorized about them; everything is acted out, giant-size. They may well satisfy a need for stories on this scale, with huge risks to be taken and immense issues at stake, that most children's fiction does not provide.

These fictions, despite — or perhaps because of — their crudity, serve a particular purpose for him at this point in his growth. They are overt fantasies about power and domination, and they enable him to become a 'master of the universe' — to take charge, in imagination, of an entire world. They encode dangerous and frightening aspects of life as enemies and monsters, and thus enable them to be fought and overcome, again and again. They express an unbounded sense of optimistic aspiration and confident reaching out into life, uninhibited by shyness or insecurity. They also represent an exaggeratedly 'male' position, at a time when Ben is busily defining himself as a boy.

The dramas that Ben invented himself had all these characteristics, and were also extremely violent. Many people — usually enemy guards — were killed in the course of a game, and there was never any debate about the killings. Every character coded as an enemy was simply a fair target, to be wiped out without a second thought. Violence was highly formalized and cartoon-like in character, but it was the *whole substance of the action*. There was never any point in the games where the main character rested, had a meal, or engaged in any other form of activity. In most of the games all the characters encountered were hostile, and there were no allies. Essentially the games might be seen as a series of encounters between the same two adversaries: the Michael hero-figure, and an Enemy that was, like the guard in *Stinging Fire*, many-headed, and needed to be killed over and over again. In other words the games seemed to fulfil the worst fears of anyone concerned about the effects of television violence, or worried about the macho character of boys' play. They were certainly disturbing in this respect to the liberal-minded adults that Ben was with.

However, it would be wrong to see Ben as a passive consumer of commercial fantasy in his liking for the *Masters of the Universe* stories and his use of them in his play. For one thing, his choice of the stories was highly active. There were many influences in his life that were presenting him with quite different material for his interior fictions, and he seemed to be asserting his liking for stories of this type against some resistance from parents and adult friends. The implicitly behaviourist view which would suggest that Ben had been conditioned or socialized into this play seems inadequate to describe the very active nature of his involvement, and the extraordinary and concentrated creative energy that he brought to it.

It seemed more than likely that the macho character of the stories, and the grossly exaggerated maleness of the *He-Man* dolls, was a major reason for Ben's interest in them. The nature of the plots, which all revolved around a quest format, seemed also to symbolize, as do quest legends and sagas in general, a preoccupation with what the male role conventionally entails, with the business of acting on the world, being powerful and achieving. For Ben it may have been particularly important to dwell on these fantasies of masculinity (though observation of boys of this age group suggests that his persistent interest was far from uncommon). Like many small boys who live with their mothers and attend infant schools staffed and run by women, Ben currently inhabits a largely female world. His deep involvement with stories of this type may be part of a process of asserting his own sexual identity.

Here is another example of Ben preparing a game plan for Michael, this time for a game called *Stinging Monsters*, which shows him setting up another quest adventure that involves considerable hazards:

> *Ben.*   This time Michael there's ten stinging monsters
> with spikes all over and you have to blow the sting
> off ... [*busily drawing the monsters*]. ... Ten stinging
> monsters won't let you pass, they've got stinging
> horns, see, there's their stinging horns. Can you do
> the next stinging monster? They've all got stinging
> horns and there's ten of them ... ten. They jump up
> from the ground when you're not expecting it.
> They've all got stinging spikes.

It was clear from Ben's tone that he expected Michael to be duly impressed by the danger that the stinging monsters represented. The risks are serious in this game, and the goals are set almost impossibly high:

> *Ben.*   But you *have* to find the key again. But the key's
> up, up, up, up. But you can't reach it. *Nobody* has
> reached it. It's in a cloud. And that part cracks
> when you touch it. ... It's got every kind of metal,
> wood, everything. You have to use your strongest
> laser.

Michael was the perfect partner for Ben's play, because he gradually assumed the role of a nervous and uncertain protagonist, who had to be cautioned, commanded and encouraged by the omniscient Ben:

> *Ben.*   But there's a platform and you'll be able to get a
> closer view of the monster and fire down at it.
> There's the ladder for you to climb up. You have to
> go whizz, whizz, whizz [*shooting noises*]. But don't
> make the monster frightened or else!
> *Michael.*   Oh there are all those monsters!

Ben.   Quick, up a ladder! Here's your gun! Your gun's up there already! Tooo! Tooo! Tooo! [*shooting noise*]. You're shooting ice now!

Even the ultimate in monsters can be confronted or evaded by Michael, urged on by a resourceful Ben.

Ben.   They're flying up to you!
Michael.   Oh *no*!
Ben.   This one's a daddy one and he's got a massive spike, bigger than any of them. ... Quick, jump!
Michael.   Where? Down into there?
Ben.   No, up! Hang onto a rope! Quick, get a stick! You're hanging on to it!. ... You jumped onto the next platform which is over here.

Ben's passionate involvement in these games was obvious in his voice, in the wild energetic drawings that he did in the heat of the drama (unlike the careful mapping that preceded the game) and was often expressed physically.

Ben.   Guess what, here's a rope! Jump right across! [*races across the yard*, *acting it out*] Guess what you're going to do! Swing across to the platform! Where the key is! And you're a really good swinger!

In this drama the Michael figure is expected to undertake almost impossible tasks, against almost insuperable odds. The ferocity of the stinging monsters with their phallic spikes, the unexpected revelation of their ability to fly, the sudden apparition of the Daddy monster, not to mention the armed guards who also pop out of odd corners at various stages of the drama, all confront Michael with an apparently hopeless task — yet again and again he is endowed with superhuman abilities and steadily led towards the unattainable key.

To an observer one of the most astonishing aspects of this remarkable afternoon of play was the rapid development of the maps that were produced during the games. The plan for the first game was very small and rather scrappy, only about three inches square. Later maps were done on very large pieces of paper (about 15″ by 25″), and most filled the entire space available. Both stages of the drawing were taken very seriously by Ben. The initial game plans, which he drew by himself, became more complex and shapely as the afternoon progressed, while the drawing done in the course of the game became more accomplished as both Ben and Michael developed more formalized systems of notation to show things as they happened in the games: the jumping, swinging, shooting and general zapping which made up most of the action. In this way it was possible to encode the key factor in these fictions, and to create maps which were no longer static but dynamic in character. They seemed to represent an interesting shift from the enactive mode of Ben's solitary play to an iconic mode of shared play, where the maps were strong symbols of the shared nature of the fictions.

In moving out of his usual play mode into this mode of play shared with an adult, Ben also made significant changes in his language. His usual style of story-telling, as has already been described, was dramatic dialogue with some commentary. Although it was not possible to make close comparisons between the language of his solitary play and that of the games with Michael, because so much of the solitary play was inaudible, it was still apparent that in moving from basically first-person dialogue to the second-person explaining/instructing style of his talk with Michael, Ben was obliged to fill in much more context, to articulate more of what he knew about this particular genre for an uninitiated player, and in general to make much more use of commentary. The maps, similarly, had an explanatory function, and were at one level a way for Ben to make public for Michael the fictions inside his head. Throughout the game Ben was constantly feeding information to Michael, and his explanatory, even didactic tone, made clear that he was strongly aware of his audience's needs. Perhaps because of the need to be particularly explicit, the stream of Ben's language was more continuous than in his solitary play, and there was less use of 'background music'.

It seems likely that these games, which Ben had not played in this form before as far as we knew, were important for what might be termed his 'symbolic development' — his awareness of the possibilities of representing meanings on paper. The exact nature of the maps, the way in which they are capable of showing not just a scene, but actually a story, seemed to be of importance. Maps can perhaps be seen as a step beyond picturing towards more formalized and abstract representation; they can encode a considerable amount of information and description. The influence of cartoon comics, of children's board games and perhaps of computer games can also be seen in Ben's story maps. These influences obviously affect children's understandings of the ways in which meanings can be symbolized, and may therefore have a bearing on their literacy development. In the case of Ben's game maps, the most striking achievement was the symbolic representation of action. In this respect the maps can be seen as an attempt to move into a second order of symbolism in dramatic play — to develop a notational symbol system for drama. To paraphrase Vygotsky, Ben had learnt that one could draw not only objects, but also action.

The week when these games took place was an important week for Ben's literacy development. He was visibly and actively engaged in making connections between spoken and written language and between reading and writing. For much of the week he was immersed in story of one kind or another — either in his own fantasy dramas, or in the stories that were read to him by his mother or by other adults in the group. Early morning story sessions, or bedtime sessions, lasted up to two hours every day. He became excited by a book (*Bear's Room* by Michelle Cartlidge) which showed a series of doors with 'Do Not Disturb' notices on them, and with his mother he made a set of notices for the doors of the rooms in his own house. He painted many pictures and dictated captions for them, watched adults writing and listened to one of the adults reading some stories that he had written. At the end of the week he dictated and illustrated his own story — a long Ananse story that was original and that he dictated confidently and fluently over a period of two to three hours.

It would be impossible to say where, in all this growing week, the games with Michael fitted in the development of Ben's concept of literacy and his sense of how stories in your head can be made public. It seems likely, though, that the playing of the games, and the making of the game maps of this fantasy world, were significant events among all the other flourishing activities.

8 Sarah's Story Book: Gender and the Beginnings of Writing

David Hutchinson

Although Sarah's story-making complements Ben's as an account of how children move towards gender identity in play, narrative and writing, it is important to see Sarah discovering her own distinctive voice. As she goes in search of the personal, her own tale, she explores the history of her culture embedded in folk tales. As she exploits the emotional depth of the stories she tells, she examines loss and attachment. In doing so she creates a virtual space for her own independence. The 'issues of language and subjectivity in which gender is crucial' are made plain in sequences which show the limitations of normative accounts of language development. As Sarah learns different ways to say what she has to say, she lets us see how we cannot ignore, neither in her case not in Ben's, emotion, fantasy, desire and power as aspects of the social processes of early literacy, and the struggles, as well as the successes, which generate them.

When our daughter Sarah was in her second year at infant school, she used to write daily in her 'story book'. This was a large format book of plain paper. The upper half of each page was used for wax crayon drawings, the lower half for writing. Sarah could write what she wanted within the 'story book' conventions as understood by infant children and their teachers. She could ask for spellings to copy from her wordbook. The teacher marked each entry with a tick and corrected a few spellings. There are twenty-four entries in all, written over some nine weeks, starting when she was 6 years 3 months old.

Reading the entries as a series is very different to reading them individually, as the teacher would have done. Sarah is beginning to find her feet as a writer (a little after she had done so as a reader). She is exploring various types or genres of writing, the linguistic forms and the subjects conventionally associated with them (Kress, 1982). These genres and their associated conventions are not formally taught, but are learned informally through the child's experience of literature — hearing reading, watching television, the child's own reading and writing. In her story book Sarah deals with three main genres: the timeless past tense narrative of the folk story tradition; present tense description; and eventually a past tense narrative dealing with actual historical events. Throughout her writing she varies her position as author between an unnamed author writing in the third person and first person authorship. At the same time as she is working with these sociolinguistic elements of writing, she can be seen to be playing with fantasy and reality in her personal life. She produces many variations on what I shall call the 'family' theme. Gender issues are particularly evident: she writes as a 'little girl' and deals thematically with personal relationships, fantasies and realities. I shall draw on a post-Freudian perspective to show one way of approaching these issues.

In transcribing her writing I have omitted the teacher's markings and corrections. The diagonal dashes denote Sarah's own editorial crossings out. There are two particular aspects I shall not comment on: I have ignored Sarah's developing concepts of sentence structure, as analyzed by Kress; and I have not dealt with the very real relation between the written texts and her accompanying illustrations.

7 Sept.	the was a little girl and she lived in a house with her mother and fater.

She writes a past tense narrative, as an unnamed narrator using the third person.

8 Sept.	there is a house with a flower around ti and a little girl lives in the house.
9 Sept.	here is a house with some flowers around ti
10 Sept.	look at the house it has a chimney and a little girl lives there.

She switches to a present tense descriptive genre, still as an unnamed author using the third person. As an author she is, therefore, distanced in some way from what she writes, a distancing which is compounded by the way she objectifies a third person 'little girl'. Sociolinguistic and personal forms of distancing are combined, defining particular positions and relations. Already a general theme seems to be emerging, centring on the house and its inhabitants, which I shall call the family theme. The positioning and relationships that she manipulates in her writing articulate this theme.

> *13 Sept.*   I like the flower and there is a tree. and tree in are garden.

Whilst maintaining the present tense description of the previous three entries, she adopts the position of a first person narrator for the first time. She can, therefore, identify explicitly with the picture she draws and describes, and implicitly with the wider family theme — 'are garden' (phonic spelling of 'our').

> *14 Sept.*   this house belongs to a little girl and it is private

She returns to the position of an unnamed author writing in the third person. Using the concept of 'belonging' she moves from pictorial description to an abstract, emotional aspect of the family theme.

> *16 Sept.*   this is the flat that we live in and this is a little girl that lives in the flat t.o and. I like to play with the little girl and her toys we play doctors and nurses

She returns to a first person narrative, which is implicit in 'we' in the second clause, explicit in 'I' later. But in this authorial position she embeds a distanced, third person 'little girl'. She is not simply switching authorial positions within a text as she has previously done between texts, but combining a first person author with the third person little girl. She achieves this complex embedding of relationships between herself, herself as author, and the family theme by a play of fantasy and reality: no other girls lived in our flats. The play of fantasy and reality which emerges here is crucial in Sarah's development of the family theme. This is the only text in the book which specifies that we lived in a flat, as in fact we did. On every other occasion the family lives in a 'house' if the place is specified at all, which I think indicates the generalizing and fantasized way in which she is dealing with the theme. So far the gender aspect of this theme has been merely implicit in the central 'little girl'. An explicitly sub-theme of children's play — 'doctors and nurses' — now invokes the exploration of gender relations in both fantasy and reality.

> *21 Sept.*   this little girl lives in this house and she has got a
> scooter and the scooter is blue and she is going to
> play with it and she she is going to ask. has brother if
> he would y̸ø̸ø̸ like to have a go fo it.

A brother appears (Tom being eighteen months younger than Sarah). Linguistically the entry is impressive in moving from the descriptive present tense of the first four clauses to a predictive use of the present tense and then to a conditional final clause. Her self-correction of 'you' in this conditional clause is fascinating. It suggests to me that she intends to write indirect speech — 'she is going to ask her brother if he would like to have a go of it' — but gets waylaid by direct speech during the first writing of it — 'would you like to have a go of it?' Any self-correction involving editing is significant for a 6-year-old writer. This instance of arbitrating between direct and indirect forms of speech within writing shows firstly that she can objectify direct experience in her writing, moving from direct spoken language to indirect written language; and secondly that she can adopt and arbitrate between alternative authorial positions, each posing a different relation to her own experience. (For a discussion of the significance of indirect speech see Volosinov, 1973.)

> *22 Sept.*   this little girl is going to her house to her mummy
> and she is going to play h̸e̸r̸ brother with her brother
> and she is play mothers and
> *24 Sept.*   this is the house that we live in and I am playing with
> my brother and we are playing mothers and fathers.

These two entries are variations on almost the same text, expressed in the two authorial positions of first and third person. 'Mothers and fathers' is the classic instance of gender-based play, confirming and developing the sub-theme begun with 'doctors and nurses'.

> *27 Sept.*   this house is a little girls house and she has a brother
> and in this priture you can see me.

Following the variation of authorial position in the previous two entries, she now embodies a personal identification within a third person narrative. She does so by referring to the pictorial text rather than keeping within the written text, but even so it is an interesting meta-textual device which must have cognitive and social significance. At this stage in the series of texts it seems clear that Sarah is varying her linguistic treatment of her author's position, developing a complex but unified theme, and doing both together in a play of fantasy and reality.

> *28 Sept.*   once upon a time there lived a witch and she lived in the wood in a cave one day she saw a monster and she thought that she would cast a spell on the monster just then a knight came by and he saw the monster.

Sarah uses a past tense narrative for the first time since the initial entry. This text is clearly within a folk story genre, using the classic timeless introduction to a world of stereotyped characters and events. No comment can be made on the thematic significance of this one entry, beyond the gender aspect of the witch and knight stereotypes.

> *1 Oct.*   this little girl is playing with her brother and they play are are playing doctors and nurses.
>
> *4 Oct.*   this is the house that we live in and my brother lives in it to sometimes we play.

She returns to present tense descriptions, again alternating third and first person positions. The 4 October entry is subtle and economical in its positioning of the author *vis-à-vis* her family. Neither herself nor the family is explicitly mentioned, but are located implicitly in 'the house that we live in'. Her brother — the only person explicitly referred to — is both highlighted and somewhat distanced by the subtle use of 'too' and 'sometimes', producing an ambiguous relationship.

> *5 Oct.*   one day I went to my friends house to play with Janice and we played kings and queens

A different form of past tense narrative is used here: 'one day' introduces a historical, factual narrative, unlike the timeless introduction and narrative of folk stories. It is the first entry that is historical and factual. There can always be a link with fantasy, of course, occurring here in the game of 'kings and queens' that they actually played. Now that there are three variants of the 'play' sub-theme — I would argue that they deal with the power underlying gender relations, in ways which young children's play can express.

Sarah also deals nicely with a problem of syntactic complexity.

She does not write something like 'my friend Janice's house', but what she does write copes well with the embedded syntactical demands of relation, possession, location and identification.

> *6 Oct.*　　once upon a time there lied a little girl and she lied in a house she had no mother.and father.

Sarah is evidently familiar with the folk story genre. She can use the appropriate linguistic conventions as a basis for stereotyped characters and events (as in the 28 September entry). Here the stereotyped 'little girl' adds a further distance to that of the third person narration, and enables her to put the little girl in an existential predicament — in some way parentless, though perhaps with economic independence! So far she has specified a range of permutations within the family:

> girl + mother and father
> girl + mother
> girl + brother
> girl + girl friend
> girl alone

This range suggests that she is using the theme to fantasize about various positions and relations within the family, including her own independence from it.

Some psychoanalytic approaches are relevant here. Bruno Bettelheim (1976) analyzes folk tales in Freudian terms, based on classic Oedipal theories and implicitly dependent on his own analytic work with children. There are two problems here: there is no critical discussion of the Odeipus complex, and no case studies are available to the reader. More recent work drawing on sociology, psychoanalysis and feminism examines these problems. For example, Charles Bernheimer and Clare Kahane (1985) have edited papers dealing in detail with Freud's classic case study of Dora, and with feminist reinterpretations of the Oedipus complex. In Freud's view sexuality developed from early bi-sexuality to the maturity of genitally oriented heterosexuality. Various reinterpretations, drawing particularly on feminist views of Lacan, argue that this apparently 'natural' development is 'normative', that is, historically and socially determined. Penis envy, for example, would not be an inevitable and universal feature of female development but a possible product of specific sociohistorical power relations.

Carolyn Steedman, Cathy Urwin and Valerie Walkerdine (1985) have edited papers which develop such an analysis in terms of language, gender and schooling. The genres that Sarah works with, and the social relations involved in the family theme, are instances of what Walkerdine calls 'practices'. Such practices produce 'positions' from which a person's subjectivity is constructed, involving both power relations and desire. These practices and positions are often diverse and contradictory, as can be glimpsed in the permutations of the family theme, and in the subjective and authorial positions Sarah adopts. Personal identity is constructed not as a single unit, exemplified by the 'normal individual'. Instead, 'a variety of potentially conflictual and contradictory identifications is possible, relating to the others in the family constellation, parents, siblings, other caretakers ...' (Walkerdine in Steedman *et al.*, 1985, p. 227). This variety of possible identifications would produce Sarah's subjectivity as a little girl and as a writer in school.

Walkerdine draws on Urwin's reworking of Lacanian psychoanalysis (Urwin, 1984), allowing power and desire to be seen not as a normative Freudian sequence but in sociohistorically specific terms. Gender differentiation, and the practices and positions that produce it, can than be examined more specifically. Steedman and Walkerdine both emphasize how primary schooling and teacher education enshrine the normative approach, through, for example, Klein and Winnicott in psychoanalysis and Piaget and Bruner in cognitive development. Broadly similar arguments could be made in the case of functional developmental views of writing, and of their use in primary schools. Kress emphasizes both the cognitive demands of learning to write and the sociolinguistic issues of power involved as a child learns about genres (Kress, 1982). But Kress works along the lines of Halliday's functional approach (Halliday, 1976), based on universal functions and developmental sequences. In such a universal functional system a person's subjectivity is defined in individual terms within a normative sequence. The individual and the power relations appear as gender neutral because of their universality. A more widely accepted approach to types of writing and their development is James Britton's typology, as, for example, surveyed for teachers in Temple, Nathan and Burris (1982). Britton's types derive from Jakobson's universalistic functions of language (Britton *et al.*, 1976, Ch. 5), and are similarly gender blind.

With such a brief discussion of a complex area I can do no more than raise some issues. But I hope that there are possible readings of

Sarah's story book which rely neither on normative psychoanalysis, nor on gender blind views of learning to write.

8 Oct.   once upon a time there lived a little old woman and she dad no little girl one day she went to a witch for advice the litte old woman gave the witch free bits of silver in year she had a little girl she was called Thumbelina ane day a frog came and he took her away when mrs frog saw Thumbelinas tears she puffed up and angry then a school of gold fish came swimming just below the lilly ꝑ pad the gold fish heard Thumbelinas crying the gold fish cut the lilly ꝑ pad then Thumbelina was attacked by a big wasp the wasp carried her of then his famll buzzed on about her Thumbelina then the wasp carried her away into the wood she wove a hammock out of grass ᵬꝰ then it began to slow Thumbelina was dreadfully cold / then she went to ask a fieldmouse then one day Mrs fieldmouse said my friend mr mole is going to vizard us one day she was walking along to mr mole than she saw a lifeless swallow then / mr mole announced that he would marry her Mrs fieldmouse began to make a wedding dress Thumbelina did not want to marry mr mole one day the swallow said to Thumbelina I am well enough to fly shall I carried /// you away came you see those flower you came chose any for your home.

Sarah retells Hans Andersen's *Thumbelina*. It was one of her favourite books, had been repeatedly read to her, and she had 'read' it many times herself. It must have taken her many days to write this text as the next dated entry is eleven days afterwards. The transcriptional demands of the story — its length and the number of spellings she must have needed — and its compositional demands can only have been sustained through her grasp of the narrative and its meanings for her. She did not have her book in school with her so it is clearly a retelling. The text of her edition (Hallmark children's editions, no date) is a simplified, somewhat condescending adaptation compared with Haugaard's translation (Andersen, 1974), but it is much longer than Sarah's rewriting. Although some literary phrases and vocabulary are retained, these and the structure of the story have been thoroughly adapted by Sarah, as can be seen by comparison with the opening of the printed version:

> Many years ago there was a woman who wished for a very
> little child. She didn't know where she could get one so she
> went to a very old and wise witch for advice. 'Here is a bit of
> barley-corn' said the witch. 'Put it in a flower-pot and see
> what happens'. The woman gave the witch three pieces of
> silver and went home and planted the barleycorn. But it did
> not grow into a stalk of barley. It grew into a lovely flower
> which looked like a tulip with its petals tightly closed. 'What
> a lovely flower' said the woman, and she kissed its yellow
> petals. Immediately the flower opened, and the woman was
> surprised to find a tiny maiden sitting inside. She was only a
> thumb's length in height and so the woman called her
> Thumbelina.

The first line of Sarah's writing restores the stronger, more pared
down folk story conventions, the timelessness and reinforced stereotypes expressing the predicament more powerfully. Wishing for 'a
very little child' becomes more specifically 'and she had no little girl',
invoking possible reasons for Sarah choosing to retell this story as
part of her treatment of the family theme. 'one day she went to a
witch for advice' is a similar paring down to the most economical
essentials. She omits the dialogue between the witch and the woman,
and indeed all of Andersen's metaphorical treatment of conception
and birth. She repeats the reinforced stereotypical phrase 'the little
old woman', restoring the resonance of the oral tradition (which
Andersen was writing out to some extent). 'free bits of silver' is a
nice south-east London dialect and accent transcription of 'three
pieces of silver'. Although she does not deal with conception, or
obscure it in a gooseberry bush metaphor, she adds a reference to a
gestation period. So Sarah cuts and paraphrases the story she knows,
restoring in the process some of the strength of the oral tradition. She
could only do this on the basis of an unconscious grasp of the
structure and emotional depths of the folk story genre.

It is interesting that Sarah ends her story with Thumbelina
choosing her new home. In the Hallmark edition Thumbelina
unwittingly chooses the very flower where the king of the flowers
lives; they then get married and live happily ever after. In the original
Andersen the swallow deposits Thumbelina on the right flower in a
preordained way, without even a spurious choice. It would be
tempting, though groundless, to see Sarah's omission of the 'happily

ever after' marriage ending as proto-feminism! But it does raise the issue of how far a child may rework a genre, and whether the normalizing power relations embodied in a genre may always be effective.

> *19 Oct.*   once upon a time there lived two little children and there names were Simon and Ann one day they when for a walk then they met a old witch the witch saw then the children tried to run away.

In the summer we had been on holiday with her older cousins, Anne and Simon. Identifying them as the children perhaps brings the timeless distancing of the folk story genre a little closer home, but not too close. A Freudian reading of this entry could identify the old witch with the stern, punishing aspect of the mother, these attributes being polarized and stereotyped to their greatest extent. Going for a walk would be a metaphor for the children's independence, which would crucially involve sexual exploration. On this sort of reading it is no accident that the two children are a boy and a girl, living apparently on their own. The witch/stern mother *sees* them, threatening retribution for implied sexual activity. That the children can only try to run away perhaps indicates the bonds constraining the children to the witch/stern mother.

> *20 Oct.*   one day a little old woman said I want a child then she got a little girl then one day she said y̸o̸u̸ you must go shopping then a witch caught her and she put her in a castle then the witch went away then a fairy rescued her the little girl was then she saw a fairy then the fairy said why s̸h̸e̸ w̸a̸s̸ our you crying so she told her the tale one day I was going to the shop then I got caught.

This time Sarah does deal explicitly with conception, though in the most literal way, when the little old woman conceives the *idea* of having a child. The little old woman could be a stereotype both of Sarah's mother Ann, and of Sarah herself as an adult woman conceiving. The distancing of age and status is achieved by the stereotyping formula 'little old woman', which is sufficiently condensed to be a projection of both Ann and Sarah. In *Thumbelina* and in the Simon and Ann story the children's independence just happens, but here it is initiated by the mother. The contradictions in the mother that the child senses are then exposed as the witch/stern mother catches and incarcerates the child. The fairy who rescues her can be seen as the opposite pole, the good mother (an identification preserved linguistically in the conventional 'fairy godmother').

Sarah uses even more complex narrative devices which may also express complex emotional depths. Firstly, she has to redraft what the fairy said from indirect to direct speech, involving in some way complex embedded positions: Sarah as author of the text relating to what Sarah as the little girl is feeling. Secondly, she uses the intriguing meta-linguistic device of the story within a story. This could be seen to condense crucial aspects of this story's focus on the family theme: the desire for independence and sexual experience, and the fear of retribution. Very early in his psychoanalytic work, Freud recognized that common fundamental processes were at work in folk tales, writing and dreams (Freud, 1900/1976, p. 345). In this case 'condensation' is one of two basic mental processes, and enables us to produce and understand metaphors. Metaphors can act as extremely condensed locations for a range and depth of meanings and emotions. Freud's theory of condensation has been developed in terms of language and metaphor by Jacobson (1971) and Lacan (1977, p. 160). Such metaphorical understanding, conscious and unconscious, would have enabled Sarah to reconstruct what was crucial for her in *Thumbelina*, and here to write a powerfully condensed story within a story. On such a reading 'going shopping' could be seen as a metaphor for both independence and sexual experience. If it was literally and only going round the shops, where does the fear of being caught by the witch come from, and the fear of being seen by the witch in the earlier story?

> *8 Nov.* once upon a time there lived a princess and the princess had a friend she was a fairy and her name is cobweb and she is nice and she lives in a tower and sometimes she comes to visi/t me.

The princess is another projection, at another remove from the 'little girl' and probably more idealized. As part of this idealization, the princess has a friendly relationship with the fairy/good mother. Sarah's idealized identification with the princess is indicated by the change from impersonal to personal authorship. Sarah played Cobweb in a version of *Midsummer Night's Dream*, so the identification could be dual, with the fairy/good mother as well as with the princess: that is, with herself as adult as well as adolescent. Whatever one's view of these psychoanalytic readings, it seems clear that such an apparently short and stereotyped text is extremely condensed, and that the condensation envelops multiple possible meanings.

> *10 Nov.* once upon a time there lived a little boy in a house with her sister and his mummy and his daddy and they all live in the same house in there house they had a book of Israel and this is what it said in Israel is a very small place and there mummy and daddy didn't live with them.

Here and in the following entry Sarah focuses on a little boy, which could be her brother and/or a projection of herself as a boy. She makes a mistake in cohesion with the gender of the pronoun ('her sister') compared with the correct 'his mummy and daddy'. (For cohesion see Kress, 1982; Halliday and Hasan, 1976). She can obviously operate cohesion correctly, so this slip is not unmotivated. It must relate in some unknowable way to the complex of possibilities for identifying herself as brother/sister, that is with gender differentiation and relations between genders.

The 'book of Israel' presumably referred to child rearing on a kibbutz. The way Sarah brings in this theme of non-parental child care indicates that she is dealing with another and striking variation on the family theme. Again a condensed passage is contained in a story within a story, perhaps with emotional depths of loss and attachment.

> *11 Nov.* once upon a time there was a little boy and he have a little baby and har name was Sheena and she was a very nice girl. one day she moved.

It would be tempting to read this as conception and birth by a male, but it may simply refer to the colloquial way in which children say of their younger siblings that they 'have a baby'. But even then I would suggest that there are multiple possible meanings here. Sheena was a friend of Sarah's who was a very nice girl, and she did move. Sarah seems to be bringing her own sense of loss into the folk story genre, or else abruptly switching out of it into an historical, factual narrative.

> *12 Nov.* once upon a time ~~there was a b~~ my brother was play in our house we were playing circus and I got stuck in the

> circus and Tom ran around shouting then mummy
> came into the room and lifted me down from the chair
> then I want into the tent Tom was going to get a chair
> and a cushion and a stool then he went in to the tent.

The editing shows how she discards the timeless and impersonal folk story genre — 'once upon a time there was a b(oy?)' — for a historically located and true narrative written in the first person. For the first time Tom is mentioned by name. Without the generic conventions of the folk story she writes a literal account, with no evident metaphors or references to her feelings on getting stuck or being rescued.

> *18 Nov.* when I went to the Christmas market and I brought a
> cat and she was very fur.y she was black and white and
> I stroked her then we went home Tom h̸a̸v̸e̸ has
> brought a toy dog.

The final text in the book continues with a historically located, true narrative. This text and that of 5 October are the only ones completely within this genre. I do not wish to imply a development through fantasy to reality, but the way Sarah works or plays with fantasy in some sort of preference to reality is intriguing. The accompanying drawing of the toy cat is the most realistic and least stereotyped drawing in the whole book. Almost all the other drawings feature a strip of blue 'sky' at the top and a strip of green 'grass' at the bottom. There is no sky or grass line here, but a creditable realistic drawing using carefully chosen appropriate colours. But fantasy and wish fulfilment emerge even here. The cat in the picture has a stereotyped long tail at right angles to its body, whereas the actual cat only had a short stubby tail, much to Sarah's dismay.

Reading Sarah's story book illustrates how in learning to write her subjectivity is also developing. Ruth Weir first showed how young children learning to speak may construct their own self-educational linguistic games in their own time (Weir, 1962). Her son Anthony's pre-sleep monologues at 2-years-old and Sarah's series of stories at 6 raise some common issues. Anthony plays with the structures and meanings of spoken language whilst fantasizing about his day, and as Jakobson writes in his introduction to Weir's study this linguistic play occurs on the 'border zone of inner speech and dream speech'. Sarah similarly plays — and works — with written language. I have outlined how a non-functional approach to that 'border zone' can grapple with some of the issues of language and subjectivity, in which gender is crucial. Although developmental theories of writing and teaching approaches cannot grasp some of these issues and may have normative effects in the classroom, there is no necessary determinism. What Sarah's story book shows above all is the range of possible positions that can be adopted during learning. Perhaps as teachers we can try to understand not only the strategies for learning that developmental approaches reveal but also the relations of power and desire that articulate them.

9 The Singing Game: An Untapped Competence

Elizabeth Grugeon

During her first weeks at school Jessica learned to play the singing games which let her join in the social life of girls in the playground. Six years later she and her friend Lucy listen to a recording of what they sang and talk about how they learned the words and the actions. From her study of this richly textured material Elizabeth Grugeon adds an original dimension to the work reported by Iona and Peter Opie in The Lore and Language of Schoolchildren (1959) and The Singing Game (1985). Here we see childhood without adults, literary, secret, social, socializing, verbally confident. The language has a momentum of its own, and is poetic in both form and content and dramatic in presentation. It also sorts out the immediate concerns of girls by being subversive, oppositional and shaping of those things which adults never address directly: excesses, origins, sex, death (cf. Rose, 1985).

Jess.   Yeah but I can remember, we sort of walked out onto the playground and everybody would be just playing clapping games and if somebody's got a skipping rope we played with the skipping rope and played games with them. ...

Lucy.   Actually, yeah, we played loads of skipping rope games. ...

Jess.   When they say play time, I mean it really really meant play time, everyone was always doing something.

Lucy.   I mean we weren't ever sort of. ...

Jess.   not doing anything, we were always making up a game of some sort.

Two 11-year-olds, Jessica and Lucy, are listening to a tape recording.

Six years earlier Jessica had made the tape of the songs which accompanied the clapping games she played on the playground in her first term at school. They speculate about how they had learned these games.

> *Jess.* I don't know how we thought some of them up, they sort of really make me, really sort of stretched our imaginations. ...
>
> *Lucy.* I mean games like 'Rover' and things, how on earth did they come into the school? We just sort of don't know.
>
> *Jess.* No, did we make them up or were they do you reckon, they just came along...?
>
> *Lucy.* I'm sure that we definitely didn't make them up, I don't think.
>
> *Jess.* I can't, I mean it's really hard. I really don't know who taught us, you just sort of knew them, didn't you?
>
> *Lucy.* I think we just heard the bigger girls saying them and if they said them. ...
>
> *Jess.* They sort of passed down almost, didn't they?
>
> *Lucy.* But I reckon that, I mean if we thought the bigger girls were saying them, we thought that we would be really big by saying them ourselves, so we just tried to copy them.
>
> *Jess.* Yeah and we. ...
>
> *Lucy.* but I don't think anybody, sort of actually went up to us and actually taught them. ...
>
> *Jess.* taught them, you just copied
>
> *Lucy.* You just sort of picked up

The oral transmission that takes place on the playground is out of the hands of adults; it is child initiated and mediated. All we can know for a fact is that it takes place between the ages of 5 and 9 (Opie and Opie, 1985, p. 2). The games are well documented by collectors of children's folklore (Opie and Opie, 1985; Turner 1978; Sutton-Smith, 1959; Knapp and Knapp, 1976; Webb, 1985) and yet their continued existence in the face of all the other distractions of the modern world remains a wonder and a mystery. There seems to be no satisfactory explanation of the nature of these rhymes, nor of the role they play in the development of children's social competence or the acquisition of literacy.

A small collection of singing games played by a 5-year-old in her first weeks at school provides evidence of the existence of a thriving oral tradition and of a particular girls' culture. Jessica's songs are typical of those which accompany clapping, skipping and ball bouncing wherever little girls are gathered together; every one of them can be accounted for by folklorists.

The ten songs fall into two groups which differ at the extremes but also overlap:

Rude or subversive	*Clapping games and nonsense*	*Women's life experience*
My friend Billy.	I went to the Chinese	I'm a little Dutch girl.
Batman and Robin in	restaurant.	When Suzie was a baby.
the Batmobile.	Hands together.	My mummy is a baker.
I'm Popeye the sailorman.		My boyfriend's name is
We break up, we break		Tony.
down.		

The first group contains songs which Jessica and Lucy consider 'really rude' and which made them feel 'really hard' when they played them. Jessica found even hearing them quite embarrassing to begin with and denied remembering Batman and Robin, 'about his supersonic ... whatever. ...' The word 'fart' is clearly too vulgar to use on a recording when you are 11, but Lucy is less delicate and claims that 'everybody used to sing that'. Some of them have been handed down from generation to generation. I'm a little Dutch girl' appears in a section of *The Singing Game* (Opie, 1985) which the Opies call 'Mimicry', games which mimic and rehearse a girl's expectation of life. Likewise, 'When Susie was a baby' can be traced back to the eighteenth and nineteenth centuries, while the vulgar Popeye rhymes have their origins in 1930s film culture and Batman and Robin are more recent TV imports. The tradition is not static; adaptation and innovation ensure its dynamic quality. No distinction is made between the antique and the new; both are played with equal gusto and irreverence. In the summer of 1986, on the playground where Jessica played in 1979, some little girls were singing 'A ship sailed from Bombay', which is a descendent of Fred Godfrey's 'Bless 'em all' written in 1916 (Opie, 1985) alongside 'She's an uptown wally and she's living in a Tesco trolley', a mocking parody of a 1983 pop song, 'Up-town girl'.

An interesting feature of children's folklore and oral tradition is that it is not kept alive by public performance or adult intervention. It is intensely private and there may be a danger in attempting to capture or exploit it. On the whole most adults seem unaware of its existence, 'Oh I don't think that sort of thing goes on any more. Isn't it supposed to be dying out?' said a deputy head teacher. Their games are most successfully a secret domain.

> *Jess.* We used to go and sort of hide away in that little dip past the, um. ...
> *Lucy.* canteen
> *Jess.* canteen
> *Jess.* and we used to play in there and sing those songs and do all the clapping games — oh well.

Lucy and Jessica had their own ideas about who did and did not know about their singing games.

> *Jess.* I reckon teachers sort of walking through the playground would have heard them and things like that but I don't, they never took much notice of them or anything, they didn't. ...
> *Lucy.* But they weren't really in the playground much were they, I mean we thought they were all too rude
> *Jess.* they had ... playground duty but the dinner ladies definitely knew about them.
> *Lucy.* Oh yeah, the dinner ladies did
> *Jess.* the dinner ladies knew most of them off by heart I mean they didn't sing them theirselves but they probably knew them, but I don't think the teachers did actually. When the teachers came along you sort of had to line up for dinner and things like that,
> *Lucy.* the teachers didn't really take much notice of you.

The dinner ladies out on the playground all year round, helping to turn the ropes, had a role in stimulating and initiating games, unconsciously helping to keep the tradition alive, one of which they had once been part.

> *Jess.* and the din ... actually the dinner ladies used to get us into a big group and do different games and sing things as well.
> *Lucy.* Yeah but I don't think. ...
> *Jess.* They weren't those, they didn't teach us
> *Lucy.* They weren't those ones because

Jess. Those were the sort of ones
Lucy. They were too rude
Jess. Yeah we sort of kept those ones to ourselves really, didn't we, and everyone sort of did them.

The dinner ladies did not enter the secret domain at the heart of the culture. Boys too were excluded. Jessica and Lucy admit that some boys joined them in singing some of the ruder songs, but more often they comment on the absence of the boys. Their explanation is the gender specificity of the songs:

Lucy. Because no, most of them were about girls though, 'weren't they
Jess. Yeah, I mean
Lucy. I mean it was, I mean you'd never catch the boys singing the one about, um, 'please will you marry me'
Jess. No
Lucy. It's too
Jess. I mean that was just sissy, wasn't it?
Lucy. Yeah, the boys would never have been seen dead doing that
Jess. I reckon, I think, um Robert sang the one about the ten foot willy
Lucy. Oh yes the boys sang *that* one, because that was the rude one and they sang 'Batman and Robin in the Batmobile'
Jess. Yeah they sang all the Batman ones and that
Lucy. but they didn't sing things like, 'When Suzie was a baby' and things like that
Jess. I don't, I can't think where the boys must have been. ... I didn't even notice what the boys were doing when we were playing our games.

This emphasis suggests the presence of a flourishing girls' culture on the playground.

Although they have been annexed by the girls for clapping routines, rhymes like 'My friend Billy', 'Batman and Robin', 'I went to the Chinese restaurant' and 'Popeye the sailorman' are not exclusively girls' property but are on their way to becoming so, since apart from occasional acts of bravado boys have no real use for them. Harnessed to the intricate movements of clapping games they are well inside girls' territory. As Jessica and Lucy have made it clear, no boys were involved in 'I'm a little Dutch girl', 'When Suzie was a baby', 'My mummy is a baker' and 'My boyfriend's name is Tony'. These are concerned with marriage, motherhood, family relationships, birth and death. In playing these games they were like the little girls Carolyn Steedman writes about in *The Tidy House* (1982), taking part in the process of their own socialization; the games help them to explore the social beliefs that have brought them into being.

The clapping games helped Jessica in her first weeks at school. She was able to participate in non-threatening group interaction, to play with language, to rehearse adult roles, to investigate and challenge social and sexual aspects of the world and to become involved in peer group relationships. The gender specificity of the games introduced her to a girls' culture. When little girls play hand clapping games, the participants establish and maintain patterns of exchange, alternating turns and synchronizing utterance, as a form of mastery play (Garvey, 1977) where what is mastered is control of one's own and one's partner's actions. It is play which demands attention and adaptation to a partner's behaviour.

This kind of play is also a vital means to socialization. The potentially traumatic situation of arriving at school without friends can be alleviated by finding a friend with whom it is possible to build a system of shared meanings and understanding, so that the world becomes a more predictable place (Davies, 1982). A particular mode of viewing the world, with its accompanying language, taboos, rituals and sanctions, is developed in interaction on the playground. Six of Jessica's games are clapping games, essentially social and cooperative, rule-governed and ritualistic but not hierarchical or competitive. Typically, older girls take on younger children as their apprentices. At first Jessica played with Sarah, Janine and Harminder, all in their second year at school. From them she learned sex-specific patterns of behaviour in what seems to have been a cooperative but exclusive girls' culture (Heath, 1983; Romaine, 1984).

The games can also be seen as discursive practices in which children can become powerful (Walkerdine, 1981). Rhymes like 'My friend Billy' and 'I gave my love an apple' are examples of girls' resistance to the relations of power in the playground. The 5-year-old girl is particularly aware of her physical weakness and powerlessness in the face of older children, and of boys in particular. Rhymes like 'My friend Billy' provide ammunition for resistance and are the means by which they may seize power in discourse. Such rhymes can render boys powerless and vulnerable, 'I gave him back his kiss and kicked him down the stairs', 'She hit it with a rake/and now it's only four foot four'. Taboo rhymes are not childish acts of rebellion but tools for resistance and criticism. In Jessica's repertoire of ten songs, three enable her to seize power by making boys, teachers and the school the powerless objects of their discourse.

Stewart (1978) suggests that from a very early age rhymes and games of this kind give children access to the means to challenge particular forms of discourse. In singing these songs little girls are not simply acquiescing in the stereotypes but learning to challenge and question them. To use a Hallidayan metaphor (1978; p. 186), the playground can be seen as the environmental determinant of the texts which have taken place on it and these texts or linguistic structures are a realization of the social structure, capable not only of transmitting the social order but also of maintaining and even modifying it. At a period in their lives when most of them can neither read nor write, children on the playground are playing with literary forms and highly textured oral discourse.

Features of the Language

When children get together to play these games, language is an accompaniment to physical activity which is as structured and rule-governed as the syntax itself. All the rhymes accompany different patterns of handclapping and each one involves an elaborate dramatic routine with actions which interpret and accompany the words:

> *Jess.* We used to do a sort of dance ... prancing about like witches.
> *Lucy.* We used to float around for ghosts

The language of all the games is emotionally charged; the relationship and interaction between participants are determined by the text; both speech and movement shape the situation. In the case of *I'm a little Dutch girl* the dialogue bears no resemblance to spontaneous conversation; it is highly formulaic in its repetitive patterning. The text is complex, monotonous and powerful; it shapes the performance; the participants are in thrall. There is no scope for originality. This is not language to get things done but language which seems to have no purpose outside itself, dominating the situation which it creates.

To begin to understand what is going on here, it helps to look at

some of the formal features of the texts which seem to control the
players so effectively. The co-occurrence of so many items which
seem to echo and repeat each other is typical of what Halliday calls
collocational cohesion. Items from the everyday world rub shoulders
with deeper psychic fantasy, snakes, witches and ghosts alongside
bakers, dustmen, schools and knitting. Long cohesive chains are built
of lexical relations of different kinds. These do not have to depend on
anything more than their association with each other. More complex
semantic structures are the formulaic ones of narrative: 'and this is
what she said' 'and this is how my story goes'. A quick look at
Batman and Robin illustrates the amount of lexical cohesion even in a
short text.

'*Batman and Robin* in the *bat*mobile' — Batman and Robin are
cohesive because of their proximity in the discourse, and their
partnership in the fiction beyond the text itself, *bat*mobile echoes
Batman, the reiteration of Batman (three times) *fart* (twice), *go* and
start as near synonyms, *start* rhyming with *fart*, *wheel and engine*
relating both by anaphoric reference and collocation to the batmobile, and to *go* and *start* all combine to give this rhyme its
particular quality of text, its particular 'texture'.

Thus there are many linked items; one collocational chain
concerns the gender differences; another, the role relationships of
school and family. The most prominent cohesive element, account-
ing for the largest number of lexical items, derives from a constant
testing and questioning of sexuality and the challenging of sex roles.
This results in an impressive chain: willy, snake, curls, belly ache,
show-off, boyfriend, underwear, fart, love, kiss, ring, necklace,
bracelet, marriage, teenager, women, baby.

This list is reminiscent of Sylvia Ashton-Warner's 'key vocabulary' (1980; p. 33) and her belief that we should introduce children to
the written word using the children's own words, what she calls 'the
captions of dynamic life'. She argues that 'pleasant words won't do.
Respectable words won't do. They must be words organically tied
up, organically born from the dynamic life itself. They must be
words that are already part of the child's being.' The strongest
cohesive links in the text of the singing games fall into this category:
'love, kiss, mummy, daddy, granny, brother, sister, baby, witches,
ghost, snakes, dying, heaven, nothing, dust, fart, willy, underwear,
supersonic, dynamite, wheel, engine, serve her right, bow her up,
show off, fall down, paralysed, don't care, jumped, swallowed,
interfere, box her ears', these are *all* 'captions of dynamic life' and
most of them not the adult mediated vocabulary of the early reading

texts they will be meeting in the classroom. These lexical items drawn from only nine short playground texts add fuel to Claudine Dannequin's (1977) contention that without them the linguistic environment of the infant classroom is impoverished.

Even this brief example of the kind of analysis that is possible suggests that what is going on in the playground is a particularly highly organized kind or oral language which is rarely found in children's normal discourse. Although scholars like Weir (1962), Hymes (1964), Bruner (1975), Halliday (1975), Sanches and Kirshenblatt-Gimblett (1976) have analyzed and recognized the meta-linguistic features of children's speech play, they are more inclined to stress the formal differences between children's productions and those of adults, especially of literate adults. What they seem to ignore is that the singing game, with its rituals, its precise regulation of language and behaviour, and the ways in which the group which creates and sustains this language has to be synchronized in its solidarity, gives children a linguistic power which stretches their competences beyond the confines of their normal speech production. This power is the capability to create extended texts, because in oral transmissions each reciter is a new author. This lies behind the children's next important move in language development, the move to literacy, which occurs in a different social context.

The language generated by ritual play could also be classified as 'antilanguage', the language a subculture uses to set itself apart from the established society by creating an alternative reality (Halliday, 1978; p. 177). It can be the language of literature and at the same time the language of social resistance and protest. The singing game can be explained as verbal art, as highly textured discourse, as antilanguage, as a language of resistance, as constitutive of a subculture and as language which transmits the beliefs of society in particular ways.

The Move to Literacy

But none of this, on its own, accounts for the continued existence of these games as an oral tradition. Another perspective might see them as part of children's transition from a predominantly oral to a written culture. It is easy to overlook or underrate that period in children's lives, when they are not fully literate and thus operate more in an oral than a literate environment. Up to the point at which they start school most children rely heavily on oral signals for making sense of their experiences. School introduces an element of discontinuity with the practices of their everyday life.

> Entry into school in our society provides ... a ritual entry into a formal apprenticeship towards adult communicative skills. But since we do not look upon the early years of language use as different but merely as a lesser form of what is to come, this ritual entry does not have the nature of its transitional experience truly evaluated. The *oral* language experience of children is looked upon as a preparation rather than a separate stage of experience, and we do not always give sufficient thought, nor recognition, to the social as well as the cognitive reorganization of experience and its processing that is necessary for the child to enter into literacy. (Cook–Gumpertz, 1981, p. 98)

At this stage Jessica and her friends were oral. On the playground they were firmly in an oral culture. They had no book texts for their rhymes but relied entirely on memory. Orality requires a different cognitive organization of experience from literacy (Ong, 1983; Luria, 1976). If there are no written texts then the material must be organized for easy recall. 'In a primary oral culture, you have to do your thinking in mnemonic patterns, shaped for ready oral recurrence' (Ong, 1983). One aspect of this orality which may well be overlooked or underestimated is the verbal memory skill which it entails. Jessica's repertoire is impressive for the sheer number and range of items she has committed to memory.

As important as the mnemonic devices are 'the existential contexts which surround oral discourse'. On the playground groups of familiar friends generate and support performance, which itself relies heavily on gestures, vocal inflection and facial expression. Oral memory depends on a high somatic component; hand and body activity characteristically accompany it. The oral lore of the playground is performance and it is inseparable from the movement which both accompanies and responds to it: hand clapping, skipping, dancing. All Jessica's rhymes entailed action of varying degrees of complexity, 'we used to do a sort of dance.' The oral word does not exist in a simply verbal context, as the written word does, but is part of an existential situation which engages the body.

Oral transmission is not a remnant of the past, a series of isolated survivals but, as we have seen on the playground, a powerful reminder of 'the resilience of distinctively oral modes in the heart of societies with centuries of familiarity with paper and print' (Levine, 1986, p. 189). Children entering school at 5, particularly those from different cultural backgrounds (Scollon and Scollon, 1981), will often be affected by a residual orality, a particular mindset which will predispose them to adopt oral rather than literate strategies in the classroom. On the playground with their peers socialization will continue to be dominated by an oral tradition which is likely to be a continuation of the orality of their homes. There may, therefore, be a marked discontinuity with the demands of the school.

Looking back on the games they used to play, Lucy and Jessica remember rather wistfully what it was like.

> *Jess.* The thing about Castle Lower was that the whole school did everything together, I mean. ...
>
> *Lucy.*We were all so friendly, weren' we?
>
> *Jess.* There were so many games we thought up but nowadays you just wouldn't do that. ... It was a load more friendly than it is at middle school and, and when you look back and see all the things you've sort of done, it was really pretty amazing. ...

What is amazing is that these games are almost invisible and taken for granted. Yet when children play them they are engaged in making meaning, in an ongoing process of interpretation which must contribute significantly to their future literate and literary competence. Playground culture is neither wholly oral nor wholly literate but is an area of overlap between the two modes, having an important bridging function. I shall leave the last word to Jessica and Lucy, without whom these explorations would not have been possible.

> *Lucy.*You just sort of picked it up
>
> *Jess.* Yeah I think, I can't remember
>
> *Lucy.*and it was probably in school. I can't remember doing them in playschool, at all
>
> *Jess.* No, actually, no, I don't think so, I mean I can remember actually a few people might come up and say what are you singing and you'd say oh it's this and they'd pick it up you know, they'd pick it up as you are going along, you didn't really sort of say do you want to learn this.
>
> *Lucy.*You must be very quick at picking things up.

Elizabeth Grugeon

1   My friend Billy had a ten foot willy
    Show it to the girl next door
    thought it was a snake
    and hit it with a rake
    and now it's only four foot four.

2   Batman and Robin in the batmobile
    Batman did a fart and paralyzed the wheel
    the wheel wouldn't go
    the engine wouldn't start
    all because of Batman and his supersonic fart.

3   I went to the Chinese restaurant
    to buy a loaf of bread bread bread
    I saw a Chinese lady
    and this is what she said said said
    My name is elli elli
    Chickali chickali
    Chinese chopsticks
    Willy willa whisky /or Rom pom pooli [*Lucy's version*]
    Pow Pow Pow

4   We break up, we break down
    We don't care if the school falls down
    No more English, no more French
    No more sitting on the old school bench
    If your teacher interferes
    Turn her up and box her ears
    If that does not serve her right
    blow her up with dynamite
    Teaching, teacher, we don't care
    We can see your underwear
    Is it black or is it white
    Oh my god it's dynamite.

5   My mummy is a baker
    My daddy is a dustman
    Yum yummy pooey, ticker tacker tooey
    My sister is a show off

142

My brother is a cowboy
Yum yummy pooey ticker tacker tooey
Turn around and pow.

6   I'm a little Dutch girl Dutch girl Dutch girl
I'm a little Dutch girl, from over the sea.

Please will you marry me marry me marry me
Please will you marry me from over the sea.

No I won't marry you, marry you, marry you
No I won't marry you from over the sea.

Why won't you marry me marry me marry me
Why won't you marry me? from over the sea.

Because you stole my necklace, necklace, necklace
Because you stole my necklace from over the sea.

Here is your necklace necklace necklace
Here is your necklace from over the sea.

Now will you marry me marry me marry me
Now will you marry me from over the sea.

No I won't marry you marry you marry you
No I won't marry you from over the sea.

Why won't you marry me marry me marry me
Why won't you marry me? from over the sea.

Because you stole my bracelet bracelet bracelet
Because you stole my bracelet from over the sea.

Here is your bracelet bracelet bracelet
Here is your bracelet from over the sea.

Now will you marry me marry me marry me
Now will you marry me from over the sea.

No I won't marry you marry you marry you
No I won't marry you from over the sea.

Why won't you marry me marry me marry me
Why won't you marry me? from over the sea.

Because you stole my ring ring ring
Because you stole my ring from over the sea.

Here is your ring, your ring, your ring
Here is your ring from over the sea.

Now will you marry me marry me marry me
Now will you marry me from over the sea.

Yes I will marry you, marry you, marry you
Yes I will marry you from over the sea.

Now we're getting married, married, married
Now we're getting married from over the sea.

[*Repeat this format with each of the following lines*]
Now we've got a baby, from over the sea
Now we're getting older
Now we're dying
Now we're dead   [*All these are*
Now we're witches   *accompanied by*
Now we're ghosts   *dramatic*
Now we're dust   *representations*]
Now we're nothing

Now we're in heaven, heaven, heaven.

7   1 2 3 together
     Up together
     Down together
     Backs together
     Fronts together
     Up, down, in, out
     Sides together
     Bums together

8   My boyfriend's name is Tony
     He comes from Macaroni
     With a pickle on his nose
     and ten fat toes
     and this is how my story goes
     One day as I went walking
     I heard my boyfriend talking
     with two little girls and two black curls
     and this is what she said
     she said I L/O/V/E/ love you

I K/I/S/S/ kiss you
I jumped in the lake and I swallowed a snake
and came up with a belly ache.

9   I'm Popeye the sailor man
Full stop
I live in a caravan
Full stop
When I go swimming
I kiss all the women
I'm Popeye the sailor man,
Full stop
Comma comma dash dash.

10   When Susie was a baby
she went goo, goo, goo, goo, goo

When Susie was a sister
she went scribble scribble
scribble scribble scribble

When Susie was a schoolgirl
She went
Miss Miss
I can't do this

When Susie was a teenager
she went help help
I've lost my bra in my boyfriend's car

When Susie was a mummy
she went cook cook cook cook cook

When Susie was a granny
she went knit knit knit knit knit
I've lost my stitch.

The Open Space

As the result of what we have seen of children telling stories and being read to, we know that they use other people's texts to make powerful narratives of their own. Before they are taught to read in school they are able to read the world by means of television pictures and pictures in books created specially for them. In doing things they make plain both their linguistic and literary competences and their social understanding of what counts as a story.

Children are important consumers of books. To exploit adults' concern to find distractions and to ensure their children's entry into literacy, publishers make books for very young children look like toys. International markets open up for gifted authors and artists and what is called children's literature takes on more and more proliferate forms.

The most remarkable books, and those which can be distinctly seen as children's, are picture story books. They combine ingenuity of presentation with a great variety of kinds of discourses. Children learn to 'play' the text as well as to investigate the pictures. In demonstrable ways these books teach many reading lessons (Meek, 1987). The authors and artists seem to go in search of young readers for whom reading is not yet a fixed pattern of textual behaviour but something to be explored as sets of possibilities, what reading might be like. This early reading is carnivalistic, when monsters and fabulous beasts, tall tales of flying children, strange behaviour on the part of adults, the existence of the miniature and the gigantic, the laws of nature suspended or amended, are all part of the scene, as are explosions of laughter from the readers. This looks like reading as play, as desire. We also know that it is play for real. Adults are pleased to join in this delight because they can see that the children are also working hard to make the text come together as a meaningful story. The accomplishment is both the reward of the effort and the desire induced by the pleasure. All children work hard to learn to read. Some who miss the carnival have to discover later that reading can be fun.

The present move in infant classrooms is to keep the pleasurable aspect of reading as long as possible as the motive for desire. To do this, many teachers are now replacing outmoded reading schemes with 'real' books, a move that is to be welcomed for many reasons, not least because it gives young readers the chance to choose from a range of discourse kinds earlier in the process of becoming competent. But we are bound to recognize that this is something more than the replacement of one set of books by more attractive titles. The change is also complicated by the paradox that lies at the heart of the history of literacy in our culture.

As Shirley Brice Heath has shown, some cultural groups take reading narrative fiction for granted as a way of extending their understanding of living. Novels are natural ways of exploring how things might be. For others literacy is traditionally seen as a necessary means of *gaining* a living, and therefore too important to be wasted on stories. So, while we want children to enjoy reading and to do enough to ensure that they will become skilled as the result of insightful practice, we may still have to take seriously the ideas that link reading with work, instrumental effort, especially in school. In addition, we have to acknowledge that all stories 'carry in their sub-texts affirmations of what it means to be a proper person and what constitutes proper behaviour' (Rosen, 1984).

The history of children's books shows plainly the didactic intent of most authors to mix the beautiful with the useful. Jacqueline Rose puts it thus: 'There is, in one sense, no body of literature which rests so openly on an acknowledged difference, a rupture, almost, between writer and addressee. Children's fiction sets up the child as an outsider, to its own processes, and then aims, unashamedly, to take the child *in*' (Rose, 1984, p. 2). There are latent messages in all texts, and those for children are no exception. There is no collection of books that can be required reading for all children, no matter what one's theory of literature may be, given the social divisions of our culture. Indeed, the less direct a child's access to a book, the more he or she is deemed to be in need of a 'message' in the text. Behind the desire of most adult writers for children to make reading pleasurable there is often a parallel desire to make children good.

Implicit in every text for the young is the author's or artist's way of attaching to words or images a desire to affect children's looking or understanding. Stories are interpretations of childhood *by* those whose selective remembrance of it is invaded by unconscious as well as conscious recollections which are then offered *to* those who are actually living through this period. When a young child listens to a story told by her grandmother, the gap between them is visible; the tale is always about 'long ago', or at least not now. But the trick of writing is to present the past as the here and now, so that a psychological reality replaces or excises the story-teller and naturalizes the events of the narrative. The author is, for a long time, hidden from children behind the apparent reality of the tale.

Because we have not yet investigated enough the way by which children 'get into' stories, or how they discover the ways in which the narrator affects the narrative, we are caught in a curious double bind. We want young readers to 'believe in' the characters; in reading this seems a natural thing to do (Josipovici, 1976). But we also want them to 'resist the blandishments of literature', *not* to take Enid Blyton as eternally true, for example, and to see it for what it is, something made with words (Miller, 1984).

We have too few good studies of how children read books written for them (Crago, 1983). Until we have more we are at a loss to know how to examine, in any way that matters, children's reading development. Take, for example, *The Jolly Postman* which has proved remarkably popular with both children and adults who might be hard put to it to explain just why it is such a success (Ahlberg and Ahlberg, 1986). There is a story in rhyme about the postman delivering letters to characters taken from fairy tales and nursery rhymes. The letters are physically in the book, actual miniaturized versions of those which we write in current social practices of literacy — an apology, a lawyer's missive, a postcard, an invitation, an advertising flyer, a letter from a publisher, a birthday card. When children of 8 or so are invited to write letters like those they take from the envelopes, they adopt the conventions of the social situation which they have chosen, certainly without being taught. They simply seem to know the rules. What we need to know is, where do they learn the rules and what acts as a cueing system for the appropriate style of reply? We can guess, but do we know? An understanding of the intertextuality of *The Jolly Postman* depends on the reader's acquaintance with nursery rhymes and fairy stories. What are we to say about other kinds of polysemic texts written for children as instances of how texts teach what readers have to learn about the nature of the thing we call literature?

Until we pursue such questions further, we must be specially grateful for distinctive adult readings of texts designed for the young. Geoffrey Williams' essay stands alone in this open space as a special example of its kind. He shows, in significant and rich detail, how Katherine Paterson works on children's understanding of boundaries and limits. He makes plain the nature of narrative in the exploration of possibilities (Bruner, 1986), while at the same time laying bare the implicit value system of the author. He does full justice to an impressive array of narrative studies, the insights of which are very rarely applied to writing for children.

10 Naive and Serious Questions: The Role of Text Criticism in Primary Education

Geoffrey Williams

Discussions of books deemed 'suitable' for children are often hampered by simplistic judgements about the contents of the plot and the life-likeness of the characters. In this episode we confront the possibility of children's books being about adults' views of what children should know. In his analysis of the narrative discourse of Bridge to Terabithia *Geoffrey Williams breaks the realist illusion of the story and shows how the author, Katherine Paterson, whose acknowledged skill lies in showing characters in stages of developmental transition, also manipulates the reader's view of social values. The essay argues that the polysemic text of a story for children can be as ideational and ideological as anything written for adults. Consequently, we are encouraged to move away from naive judgements of suitability (which book?) and to take on the task of 'constructing powerful critical theory and critical practice, which is enormous but inevitable.'*

Those of us who read stories with young children quickly learn that the interpretation of narrative is not a simple matter. By the time they enter school children's skill in the social use of language is so great they are often able to go well beyond what adults think are the plain senses of texts. Children so often surprise us by what they notice (or fail to see) in discourse or pictures.

The precocious are not the only children to surprise. I shall always hold as an image of children's interpretative ability an occasion when 9-year-old Greg, struggling to learn to read in a special education class, was talking about Anthony Browne's *Hansel and Gretel* with a friend. At the end of the book, as he looked at the picture of the reconciled family, he said very excitedly, 'I bet, I bet the stepmother was the witch. Would you bet? It was the richness of the text which made his dizzy interpretative leap possible. The ironic relationship between language and pictures gave him space for his interpretative play, just as the cohesive repetition of images assured him that this was a genuine story in the making of which he could participate. Children's fiction so often *invites* interpretative work because texts are open to subtle interpretations of narrative form and patterns of value, even when the language seems plain enough.

Educational discourse about children's fiction, however, rarely acknowledges either the subtlety, openness or complexity of text. Despite vigorous general discussion of the appropriateness of some titles for children, in primary education we have been rather better at listening to children's interpretations in order to guess about their ability to comprehend than at investigating the complexity of the texts themselves. Yet the *form* of texts from which children are invited to learn to read is crucial to an account of what it is to comprehend them. A theory of how written texts mean which neglects form would be so seriously reductive as to be worthless.

Criticism of children's texts could contribute very usefully to debate over contemporary definitions of literacy and literary competence and to debate about what counts as reading development. For example, with more interpretative explorations of multiple senses in children's texts available it would be possible to address the complex problems of comprehension in new ways. 'To interpret a text', Barthes remarks in *S/Z*, 'is not to give it a (more or less justified, more or less free) meaning, but on the contrary to appreciate what *plural* constitutes it' (1975/6, p. 5). Critical discussion of the multiple senses of fiction for children is discourse on which teachers might draw to help children expect multiple senses in all narrative, and to learn to discover some that are latent for themselves. The point is not to teach literary critical concepts such as irony to primary children (cf. Scott, 1982) but to deny the *possibility* that a narrative text could have a single meaning and to change pedagogy appropriately. Power relationships between teacher, text, author and young reader, not to mention standardized test constructor, would be changed considerably if criticism of children's texts were to be more readily available.

The issue has general significance in primary education because the interpretation of narrative is more than an aspect of literary competence. Interestingly it is Kermode, the professor of English literature, who remarks in his discussion of narrative 'secrecy' that problems of interpreting: 'seem to be problems of importance for, broadly conceived, the power to make interpretations is an indispensable instrument for survival in the world, and it works there as it works on literary texts' (1979, p. xi). Dominant models of comprehension, as they are constructed by reading schemes, would certainly be forced to change if interpretative debate about texts were more a part of discourse about reading development. The 'power to make interpretations' is not readily developed when only one interpretative possibility is allowed for the texts children encounter.

Neglect of the significance of interpretative criticism, and of *form* in particular, arises largely from an assumption that primary-aged children read only for plot and that therefore the sensibility of the literary critic in investigating form is unnecessary, even irrelevant, to texts for them. Children are intensely interested in plot but whether that is all that is important in their reading of narrative is very questionable. The analogy of children's oral language development, an analogy which has proved so fruitful for reconceptualizing reading processes, is also useful in considering the role of text criticism in primary education.

In learning to speak children learn much more than the phonology, lexis and grammar of a language. They also learn much about the social conventions, ways of thinking and behaving of the society in which the language functions. They may learn, too, ideology from those with whom they talk earliest and most often (Hasan, 1986). In Halliday's (1975) phrase, they learn how to mean within a culture.

The taken-for-granted form of the texts children read, it can be argued analogically, carries important messages about social values: that is to say, narrative form may be as influential as plot, setting and dialogue. That young children may not be consciously aware of relationships between form and patterns of value in a story is of no more educational significance than their lack of self-consciousness about the nature of rules of conversational turn-taking. Indeed, as in everyday talk it may be that what is taken for granted is even more important than what is made obviously significant.

It is surprising, therefore, that text criticism which is attentive to text form has received such limited attention in discussions of reading and social development in the primary school. The text criticism most readily available to primary teachers has, largely, been brief notices or reviews which point to thematic suitability of texts to age, scope for readers' involvement in the plot and accessibility of characters to readers' 'identification'. Such notices and reviews are obviously very useful, especially given the range of curriculum issues and rate of change to which primary teachers have to attend, but they are significant rather than sufficient aids to judging texts for children.

The significance of texts as social constructs, children's texts especially, is very often carried more by what they do *not* reveal explicitly in plot, setting or dialogue than by what is made plain. Narrative, like oracular pronouncement, as Kermode (1977) argues, does not always speak its senses directly but requires interpretative work to discover what it might be construed to say for a particular social and historical context.

The educational task for text criticism is enormous, but perhaps no more urgent than in the case of 'realism' fiction which offers language as a representation of life. Such texts are most frequently the object of claims for the ability of narrative to transform lived experience. If narrative is as powerful as these claims suggest, what the language of realist texts offers readers is of some importance for education, Jacqueline Rose argues: 'Even if it is not the intention, it is the effect of writing which presents itself as "realistic" that the premises on which it has been built go largely unnoticed, because it appears so accurately to reflect the world as it is known to be' (1984, p. 62). Realist texts are never as ideologically innocent, whatever their social setting, as the stories they tell seem. Usually written as readerly texts (Barthes, 1975), these novels direct attention to the resolution of major, easily recognizable and often emotionally very moving conflict but they *also* simultaneously construct other patterns of value which are active in building up ideology and which need to be opened to interpretative discussion.

Much reviewing of realist texts seems content to check for narrative trouble over 'didacticism', values in terms of verisimilitude and stylistic trouble in terms of accessibility. So long as, it would seem, a text tells a realistic story, tends to be mimetic in narration and unstereotypically represents the experience of a range of characters in the setting it portrays, it is acceptable. Sometimes a realist story may even be said to have its inevitable, 'true' resolution if the author does not didactically interfere with it.

In the remainder of this chapter I should like to argue, by taking some examples from the Newbury Award winner, *Bridge to Terabithia* (Paterson, 1978), that features of text other than plot, character, setting and dialogue are active in constructing values, that these values can at least be partly understood through a consideration of the form of narrative discourse, and that such a consideration presents problems of didacticism in children's texts in a new way.

Form of discourse seems, on this analysis, to be an important issue for both criticism and pedagogy which is yet to be explored in detail in primary education.

Bridge to Terabithia is a realist text about which the question of didacticism has often been raised. Most writers hold that the text is not didactic overall though there may be occasional didactic lapses in narration. Anthea Bell (1982), for example, in examining a case of obvious foreshadowing writes:

> It is as if, just for once, didacticism had got the better of the author, and she then realised it did not ring true. I have dwelt on this passage not from a wish to pick unfairly on what seems to me Paterson's one real lapse, but because it *is* just for once, and it *is* her one real lapse. The book stands perfectly well without it.

Katherine Paterson herself remarks, 'I don't even really mind being called a didactic writer because I think teaching is a wonderful thing.' However, she qualifies the remark with a view which finds wide acceptance in children's literature:

> The problem comes, of course, when the story is not paramount; in fiction the story must always be paramount. Any teaching must grow *naturally* out of the story and not be something that you figured out in your head and are determined to get over to the kiddies. That never works. Readers of whatever age are too wise. (in Jones, 1981, p. 196, emphasis added)

The sense seems almost to be of a writer as amanuensis to the values of a story: it is the story 'naturally' (by its verisimilitude) which teaches. The view is important for what it implies about interpretative authority and, eventually, for what might count as useful interpretive work with a text by children and teachers. It deserves a second consideration with *Bridge to Terabithia* as example.

Leslie, the only child of two successful writers, moves with her parents to Lark Creek, into an old house next to the small farm occupied by the Aarons family. Jesse, the only son, has two older and two younger sisters. Jesse meets Leslie early one morning when he is training for the school footraces by running around a cow paddock. After an initial period of shyness and reserve on Jesse's part the two children become close friends and create a 'secret kingdom',

Terabithia, in a forest on the bank of the creek opposite their homes. Their way across the creek and into the kingdom is a rope tied to a tree. Leslie helps Jesse see other possibilities for life, especially for the use of his talents in drawing, thus helping him to overcome the oppression of his unsympathetic family. Jesse, as Leslie tells him, becomes her only true friend and helps her cope with the prejudice and suspicion of the other children in this small rural community. Jesse's artistic talent is also supported by the school music teacher who one day takes him to the Smithsonian in Washington. While they are away Leslie attempts to cross the creek on her own and is drowned when the rope breaks. Jesse seems to pass through all the major signs of deep grieving: confusion, denial, guilt and rage against Leslie for 'abandoning' him. He eventually succeeds in accepting her death and in bridging the gap in his life by welcoming the younger sister of whom he is very fond as the new queen of the secret kingdom.

This counts, I think, as a plausible retelling of the story. It resembles the language (though nòt the length) of annotated bibliographies and it might be of some limited use to a teacher wishing to decide whether or not to follow up the reference as a possible text for classroom reading. As interpretation it is so very inadequate as to be misleading, a reading of only the surface sense. A casual reader of the novel will *always* find, in retrospect, that the account is deficient because the terms of address are dependent on the conventions and illusions of the story. They are irremediably and conventionally limited in dealing with questions of value.

In what terms is an educationally useful interpretation of a realist children's book to be constructed? Difficulty in answering the question reflects the lack of much critical discourse about text for young children. It is at least possible to be clear about what will no longer suffice. Terms such as 'representativeness' and 'response' seem unlikely now to advance analyses very far and methods more disruptive of narrative illusions will be needed if more of the story is to be revealed. Robert Leeson, who recently used these terms in *Reading and Righting*, has refreshingly argued for more attention to social questions in children's literature but he has proposed that questions of social value should be addressed through 'do-it-yourself' discussion in which consideration of the 'narrative thread' of a story should be prominent (1985, Ch. 15). Confusion seems to arise in a search for an adequate social criticism over differences between a social context for critical enquiry, rights of readers to engage in it and the language in which it might be conducted.

Presumably it is quite feasible to construct critical analyses of a story from many different perspectives: psychoanalytic, historical, stylistic, structural. Some critical approaches will be more useful for addressing social questions than others but any of them can be the result of collaborative work; in the case of children's texts they will all have to take account of an intention (of writer, publisher, purchaser, teacher, reader) to make a children's story; and for each critical approach the senses that children say they find in a text will be very important. What seems clear, though, is that an educationally helpful criticism cannot afford to be unsystematic, atheoretical or confined to 'conventional' reading from whatever perspective it is developed. The educational significance of a text ought not to be confused with its personal significance to individual readers (or groups of readers). The latter is something criticism should presumably attend to very closely but not be co-extensive with. Criticism at least needs to make the terms of its analysis explicit if it is to assist teachers in making a serious contribution to the development of children's reading and social understanding. If criticism is confined within the conventions of a story it will necessarily be unsystematic, unintentionally diminishing of the language, form and status of children's books and vulnerable to the accusation of being 'merely' personal. In particular, ideological questions may be reductively discussed as matters of personal preference.

The task of constructing powerful critical theory and critical practice with regard to children's books is enormous but unavoidable. Both theory and practice must be attentive to story but able to go beyond to 'read out', in Seymour Chatman's phrase, the discourse in ways which reveal some of the value assumptions on which a story is built. Analyses of form, particularly of elements of form which are consistently foregrounded in support of a theme, seem a reasonable place to start (Hasan, 1971). Even a general analysis of narrative form is likely to be very revealing of social values, though at a delicate level of lexico-grammatical analysis it may be possible to argue for ways in which the language of a text itself functions to construct ideology. In this discussion I shall attend only to general aspects of form. The assumption that one could argue the case of the text's ideology at a more detailed level, lexico-grammar for example, is implicit but not substantially addressed.

Analysis of text form may seem a violent procedure to use with stories for children requiring, as it does, the setting aside of the illusions of a story. We have some support at least in classical Greek mythology for the use of necessary violence in critical practice. As

Kermode remarks in considering interpretative method generally, it is fortunate for the practice of hermeneutics that Hermes himself is the god both of messages and also of thieves and tricksters who may practice violence. (In the case of *Bridge to Terabithia* we can hope for Hermes' favour since he presides over this text very closely: he is not only the god of messages but also of young athletes and the guide of souls to the infernal regions. He, himself, also performed a remarkable feat as a young child amongst a herd of cows.) Analysis of form requires a minor violence, a breaking of the illusion of character and authentic voice, of 'natural' event sequence and the credibility of the narrator if the plurality of a text's value constructs is to be understood.

The plurality of functions of the narrator's voice is one indication that the language of *Bridge to Terabithia* is not innocent. Take, for example, the sentence: 'Like a single bird across a storm-cloud sky, a tiny peace winged its way through the chaos inside his body.' A gentle, but not innocent, image. Who speaks this sentence? Genette, in *Narrative Discourse* (1980), demonstrates the fruitfulness of distinguishing between the questions 'who speaks?' and 'who sees?' for understanding the multiple functions of a narrator. The sentence occurs when Jesse is alone in the forest: we 'see' from his point of view but he, clearly, neither speaks nor thinks these words. Instead, the reader is addressed directly by the narrator whose voice fulfils multiple functions. As well as advancing the plot by signalling a change of emotion in the protagonist, the narrator creates cohesion with a slightly earlier sentence in which a bird is described as a part of the 'virtual' world, not metaphorically as here. Two days after Leslie's death Jesse had returned to Terabithia. He picked some spring flowers from the forest and wove them into a wreath:

> A cardinal flew down to the bank, cocked its brilliant head, and seemed to stare at the wreath. P. T. let out a growl which sounded more like a purr. Jesse put his hand on the dog to quiet him. The bird hopped about for a moment more, then flew leisurely away. 'It's a sign from the Spirits,' Jess said quietly, 'We made a worthy offering.'

After forcing himself to walk deep into the forest, the imaginary land of Terabithia, Jesse, in a marked change of register from the language he used on first entering the kingdom, says: '"Father, into Thy hands I commend her spirit." He knew Leslie would have liked those words. They had the ring of the sacred grove in them.' The move between the two bird images, carried by the multiple uses and ambiguities of 'spirit', is significant. The description of the cardinal is still within the terms of the kingdom created by the children but by the second use of the bird image we are no longer *only* reading images appropriate to children's worlds of play: our attention slides very gently, carried by relief perhaps at this moment of emotional release, into a particular structure of values and belief about grace and divine intervention. The discourse glides from realism into allegory and back to realism, kept deftly relevant to the plot by the multiple roles of the narrator's voice. 'Peace' as subject of the verb, the actor metonymically acting across the chaos, makes the release a gift (of the Spirit). Jesse is acted upon, no longer the source of his own release, nor released by human intervention, but the source is not directly named: anonymity protected by metonymy.

The original example seems, at first reading, innocently resonant of the creation myths of many cultures, as merely a literary device. But the narrative is not innocent, it is not *just* a transparent description of events. It relies on more than a first level of signification to achieve its effects. In this simple event the cohesion achieved by the double use of the bird image and the double function of the narrator's voice becomes a way of constructing Jesse's emotional release as given by a metaphysical source and a way of hinting at the nature of that source.

The use of the narrator's voice in multiple functions for ideological purposes is a prominent feature of this text. For example, shortly after the bird and spirit passages, the narrator's voice occurs again in direct address to the reader: 'Now it was time for him to move out. She wasn't there, so he must go for both of them. It was up to him to pay back to the world in beauty and caring what Leslie had loaned him in vision and strength.' Here what Genette has called the ideological function is more obvious. The third sentence seems overtly didactic, an expository break in the 'narrative contract'. But the problem is not that didacticism intrudes from outside the story as though it were a product of some temporary clumsiness in the writing. Rather, an ideology of individual responsibility to share the gifts of grace is present throughout the text and is made explicit when the narrator speaks directly at this point. The text is not momentarily flawed by the sentence: the sentence hints at a secret which is present throughout the narrative, a secret which is veiled by verisimilitude.

Jesse's task is 'to move out'. The infinitive form of the verb is necessary. He has to cross the specific border of the imaginary kingdom and the immediate problem of his loss, but the general and desirable state that he moves *to* cannot be specified by the narrator's direct address if conventions of narrative are to be maintained. Only the plot can exemplify, can give a specific reference of event, dialogue and setting, as we shall see in a moment it does. Thus the function of the narrator's voice must change and the ideological work be carried out by event and dialogue. In this case reported speech does much of the ideological work. The grammar, especially through changes in transitivity and pronomial relationships, foregrounds the change in Jesse's emotional state: 'As for the terrors ahead — for he did not fool himself that they were all behind him — well, you just have to stand up to your fear and not let it squeeze you white. Right Leslie? Right.' Jesse muses, engages in imaginary dialogue. By a blending of the voices of the narrator and characters the reader is offered a single. 'natural' value position about the exercise of responsibility.

Much ideological work is achieved through the construction of borders (Hermes again). The borders are physical, psychological, sexual, linguistic and class. The way the text patterns the crossing of these clear borders is very powerful ideologically precisely because the pattern is so consistent. Binary oppositions are, of course, commonly created in narrative and, therefore, characters can commonly be said to cross borders as the starkness of opposition is faded by the discourse. Jonathan Culler, in discussing Levi-Strauss, notes the 'structuring process of reading which, in order to make the text signify, organise its elements into oppositional series which can then be correlated with other oppositional pairs' (1975, p. 52). Border crossing works, though, in a rather more explicit way in *Bridge to Terabithia*. The metaphor which signifies the change in Jesse, that of 'moving out' across the psychological borders of his deficiency and despair, relies for its significance on the way many other borders are crossed at earlier stages in the text. The borders are not only a structuring process of reading, they are also a structural feature of the writing which foregrounds desired values.

The prolific use of borders contributes much to a sense of verisimilitude, to the idea that 'moving out' is natural. It is worth noting a few general examples. On the first occasion of the children's meeting, as Jesse runs around the cow paddock, Leslie sits on the fence between the two properties, 'dangling bare brown legs' and calls to him. Jesse is troubled by her ambiguous dress: 'The person had jaggedy brown hair cut close to its face and wore one of those blue undershirt tops with faded jeans cut off above the knees. He couldn't honestly tell whether it was a girl or a boy.' As she moves across into his field and introduces herself, her androgeneity is again noticed: 'she even had one of those dumb names that could go either way' (p.26). When school opens, Leslie's lack of traditional feminin-ity in dress and lifestyle are greeted derisively by the other children. She persists in offering her friendship to Jesse despite his embarrass-ment at her inappropriate behaviour. On the first day of the footraces in the school playground, for example, Leslie moves down from the girls' playground to join the boys. In the first example of active border crossing by Jesse, after days of rejection, she is invited to run. She wins the races, ending male dominance of the event and therefore their interest in it. What the discourse makes prominent in the race is Leslie's act of crossing the finishing border ahead of Jesse:

> He felt it before he saw it. Someone was moving up. He automatically pumped harder. Then the shape was there in his sideways vision. Then suddenly pulling ahead. He forced himself now. His breath was choking him and the sweat was in his eyes. But he saw the figure anyhow. The faded cutoffs crossed the line a full three feet ahead of him.

Similarly, when Leslie later mistakenly breaks the codes of seating in the school bus she is saved by Jesse who both physically crosses the border into the seventh grade bullies' area and deliberately insults one of them in order to deflect attention from Leslie: the insult again draws attention to the significance of the act itself.

These events all seem plausible enough, 'natural' enough in the setting and they capture sympathy for both of the children. How-ever, the pattern of the discourse is not natural in the sense of inevitable. What the form foregrounds, brought into relationship with foregrounded elements of other events, builds up a sense of a message. The sense of a purpose in the discourse form contradicts the idea that it is the *story* which is the active agent of the message construction. The writer is not an amanuensis of the story's intent or its values: the discourse is a function of the writer's ideological position in relation to the story. Her position, not the story, influences the form and constructs the message, irrespective of whether the position is consciously held and explicitly articulated or not. The resolution is to this extent problematic, not inevitable, even for this story.

There is an apposite example of the way in which text form foregrounds a particular value position in the episode in which the children first decide to create the magic kingdom of Terabithia. The *act* of crossing the creek on the rope precedes their decision and is described in some detail. They first swing back and forth on the rope and then decide to use it as the magical means of entry to the secret place. Here borders have a special significance. Swinging on the rope gives Jesse a feeling of floating, of drifting cloudlike so that: 'Intoxicated with the heavens, he couldn't imagine needing anything on earth.' His feeling is immediately grounded by Leslie: '"We need a place," she said, "just for us."' First he is (dis)placed, psychologically and physically between heaven and earth; then (re)placed while he is in mid-swing, in the act of first crossing the all-significant border from the ordinary to the fabulous world by the agent of his spiritual change.

Linguistic as much as physical borders play an important part in structuring the text. Leslie provides the appropriate linguistic register for the children's speech in the magical kingdom, a register to which Jesse has no access: 'When Leslie spoke, the words rolling out so regally, you knew she was a proper queen. He could hardly manage English, much less the poetic language of a king.' Even reading the second sentence as reported speech, the passage draws attention to a general linguistic difference between the two children, inside and outside the magic. It adds force to the sense of Jesse's emergence not only from grief but from his 'old self' when he, much later, quotes the Crucifixion statement and can be sure of Leslie's approval: '"Father, into Thy hands I commend her spirit." He knew Leslie would have liked those words.' The difference in the children's speech having been given such prominence, the feeling of him moving over from a sense of linguistic deficiency is the more powerful.

Jesse's crossing of psychological borders is, of course, of particular importance. Sometimes these are as delicately suggestive of changes in the tenor of relationship as the wink he gives his sister May Belle when they discuss the probability of Santa Claus knowing the way to their house. His move is soon given its counterpoint in Leslie's wink across her parents' heads to relieve his anxiety about the safety of their shared secrets. His adventure in a new field of positive relationship in his family is supported by Leslie joining him by crossing a similar border in a similar way. Sometimes, however, his psychological border crossing is more thematically important. In those cases it is more marked by metaphor and more explicitly indicated by either the narrator or one of the characters. The play of language between killer whales and Janice Avery, the school bully whom the children successfully humiliate, provides an example. To begin the discussion of ways of preventing the bullying Jesse has to interrupt Leslie's reading of a magazine article about the preservation of killer whales. Jesse asks:

> 'Getting any good ideas?'
> 'What?'
> 'I thought you was getting some ideas on how to stop Janice Avery.'
> 'No, stupid. We're trying to *save* the whales. They might become extinct.'
> He gave her back the book. 'You save the whales and shoot the people, huh?'
> She grinned finally. 'Something like that I guess. Say, did you ever hear the story about Moby Dick?'

In itself this is an early example of Jesse moving to take initiative, to make a sympathetic judgement about another person's needs. Much later in the story, after the success of the plot to humiliate her, he continues the analogy:

> Leslie looked stricken. 'You're not sorry we did it, are you?'
> 'No. I reckon we had to do it, but still —'
> 'Still what?'
> He grinned. 'Maybe I got this thing for Janice like you got this thing for killer whales.'

The construction of the implicit metaphor in the first passage allows a gap, a division of interest to be delineated without disturbing the sense of intimacy between the two children. The movement between intimacy and difference is what allows Jesse later to cross a highly significant border of empathy and suggest that they should actually help Janice Avery when she is in trouble. Leslie has found Janice crying in the girls' toilets and gleefully reports her discovery:

> He looked at her. 'Well,' he said. 'What should we do?'
> 'Do?' she asked. 'What do you mean what should we do?'
> How could he explain it to her? 'Leslie. If she was an *animal* predator, we'd be obliged to try to help her.'
> Leslie gave him a funny look.

To use Genette's distinction between speaking and seeing again, we may ask who speaks the rhetorical question. The apparently reflective moment of reported speech, 'How could he explain it to her?', is also a moment of the narrator directing attention to the cohesion of the metaphor, of standing aside from the movement of the plot and pointing to the particularity of Jesse's move, to his crossing the gap. The words are not just the innocent utterance of a musing character but a site for a narrative bridge between his passivity and new sense of empathy.

In the final chapter Jesse admits May Belle to Terabithia. After she is trapped by vertigo on the branch he has temporarily laid across the creek, Jesse rescues her and builds a safe plank bridge from lumber he is given by Leslie's father. Terabithia is thus opened both to May Belle, the new queen, and possibly also to the youngest sister, Joyce Ann. The significance of these events is evident enough in one sense. Jesse has emotionally 'moved out' without disturbing his first allegiance to the secret Terabithia. The events signify reconciliation, triumph over grief and a new strength of character.

The form of the discourse, however, highlights other values for which it has earlier prepared the reader: not *only* the hope of reconciliation and renewal (see Paterson, 1981), but this possibility specifically as the result of his movement away from the restrictive values of his familial world towards openness to the metaphysical 'magic' of the kingdom and a (metaphysical) gift of peace. The terms on which the resolution is effected are ideologically significant, as they must always be. These terms are established not by a simple, univocal address by the narrator which explicates a 'message' for the young reader but by consistently arranged elements of form in the discourse which work to make the particular resolution necessary and therefore apparently natural. In the case of *Bridge to Terabithia* I have suggested that pervasive use of the narrator's voice in multiple functions to mask the source of address to the reader, the consistent use of borders of various kinds to create a sense of both isolation and movement, and the foregrounding of acts of border crossing in the arrangement of discourse (as against story) time are particularly significant ideologically.

It is quite possible to make a critical interpretation of the text as a realist description of the rejection, friendship and grieving of a young boy: the plot, therefore, as a (more or less) representative example of a significant aspect of human experience, and Jesse as a character with whom young readers can (more or less) identify. If the text is read in this way, critical analysis will almost inevitably proceed to address questions of representativeness and response.

Much can be gained educationally from engaging in another sort of interpretative activity. Disrupting the narrative illusions through a consideration of discourse form allows questions of value to be addressed in a different way and the methods through which these values are conveyed to be understood in different terms. Jesse, as a site in the text through which acts of border crossing are highlighted becomes, to this extent, also a text site for the enunciation of ideology. The text structures as acts of perception and selection, and not just the 'representativeness' of event and character, carry the ideology. Criticism concerned with social values in children's books, as much as any other literature, needs to address questions of discourse form.

When questions of discourse form are addressed a plurality of meanings becomes more available and the danger of novels being simply classified as ideologically agreeable or not according to their verisimilitude is lessened. Reading a novel with children also becomes more obviously a collaborative activity in which multiple senses can be welcomed and tested against the text: it is not, obviously, a matter of teaching the sense of a novel which a first reading suggests. The naturalness of the story becomes problematic and, as one consequence, 'comprehension' as part of the primary school's reading programme is opened to critical debate, redefinition and pedagogical reform. Texts might then be given the attention they require for reading development in primary education to be understood more fully.

A rather different view about the significance of form in children's literature, which argues the ideological impotence of changes in form in children's books has recently been suggested by Jacqueline Rose. After noting that 'recently there has been increasing focus on the shifting registers of language in relation to children's books' she argues that analyses of questions of narrative form are insufficient for overcoming the central problem she identifies in children's literature as: '... the constant association of language in all its forms with a register of truth' (1984, p. 140). Apart from the vulnerability of this statement as a general claim about children's literature, it does seem rather to underestimate the force of the questions which children themselves can, and often do, ask about narrative form. Children do not come to written narrative without a background in the social uses of oral language: questions about who is speaking, to whom, for what purposes and in what tenor of relationship arise very often for them in social interaction and it is therefore not surprising that they raise similar questions about written narrative. The difficulty is that so much of what they may learn about reading in school may teach them that these questions are not worthwhile, necessary or at worst even possible.

Forms of narrative, realist or otherwise, which actively invite these questions are not in any simple association with a 'register of truth' and issue nothing which resembles a 'command' to identity (*ibid.*, p. 141). Such forms are of considerable educational importance in helping children to raise such important interpretative questions even in texts where they are not invited to do so.

Rose's view also perhaps underestimates the way in which narrative language can itself raise questions about the veracity of its references. Even within relatively simple realist form the discourse itself can raise doubts about the social uses language is put to in the virtual world it constructs. Such widely differing books as Jan Mark's *Handles* and Paula Fox's *One-Eyed Cat* both achieve this. There is, again, no *necessarily* simple relationship between language and a 'register of truth' even in realist fiction and the complexity of the relationship provides room for interpretative distance and challenge *by children*. The narrator in Kundera's *The Unbearable Lightness of Being* remarks, with only slight exaggeration: '... the only truly serious questions are ones that even a child can formulate. Only the most naive of questions are truly serious. They are the questions with no answers' (1984, p. 139).

At the conclusion of *Bridge to Terabithia*, when Jesse finished building the bridge, '... he put flowers in her hair and led her across the bridge — the great bridge into Terabithia — which might look to someone with no magic in him like a few planks across a nearly dry gully.' A socially and educationally productive criticism in children's literature must often ask questions which set aside narrative conventions and therefore hover on a border between a view of the magic and a view of the planks. It cannot afford to be permanently grounded on either side. Some of its unconventional questions are, fortunately, similar in naivety and seriousness to ones which children ask about forms of written text before familiarity with the magic removes the need to ask them. The similarity is sufficient to encourage an hypothesis that critical work with children's stories can help us understand more about how narrative conventions are learned and what they teach, not just in realist texts but in all narrative for children.

Acknowledgement

I would like to thank Margaret Meek for our conversations about criticism and children's literature during the preparation of this chapter. Responsibility for the views expressed here is, of course, entirely mine.

Part 4 Reading: Retrospect and Prospect

The next four chapters provide a vantage point from which to chart the concerns which may be significant in teacher education courses into the 1990s. They document some of the ways in which thinking about reading has changed. Some of the features of these changes correspond with the themes of other contributors.

Cliff Moon shows how teachers have moved from an acceptance of what the experts tell them. They now question a view of reading as a progression from letters to words and then to sentences. The role of powerful texts has been reaffirmed. These are social changes, as powerful as any described by cultural historians (Williams, 1981). Moon's own work has done much to give teachers confidence that what they see children do as they read must count as evidence of the actual process.

Cary Bazalgette, aware of these changes and of the cultural context in which literacy is learned, introduces new themes and perspectives. She argues that notions of reading must now be widened to take in images, signs, signals and codes. She extends the notion of *literacies* that Gillian Beardsley's novice readers showed us in the Post Office (p. 83). The competences that children draw upon in their reading of literature may have their origins in the kinds of talk they engage in around *Blue Peter*.

It is clear that teachers need to know that their experiences in the teaching of reading are neither singular nor deviant. The work of Heath (1982) and Street (1984) could give students and teachers powerful case studies and tools to analyze the sites where reading and writing are taught and learned. We could still look more closely at social practices in classrooms, using Bazalgette's kinds of analyses of how cultural practices are shifting. The very terms we use may need to be inspected. Moon's sensitive account of *Titch* reminds us that literature, and what exists to be read, must be a constant theme.

Now that the role of parents in relation to their children's education is being both negotiated and analyzed, we should remind ourselves that the variety of the potential in parents' contributions is greater than we have yet taken on board. We tend to assume that partnership is good, easy and valuable — if only people will engage in it. But the exact nature of good collaboration has yet to be explored.

Barry Stierer uses the context of a large-scale research project to examine some of the fine shifts disguised by a global term like 'parental involvement'. Evelyn Gregory works on a smaller canvas to reveal how her enterprise in East London shows how literacy is culturally and socio-economically sited. She uses an anthropological tradition and a story-teller's voice to bring out reading and writing as 'part of the texture of everyday living'.

11   Reading: Where Are We Now?

Cliff Moon

Moon's account of shifts in thinking about reading is an example of how a gifted and experienced practitioner draws upon new theories and perspectives, making them his own by weaving them into his classroom practice. The young teacher's account in Mills' article (p. 29) reveals how Moon's own reflections have enabled others to grow and change. This is what makes good reflective teaching, and teacher education, into an interpretative community where teachers are able to look and listen, and match what they read and hear with what they see.

Here is a true story. A year ago we bought a border collie puppy and started to train him. One of our earliest problems was that he frequently scaled the stairs but refused to attempt the descent which meant that he was often stranded on the landing. One evening we left our 16-year-old son to 'puppy-sit' for a couple of hours and on our return we found that the stairs problem had been solved. How? It appears that Colum, who is not a psychologist, had deduced that puppies who needed to learn to come downstairs must do it step-by-step but from the bottom-up, not the top-down. He put the puppy on the bottom step and coaxed him down one step, then on the second step and down two steps, third step and so on, working his way further and further up the stairs. I recounted this incident to a psychologist colleague a few days later and she promptly said, '*chaining* — a procedure frequently adopted by teachers of physically handicapped children.' Apparently if you want to teach a spastic child, for example, how to take off his socks, you first place a sock on the very end of the child's toes and let him snatch it off. Then you work further and further back until he can take off the sock himself from the ankle down.

The more I thought about this entirely logical method of skill learning the more it appeared an apt parable for the way language is learned. Not just language, of course; it can be argued that this is how we learn anything and everything. In other words we must go to the end result at the beginning so that we can see how and why our learning will take place. In many circumstances this first step towards learning something new is termed 'play' and in returning to language-learning in particular we can see that the baby's gestural turn-taking with its mother and its early babbling are really playful explorations of an observed phenomenon, conversation (Trevarthen, 1974). For some years we have witnessed evidence of parallels in reading where an essential stage of development appears to be the child 'talking through' a story in his or her own words but using a surface form which is more akin to the conventions of written than oral language, an activity which is often referred to as 'talking like a book' (Clay, 1972; Fox, 1983). Recently we have seen how children in every literate culture do the same with writing (e.g., Goodman, 1985, p. 62; Ferreiro and Teberosky, 1983, ch. 6).

After recounting these incidents at a Teachers' Centre talk I was challenged by a remedial reading teacher of many years' experience, who claimed that learning to read was a step-at-a-time learning process starting with sound/symbol relationships building to whole words and finally to the identification of whole words in meaningful sentences. Having read about the work of Piagetian researchers like Emilia Ferreiro I had to agree that learning to read was indeed a step-at-a-time process but that much depended on which steps we were talking about and whether you started at the top or bottom of the stairs. The only drawback to my parable is its inverse relationship to the 'top-down'/'bottom-up' terminology used by reading theorists and the useful model of the communication process provided by Gordon Wells (1981, p. 69). Learning to read, like learning to swim, walk or ride a bike, is a question of completing the whole act first, however imperfectly and approximately, and refining the parts later through experience and practice.

From Oral to Written Language

Donaldson (1978) provides one of the most accessible accounts of developments over the last thirty years in our understanding of how children learn oral and written language competences. Quite properly she does this against a background of evidence about how children *learn*, full stop. The story begins with the behaviourists' claims that learning to talk (and read) was a comparatively simple question of Stimulus-Response conditioning and in terms of reading instruction this logically led to flash-cards, look-and-say schemes and word recognition tests. The position with regard to oral language learning changed in the 1960s with Chomsky's elegant theory which sought to explain oral language-learning precocity (compared with other kinds of learning as outlined principally by Piaget) in terms of a genetically transmitted grammatical predisposition which was unique to humans. A simple illustration, frequently quoted, is of the child who says, 'I rided my bike' or 'I goed to bed'. The child did not learn 'rided' or 'goed' by imitating adults and being rewarded for his or her utterance. The child arrives at 'rided' and 'goed' by means of a kind of filtering programme. The child can only imitate within the constraints of his/her own grammatical control, and in this instance has overgeneralized a rule that all English verbs in the past tense are marked by an 'ed' ending. At the time Chomsky had little choice but to isolate language learning from other aspects of early learning because children's linguistic competences were seen to be emerging much earlier, and at a much more sophisticated level, than the rest of their cognitive development.

Events in the late 1960s and early 1970s changed all that. First, a corpus of psychological research led by Bruner, Donaldson and others cohered to demonstrate that when Piagetian investigations were reworked within a framework which recognized the 'child's-eye-view' then the results were different. Donaldson (1978) describes in some detail how this came about. The result was that the gap between language-learning and other kinds of learning narrowed substantially. Language-learning was not as significantly different from other learning as Chomsky had supposed. Second, experiments with chimpanzees, dolphins and other intelligent mammals suggested that language-learning was not unique to humans because animals taught sign-language (or other symbolic representations of meaning) were able to generate novel 'utterances'. This continues to be contested but whether or not the original proposition is supported, the effect was the same at the time — it led to renewed research activity directed at how young children learn oral language.

By 1972 the picture was clearer. Language-learning took place within interpersonal contexts and the *only* genetic predisposition seemed to be a social one: the propensity of the child to *interact* with significant others. Some researchers even tracked the eye, head, arm and leg movements of new-born babies in the presence and absence of their mothers. Macnamara's (1972) seminal paper, to quote Donaldson, 'stood Chomsky's argument upon its head.' The time was right for longitudinal, naturalistic studies of oral language acquisition based on the *interactionist* position; this is precisely what Gordon Wells attempted in the *Bristol Language Development Project* (Wells, 1981, 1985 and 1987).

From the accounts of this research three clear points can be drawn. Firstly, parents do not *teach* their children to talk. Instead, children are *immersed* in oral language in use. It happens all around them, haphazardly, frequently incoherently, yet they listen to it, order it, make sense of it, generate their own rules for it and, in their second year of life, they begin to use it themselves in well organized, highly efficient ways which they have never even heard. What could be more functional than 'daddy home' and 'mummy milk'?

Wells (1985, pp. 415–16), in summing up the results of this study of 128 children, claims that:

> Those [parents] whose children were most successful [at learning to talk] were not concerned to give systematic linguistic instruction but rather to ensure that conversations with their children were mutually rewarding. They assumed that, when their child spoke, he or she had something to communicate, so they tried to work out what it was and, whenever possible, to provide a response that was meaningful and relevant to the child and that invited further contribution.

This leads naturally into the second point: parents do not correct their children's verbal 'mistakes'. The child who says 'I rided my bike' is not greeted with 'No dear, the word isn't *rided*, it's *rode*, R.O.D.E. RODE. Say after me *I rode my bike.*' What a parent typically says is something like, 'Oh, did you? Where did you go?' In other words parents attend to what the child *means*, not to the surface features of vocabulary or syntax.

Thirdly, oral language-learning takes place within contexts which are purposeful and meaningful. Children and their parents do not have conversations about nothing; they converse about real things in the real contexts of everyday events which matter to them.

In concluding that the development of communication is fundamentally interactional, Wells (1985, p. 397) states:

> At each stage, the child endeavours to communicate using the resources currently available to him. The adult with whom he is interacting interprets his behaviour in terms of her own cultural and linguistic framework and responds in a way that both reflects to the child the perceived significance of his behaviour and, in the form and context of that response, provides information about the communication system and its relation to the world that enables the child to supplement and modify his communicative resources.

So children learn to communicate by communicating just as they learn to walk by walking and presumably, read by reading and write by writing.

Admittedly these are only three conclusions from Wells' work which have a bearing on learning to read but they are central to our further exploration of what is important in the learning-to-read process. They can be spelt out in the form of questions.

1 Can reading be *taught*?
   Would it be more useful to think of *learning* rather than *teaching*?
   Is *immersion* in written language a way of getting right the conditions for learning?
   If so, what would *immersion* consist of in the home or in school?
2 Should 'mistakes' be corrected when children are learning to read?
   Can we distinguish between 'mistakes' concerned with surface vocabulary and syntax and those concerned with meaning?
   Do we attend to what the text *means* when children are reading?
   Do children?
3 Are early learning-to-read situations purposeful and meaningful?
   Do the texts we use convey important messages and meanings? Are children encouraged to learn to read by reading — the whole activity not merely parts?

We have reached a point where the theoretical and research bases of knowledge about oral language acquisition and consequent implications for literacy learning can lead to radical reappraisal of what we do to help children learn to read and how we might best go about it. Writing in a UNESCO journal, Cohen (1985, p. 44) states:

> We must analyse in detail the procedures followed by children in mastering language and then create around them the conditions and environment likely to facilitate their progress in the written language, exactly as is the case in the spoken language.
>
> It is not a matter of the adult teaching but rather of the child learning, which is quite the opposite.

The Reading Process

Moving from the learning of language competences in general to reading in particular is facilitated by the above quotation from Wells where he says that 'the child endeavours to communicate using the resources currently available to him.' The one preoccupation which has dominated studies of the reading process for the last twenty years is the attempt to delineate what the learner brings to the task in terms of linguistic, social and attitudinal experience. Kenneth Goodman, as long ago as 1963, showed how oral reading miscues reflected the linguistic resources available to the learner. The work of people like Margaret Clark, Marie Clay, Don Holdaway, Jessie Reid and Frank Smith focused attention during the 1970s on similar and related issues. Goodman (1973, p. 12) made the point that:

> Because we have not properly respected language, we have tended to think we facilitated learning to read by breaking written language into bite-sized pieces for learners. Instead, we turned it from easy-to-learn language into hard-to-learn abstractions.

More recently Goodman (1985, pp. 61–4) has offered three key reasons why literacy development in young children has been unappreciated:

1   Lack of a comprehensive theory to explain how literacy works and how it is developed by children.

2   The consequent dependence on arbitrary and unscientific instructional programmes by schools.
3   The maintenance of a narrow tradition of literacy for the élite even in the most technologically advanced countries.

His recommendations for combating these problems are summarized below (see pp. 184–5).

At first the emphasis was on the psycholinguistic processes at work in reading development, with Frank Smith making the largest single and most widely recognized contribution. It is worth remembering that Smith was a one-time student of George Miller whose work on information processing was published in the late 1960s. Miller argued that we can only cope with seven (plus or minus two) discrete units of information at any one time. Smith later developed his 'bottle-neck' theory which is an elaboration of Miller's ideas but is specific to the reading process. He used it to demonstrate that reading by decoding is impossible because readers cannot retain sufficient phoneme/grapheme correspondences, or even whole words, in memory long enough for synthesis into meaningful chunks to take place. Smith has consistently maintained that reading can only be achieved by moving from whole-to-part, not part-to-whole.

A common objection to psycholinguistic perspectives on reading is that the process is different for novice and for competent readers. Goodman has strongly contested this view throughout his career and we must note that Goodman's theories are rooted in naturalistic research and observation of children who are experiencing difficulties in learning to read. This view that the process if fundamentally similar for *all* readers, whatever their stage of development, is supported by a growing body of research and has obvious implications for teachers everywhere. Two recent examples can be cited to illustrate the point.

Meyer (1982) investigated the effectiveness of word-analysis and word-supply correction procedures when fifty-eight 'remedial' readers aged between 7 and 14 years read aloud. One group received seventy lessons of twenty minutes' duration over a four-month period in phonic synthesis and were encouraged to use these skills when they encountered unknown words during oral reading. The other children were merely told the words they did not know or read incorrectly. A battery of tests was used to measure the gains in reading attainment at the end of the project and Meyer concludes: 'Simply telling the students what the correct word was elicited gains as impressive as those associated with having students essentially reformulate how they should have "attacked" the mispronounced words' (p. 553). Backman (1983) investigated the role of phonic segmentation, blending and discrimination in the reading development of children who had learned to read prior to formal school instruction and concluded that none of these skills appeared to be true prerequisites for beginning reading.

What can be inferred from research findings like these is that where attention is directed towards maintaining the meaning of the whole rather than towards identifying constituent parts then teaching and learning will be more efficient and effective. Home-school projects like 'paired reading', reported elsewhere in this book, may well be so successful because they also focus attention upon the meaning of the whole.

A second example concerns attempts to teach whole word identification in isolation and in sentence context. Nemko (1984) studied two groups of forty-eight 6-year-old children who were taught and subsequently tested according to the two respective conditions. The most significant finding was that children who were taught words in isolation were most successful at identifying them in isolation. Nemko summarizes: 'If children trained in isolation identify significantly more training words only when tested in isolation and not when tested in context, then training in isolation would have little implication for classroom reading instruction, as the act of reading involves more than the identification of isolated words' (p. 467). Put another way, teaching which relies on behaviourist flash-cards and 'sight vocabulary' training *is* successful but only in enabling children to do what they are being trained to do — identify isolated words out of context.

So what is this process which is common to all readers, regardless of proficiency? Goodman (1973b, p. 31), in describing reading as a 'psycholinguistic guessing game', defines reading thus:

Reading is a selective process. It involves partial use of available minimal language cues selected from perceptual input on the basis of the reader's expectation. As this partial information is processed, tentative decisions are made to be confirmed, rejected or refined as reading progresses.

This brings us to more recent studies of young children's conceptual development in reading and writing. Ferreiro and Teberosky (1983) and Ferreiro (1984) report a variety of Piagetian-style investigations carried out in Switzerland, Argentina and

Mexico whilst researchers in France, Israel, Canada, Spain and the United States have subsequently confirmed their findings. Basically we must accept that children begin to learn how to read and write long before formal schooling commences. As soon as a child's eyes can focus on print in the environment (food cartons, TV adverts, etc.) then that child must be forming hypotheses about what the print is for, why it is there and how its symbolic system works. Once the child can ask questions, direct evidence of this conjecturing can be examined. A wealth of such evidence is to be found in the tape transcripts of the Bristol Language Development Project. Allan, for example, was aged 2 years 3 months when the following conversation took place with his mother as he drank Cherryade at the kitchen table:

> *Allan.* And what does that says there?
> *Mother.* That's 'Cherryade'.
> *Allan.* Look — that's that — same as that, look.
> *Mother.* No it isn't. It says 'Family Size'.

And Susan, aged 3 years 3 months, was looking through her mother's hand-bag when she asked:

> *Susan.* What does that say?
> *Mother.* That's all the list of mummy's addresses.

But children's literacy development begins much earlier and forms a continuum which embraces the point at which teachers usually say a child has started reading or writing independently. Researchers like Emilia Ferreiro have found that young children frequently hypothesize that a word must have three or more letters for it to be 'readable', that 'readable' text must consist of different letters (not a string like *mmmmm*, for example) and that the length of a word must relate to the size of the object to which it refers.

The knowledge children bring to reading is substantial and barely impinges upon traditional accounts of what is deemed necessary for 'reading readiness'. Schools usually depend heavily on books for early reading instruction yet both Goodman and Altwerger (1981) and Haussler (1984) have found that children entering school are much more proficient at handling print on cartons, signs and TV than print in books. The most disturbing conclusion from Ferreiro and Teberosky is that whereas Argentinian children with well developed concepts about literacy prior to school entry made good progress during their first year in school, children with less well developed concepts were not helped by the teaching they received. Even worse, their development was frustrated because, in Ferreiro and Teberosky's words, 'the instructional method has a restraining effect on children's creative possibilities (experimenting and testing new ideas with all the risks and errors this implies) and establishes a total dependency on the teacher' (p. 242). What was the 'instructional method' in those South American schools? The systematic teaching of phoneme/grapheme relationships and isolated whole word recognition.

At first sight it might appear that research reported by Evans and Carr, (1985) confounds the evidence presented above by concluding that 'linguistic ability facilitates beginning reading only after a threshold of print-specific skills is acquired' (p. 327) but what is claimed as a comparison between 'individualized language-experience' and 'decoding-orientated basal reader' approaches turns out instead to be a comparison between phonics and look-say methods of early reading instruction. This is somewhat misleading, and it is interesting to note that Ferreiro and Teberosky (1983) include *both* look-say and phonic methods in their indictment of instruction which restrains children's creative possibilities. They both stem, in fact, from part-to-whole models of the reading process.

So far we have concentrated upon the linguistic and conceptual resources which young children bring to the reading act but recent studies have stressed the importance of understanding the various perceptions of literacy which have been absorbed into the child's consciousness. Heath (1983) describes differences in the early socialization of children from different communities in one North American township, and a remarkable collection of papers edited by Goelman *et al.* (1984) includes several examples of this recent line of ethnographic investigation. Heath (1980 and 1982) has been particularly interested in the wider educational effects of activities like story-reading sessions with pre-schoolers. Not only do such children internalize knowledge about written language forms and the representation of meanings in story books but they also begin to cope with disembedded language and learn how to be 'question-answerers' in relation to books. In short, children who are read to at home have higher chances of becoming early fluent readers *and* of making good progress within the general educational milieu. Dombey (1983) provides a perceptive account of the various levels of learning which are brought into play during a bed-time story session with a 3-year-old girl. Anna, she says, is learning about written story and written language among many other things as her mother acts simultaneously as mediator and model.

At present the reading process is viewed as multi-faceted and interactive. The child who is born into a literate society begins to develop reading and writing competences from a very early age, the mode and direction of those competences being largely determined by opportunities for exploring them, perceptions of their functions and socially learned attitudes towards their value. Where reading has been seen as a simple skill-learning exercise, the educational implications were correspondingly simplistic and resulted in inflexible programmes of work which, if they were unsuccessful, suggested that the learner rather than the programme was at fault. Given our present level of knowledge about the process and of what children already understand before they enter school, a radical reappraisal of the teacher's role is long overdue.

Teachers and Schools

When Shropshire County Council published a report on how reading was taught in its primary schools (Hodgson and Pryke, 1983) it was immediately clear that pedagogy was lagging some thirty years behind theory. This problem is certainly not restricted to Shropshire as several small-scale replications in other areas have unveiled. Nor can teachers be blamed when so few opportunities for genuine in-service education exist. To explore fully every implication of what has been raised in this chapter is not possible for fairly obvious reasons but in order to telescope my comments I shall employ the distinction which introduces a collection of personal accounts by six class teachers, none of whom used reading schemes or rule-based approaches to teaching reading (Moon, 1985). The distinction is between *resources* and *teaching methods*, although it is obvious that a teaching resource embodies or implies a methodology relating to its use.

Resources

At the time of writing *The Times Educational Supplement* is running a series on primary schools which are recognized for their good practice. Comments like 'real books are used instead of reading schemes' appear weekly as a matter of course. Yet at this same time five major educational publishers in the UK are preparing to launch new reading schemes within the coming months. The question I often put to teachers is, 'Who needs reading schemes?' When you consider that schemes are a relatively recent phenomenon and that even now many children learn to read without them either before they enter school or at schools which have rejected them, then it is clear that teachers, not children, need reading schemes.

But why are they under attack from so many quarters? Simply because they separate literacy-learning from the natural contexts within which it should occur and, where they embody a model of the reading process which is less dynamic than that outlined above, they sacrifice linguistic relevance to artificial surface formulations. When Wade (1982) compared a typical reading scheme text with a John Burningham picture/story book he drew attention to: 'the potential conflict in the minds of children caused by any reading which promotes arbitrariness instead of pattern, disconnection rather than coherence and emptiness rather than fulfilment' (pp. 33–4). But this is an old story. At the turn of the century a psychologist was calling for the disappearance of schemes, largely on the grounds that 'no trouble has been taken to write what the child would naturally say' (Huey, 1908). Knowing what we now do of the oral language expertise and written language expectations which young children bring to print, the presentation to them of texts designed on the basis of controlled vocabulary, phonic regularity or word repetition rather than on recognizable language in use is a practice which is rapidly becoming totally untenable.

Spencer (1976) spelt out the two-fold mismatch between the books which children are given to read for themselves when they commence reading instruction and the books they have had (or are having) read to them *and* the stories they compose themselves from an early age. She called for the integration of children's literature into the literacy-learning process and this call was later answered by Bennett (1979 and 1980) among others.

By 1981 the Schools Council's primary reading project had been published (Southgate *et al.*, 1981) and, at the end of the chapter 'The Books Teachers Use to Teach Reading', the following question was asked: 'Are the basic reading schemes being used the ideal reading materials either to grip the children's interest or to increase their reading ability and fluency? Are these schemes such as to convince children that reading is a desirable pursuit?' (p. 122).

Stebbing and Raban (1982) analyzed children's oral reading miscues and recall rates after reading comparable stories from two reading schemes, *Through the Rainbow* and *One Two Three and Away*. There were differences in qualitative miscues and recall, both favouring the *One Two Three and Away* story. In discussing their results the authors say this of the *Through the Rainbow* text:

> Although the text has a fictional surface, it is in fact a narrative without structure. There is no plot requiring resolution.... There is no introductory 'Once upon a time...' or anything suggestive of development.... The characters are insubstantial and little occurs in the train of events to make the reader wonder what will happen next. (p. 159)

Note that their comparison was of two established reading schemes, not of a scheme and a 'real book' which might have provided a more marked contrast.

Bruner (1984) points out that reading schemes seldom, if ever, contain material to which the child can respond emotionally yet that is the one experience which reading is best able to offer. By denying children access to this realization we are surely acting in bad faith. He concludes that we should make reading: 'an instrument for entering possible worlds of human experience' (p. 200).

There is sufficient evidence from Southgate *et al.* (1981) and the Assessment of Performance Unit reports (1981 and 1982) that large numbers of children are learning to dislike reading as they acquire reading competence in our primary schools. This must be due, in part at least, to the *content* of what they are expected to read otherwise HMI (1982, p. 9) would not have called for greater attention to the teaching of literature in primary schools to combat negative attitudes to reading.

Meek (1982, p. 11) asserts that: 'What the beginner reader reads makes all the difference to his view of reading.' Even a cursory examination of some of our most recent reading schemes demonstrates that they are not designed to assist the development of positive views of reading nor are they designed against a background knowledge of the experience and expertise children bring to reading. They could even be partly responsible for that thirty-year lag between pedagogy and theory noted in the Shropshire report.

The sting in the tail must surely be the investigation carried out by Southgate and Lewis (1973) in six primary schools which firmly believed in the value of their chosen scheme. Observation of children aged 5–6 years showed that during the time designated by the teacher as 'reading and language time' only 7 per cent of the children's time was spent on the scheme itself whereas 48 per cent of the time was spent on other reading and writing activities and 45 per cent on extraneous or diversionary activities. All the children made average progress in reading over the year. I have often suggested to teachers that if that progress was generated by the tiny proportion of time spent in contact with the scheme then reading schemes must indeed have magical properties which flow into the bloodstream when touched! Isn't it far more reasonable and realistic to suppose that the children's progress came from the seven-times-greater amount of time they spent on 'other reading and writing activities'?

Methods

Some indication has already been given as to appropriate and inappropriate teaching strategies for helping children learn to read (e.g. Backman, 1983; Cohen, 1985; Ferreiro and Teberosky, 1983; Meyer, 1982; Nemko, 1984). The six teachers who wrote personal accounts of their classroom practices (Moon, 1985) all advocated a language experience approach which often embraced, but extended far beyond, the *Breakthrough to Literacy* materials (Mackay *et al.*, 1978). Hall (1985) has put in a plea for committed teachers to 'keep language experience alive and thriving' because it is:

> based on the premises that the learner is an active user of language, that learning is promoted through personal involvement, that communication of meaning is the purpose and heart of language learning, and that the learner's products are valued and valid materials for literacy learning. (p. 5)

Goodman's (1985, p. 64) recommendations for combating the three problems outlined earlier in this chapter can be summarized as follows:

1 Schools should build on what children already know about written language, expanding the range of functions they already have. Children should be surrounded by functional and meaningful written language — books, magazines, newspapers, and should be encouraged to keep diaries, write letters, make lists and charts, record information, etc.

2 Schools should move away from subskill learning activities,

memorization and tests, using functional materials instead to continue their literacy development. Children should choose what they want to read and write about.

3   Schools should abandon any traditions of literacy for an élite and develop ways of accepting *all* children into the literate community.

In a recent article (Moon, 1985) I suggested that an 'alternative reading curriculum' could be devised around a *provision* model, thereby placing the responsibility for learning firmly with the learner but putting the onus on teachers to design and organize the conditions for that learning:

Teachers provide — evidence (print of all kinds)
— opportunities (time to read or browse)
— resources (environmental, functional print)
— encouragement (*all* children are readers)
— models (teachers, parents, older children seen to be reading)
— practice (share books with parents at home)

But possibly the best detailed account of what might constitute an ideal reading curriculum in the present climate is that set out by Somerfield *et al.* (1983) for Coventry LEA.

Frequently the debate on methodology centres on accuracy of reading, and Goodman's work has often been disregarded because many teachers associate the term 'psycholinguistic guessing game' with sloppiness. Anderson *et al.* (1984) found that 264 9-year-olds were better able to recall what they had read if there was an emphasis on meaning rather than on accurate oral reading. Donaldson and Reid (1982) have claimed that there is no conflict between 'informed contextual guesswork' and 'getting the words right' because the one will lead naturally to the other just as the oral language learner gradually differentiates and refines vocabulary and syntax. As Meek (1982) succinctly puts it, 'the first thing is not to get the words right but to get the story right.'

Finally, it seems necessary to add a word on the practice of hearing children read aloud. It is difficult to see where it fits into what has been outlined so far yet it is widespread and appears to be one of the mainstays of reading instruction despite its doubtful pedigree (Arnold, 1982). I have claimed (Moon, 1985) that 'reading aloud might be the best way to prevent children becoming readers' because it slows down reading and forces the reader to concentrate on surface features and intonation at the expense of comprehension. The way forward may be to relegate reading aloud to the 'longer but less frequent' pupil-teacher conference advocated by the Schools Council report (Southgate *et al.*, 1981) as one among a variety of activities and that when it is engaged in the teacher's purposes must be clear. One purpose could be to carry out some form of miscue analysis in order to determine the reader's strategies; another could be to help the child become an effective and independent reader. To achieve the latter NATE Primary Committee (1984, pp. 20–1) suggests a priority order for teacher intervention when a child meets an unknown word:

1 Suggest alternative text if proportion of unknown words is higher than one word in twenty
2 Tell child the word if it is a special noun, name, etc.
3 Ask child to guess what the word might be considering sense and context. Refer to illustration if there is one.
4 Ask child to read to end of line or sentence then back-track, OR re-read from beginning of sentence.
5 Teacher reads aloud with exaggerated intonation, omitting unknown word.
6 Quiz child about what the word could be; discuss alternatives in the light of sense and context.
7 Teacher draws attention to initial consonant and links with 6.
8 Draw attention to syllables and known words within the word and link with 6 and 7.
9 Tell the child the word.

Useful transcripts which provide models for the 'longer but less frequent' pupil-teacher conference have been prepared by Baker (1984 and 1985). These *include* children reading aloud but much more besides and they are potentially more conducive to the formation of positive attitudes towards reading than are more traditional approaches.

Conclusion

The aim of this chapter has been to provide an overview of recent insights into what learning to read entails and how teachers might begin to translate those insights into practice which will support rather than hinder children's development as language users in general and readers in particular. The ground covered is far from exhaustive but a number of key issues have been raised and the sources drawn upon provide starting points for further study.

12   A Symbolic Challenge: Reading Helpers in School

Barry Stierer

When parents cross the threshold of school their presence is construed in terms of their symbolic interaction with the teachers inside the building. Different social relations, different ways of talking about children, different presentations of the self ensue. When 'helpers' are present in the classroom their role is an ambiguous one, especially when they hear children read aloud. Are visiting volunteers a help or a threat? As the result of his research Barry Stierer discovered the extent and kind of help parents offer. He examines some of his evidence and finds that the visitor-volunteers are helping to promote and sustain certain important changes in the relations between home and school.

It is 9.40 a.m. The thirty-two 6 and 7-year-olds in Ms Usher's class of top infants have just returned to the classroom from morning assembly. Having collected materials for practical mathematics work or for topic work, they are settling to their tasks either singly or in twos and threes. Ms Usher is sitting on a chair at the carpeted corner of the room discussing practical maths work with a small group of children. There is a low level of industrious chatter around the room. Through the door comes a woman in her early 30s, smartly dressed in skirt and sweater. She has a half-businesslike, half-embarrassed look as she glances at her watch and proceeds toward Ms Usher's chair, making great — almost theatrical — attempts to be unobtrusive. Ms Usher notices her approaching, interrupts her chat with the children sitting on the carpet and stands up. Both women smile. Sarah Pullen's mother has come to help with reading, as she does every Tuesday morning.

Mrs Pullen takes a ring binder from a bookcase and installs herself on the periphery of the classroom. She opens the binder and turns to the copy of the class list with her own name neatly printed at the top. Leaning forward she quietly asks a nearby child to fetch the first pupil on her list. Thus summoned, Stephen collects his current 'reading book' from a drawer and pulls up a small chair alongside Mrs Pullen, where he reads aloud for about ten minutes. From time to time Stephen gets stuck; Mrs Pullen tells him the word giving difficulty and he continues. Occasionally the story prompts Stephen to tell Mrs Pullen something about himself or to ask Mrs Pullen a question. She responds to these digressions with relaxed and amused interest, and they sometimes chat for several moments before returning to the story. When Stephen reaches the end of a section Mrs Pullen gently stops him, thanks him and asks him to fetch Nicola on his way back to his table. In the interlude she makes a note of the words which Stephen had found difficult next to his name on the class list in her binder, and exchanges a furtive smile with her daughter Sarah, who has managed to make respectable progress with her topic work despite her mother's presence in the classroom.

Ms Usher receives unpaid help with reading from three other volunteers on a regular basis: one is another parent, one is the parent of a former pupil of Ms Usher's, and one is a trained teacher who is at home nearby with small children and helps out at school when her own children are at playgroup in order to 'keep her hand in'. Most of Ms Usher's colleagues in the school also welcome the help of reading volunteers, although there are a few teachers on the staff who strongly oppose the practice.

The above scenario represents a composite picture of 'typical' practice in schools which receive help with reading from volunteers, culled from evidence collected for the Parental Help with Reading in Schools Project at the University of London Institute of Education between 1983 and 1985. Parents and other adults help with reading on a regular unpaid basis in over half the primary schools in England, and the number is steadily rising (Stierer, 1985). In a large number of these schools helpers are welcomed in a spirit of openness and partnership and, despite some practical drawbacks and misgivings in principle, are felt to assist schools in their pursuit of many objectives.

Commonsense good practice ... or misguided dereliction of duty? Enlightened entrepreneurialism ... or unprincipled volunteerism? Personalized reading practice ... or delegating pedagogy to the laity? Breaking down barriers ... or perpetuating élitism? All these viewpoints, and many others, were expressed by teachers during the research, which included a national postal questionnaire survey, personal interviews with staff and volunteers in over thirty schools, and observations in classrooms and remedial units. The task for the project was to unravel the diversity of practice and opinion on this subject in order to raise the level of the debate. One thing, at least, is clear: teachers taking part in the study, regardless of their own approach, needed no coaxing to acknowledge the important issues raised by volunteer help with reading. It is a vexed subject, which arouses great interest and strong feeling. It is also directly related to major changes in schools: changes in the relationship between home and school, changes in teachers' notions of their own professionalism, changing ideas about the teaching of reading and the changing political context in which teachers work.

Relations between Home and School

Any observer of primary education in England could not help noting that primary school teachers are becoming increasingly outward looking in their approach and in their thinking. This change takes many forms: it influences the quality of rapport and communication between teachers and parents, and it affects teachers' notions of their role within the community.[1] Because the teaching of reading occupies such a volatile position in the relationship between home and school, volunteers' help with reading was felt by many teachers to serve a *practical* role as well as a *symbolic* one in a changing relationship between teachers and parents.

The practical role is achieved in at least two ways. First, teachers are tending more and more to include 'parent education' among their responsibilities, i.e., preparing parents to make a more active and publicly recognized contribution to their children's education. Supervising parents' help with reading at school is felt by many teachers to facilitate this objective, by providing parents with a deeper understanding of the nature of the reading process and of the school's views on how young readers can best be helped.[2] Second, some teachers expressed the view that inviting parents to work alongside themselves in the classroom enabled parents to exercise their rights as educational consumers to observe first-hand the education their children were receiving at school.

The symbolic function of volunteer help with reading centres on the increasingly favoured idea that inviting parents and others into the classroom to help with reading communicates something important about the school to the 'outside world'. The practice is widely felt to help break down the barriers, anxieties and 'mystifications' which often surround the work which goes on inside schools. Large numbers of teachers continue to feel that reading is too important to be left to untrained, unpaid helpers, and they tend to deploy volunteer help in so-called 'non-academic' or 'extra-curricular' areas. However, more and more teachers are coming to the view that one of the main benefits to be gained by inviting outsiders into the classroom would be undermined if the *important* aspects of school life were to be identified as off limits to school helpers. The opening up of school reading is central to the desired relationship between home and school for a growing number of teachers.[3]

Teachers' Professionalism

The teaching of reading occupies a key position in teacher's conceptions of their professional responsibility. The issue poses a practical challenge because the use of volunteer reading helpers involves both a qualitative and a quantitative extension of teachers' professional responsibilities. Qualitatively, opening up the classroom to reading helpers may require teachers to give advice, guidance and support to parents and other adults, often of a highly personal kind. Some teachers consider such a role to be more consistent with that of a social worker than of a teacher. Quantitatively, the establishment and maintenance of a school-based reading helper scheme demands a sizeable commitment of time and energy on the part of teachers. Long hours may have to be spent liaising with helpers (at school, by letter and by home visiting), preparing materials, setting work and so on. However beneficial volunteer reading help may be, such a significant addition to the work load is regarded as unacceptable by many classroom teachers who are inadequately paid and whose work pressures are already considerable.

The issue also poses a symbolic challenge. To invite a 'non-teacher' into the classroom to help with reading is to suggest on one level that adults without the benefit of specialized training and experience are capable of contributing positively to young children's reading progress. Such a suggestion blurs the crucial difference, which teachers as a profession have long sought to assert, between themselves and others. This suggestion is particularly challenging in the reading area, which sometimes assumes a pseudo-scientific aura bolstered by talk of 'phonics', 'reading ages' and so on. For this reason some teachers taking part in the project spoke of the dangers of the profession becoming diluted by the work of untrained volunteers.[4]

On the other hand, there appeared to be growing sympathy among teachers for the view that their professionalism might be *enhanced* by enlisting, training and supervising volunteers. The task of communicating clearly and concisely to an outsider one's objectives and methods in the classroom demands highly complex professional skills. Some teachers even went so far as to suggest that their work with volunteers was an effective way to promote teachers' professionalism in the eyes of the public.

All teachers taking part in the study drew a line of professional demarcation between the work of volunteers and their own work as teachers. *Where* they drew that line differed enormously, however. At the most general level the profession is divided between those to whom the help of volunteers is — with some qualifications — acceptable, and those who draw the line at any work within the school considered to contribute formally to the teaching of reading. In most cases this latter group of teachers supports the practice of volunteer help with activities within the school regarded as non-academic, such as cooking, library management and swimming,[5] and many support the principle of parental help with reading at home. However, any school-based work regarded officially as the teaching of reading — and this includes hearing children read for many of these teachers — is seen as the professional responsibility of paid, trained and experienced teachers.

More specifically, among the sub-group of teachers who do enlist the help of reading volunteers, work with the 'less able' emerged as the area of teachers' responsibilities which they were most reluctant to share with helpers. In most cases the help received by volunteers was perceived as an opportunity for teachers to give more specialist attention to less able children themselves, while at the same time enabling better readers to gain reading practice with an adult on a one-to-one basis. Only in very rare cases were schemes devised to enable poor readers or beginning readers to receive regular individual attention from unpaid helpers, and in some of these cases volunteers were recruited to compensate for the partial or complete loss of paid remedial staff in the school. Although the view was sometimes expressed that volunteers were ideally suited to help struggling or beginning readers, teachers involved in such schemes tended to be more defensive about their use of volunteers than teachers deploying the help of volunteers with average and above-average readers.

The Teaching of Reading

The specific way in which reading helpers were used in schools was often a useful and interesting index of the view taken by schools of how reading should be taught and learned. For example, a nearly unanimous 98 per cent of headteachers in schools with reading helpers reported in the postal survey that children read aloud to helpers, regardless of the other reading-related work, if any, with which volunteers assisted. This statistic underlines the more general finding of the research that teachers continue to set tremendous store by the familiar classroom activity of hearing children read, whether they receive reading help from volunteers or not.

A number of teachers aim to ensure that every instance of oral reading is 'diagnostic' and therefore dependent on their own specialist skills. This function appeared to consist largely of regulating the speed with which children progressed through books, and of granting permission to move from one book in the reading scheme to another. However, many view the activity exclusively as reading practice, or believe that some instances of oral reading can legitimately be used for practice (and therefore handled by volunteers) while other instances can be taken by teachers for diagnostic purposes. A sizeable proportion of teachers welcome the relief from the pressure to hear children read frequently, as well as the opportunity for their pupils to have a sustained oral read on a one-to-one basis and to talk in a relaxed way about the books they are reading.

This use of volunteers to hear children read was, however, observed to have a varied effect on teacher's notions about reading. Many teachers reported that their ideas about the texts suitable for promoting young children's reading changed as a result of their enlisting the help of volunteers. Most often these changed ideas centred upon a move away from heavy or exclusive reliance on graded reading schemes in favour of 'real' books, i.e., picture books for younger children and quality literature for older readers. However, in other cases volunteer help was used simply to boost the frequency with which children were heard to read, thereby perpetuating mechanical models of reading pedagogy. This stemmed in part from a reluctance on the part of some teachers to overload volunteers with too much 'theory' about the importance of the quality of relationships and interaction while learning to read, but more typically it stemmed from a strong belief in the direct relationship between frequency of oral reading and rate of learning progress.

While hearing children read is the dominant pattern of volunteers' work, it is certainly not the only pattern. In the many schools where volunteers help with other reading activities, in addition to oral reading, a wide range of such activities were mentioned, including reading stories to children, helping children select library books, talking to children about their books, helping E2L pupils with English and mother-tongue work, and supervising reading games, comprehension work and phonic work.

Political Issues

The practice of inviting reading volunteers into the classroom raises issues about the political context in which teachers work. One of these issues has already been mentioned, i.e., the significant extension of teachers' responsibilities represented by increased use of reading helpers. When the nature of teacher's contractual duties is being fiercely debated and perhaps permanently redefined, the quantitative and qualitative additions to teachers' work load inherent in reading help schemes require serious consideration.

A substantial proportion of teachers indicated that their initial reasons for turning to volunteers were related to cutbacks in remedial provision and ancillary support. There was also a widespread sense that the growing emphasis on individual attention in primary education had rendered class sizes of even twenty-five or less inadequate to perform the job satisfactorily, and that volunteers represented the only solution. This notwithstanding, many teachers discovered that considerable educational benefits derived from the practice.

Despite a widely felt sense of compromise associated with the practice of volunteer help with reading, there was an equally strong view that teachers' use of volunteers did not ultimately represent a cheap alternative to adequately resourced schools. Teachers repeatedly expressed the need for more training to deal effectively with parents and other helpers, and for more time to coordinate and supervise the work of volunteers. Increasing use of volunteer reading helpers was seen as an argument for *more* funding and training rather than less.

Anxiety was also expressed that an important gap may be developing between schools with reading helpers and other schools, which parallels the gap between schools with and without an active body of parent fund-raisers, already documented by Her Majesty's Inspectorate (1985). Although there was some evidence to sustain this anxiety, insofar as volunteer help was more often found in schools with middle-class catchment areas, a surprisingly high number of schools in inner-city areas with large proportions of ethnic minority pupils reported that parents and other local people helped regularly at school.

Practical Problems and Possible Solutions

Irrespective of these conceptual issues, many primary school teachers, for whatever reasons, are determined to open their classrooms to volunteer reading helpers but have found their efforts thwarted by a number of practical difficulties. These are by no means trivial, and have in some cases brought about the demise of the scheme. The most frequently mentioned practical problems are summarized below.

Selectivity

Many teachers indicated their intention of implementing an open-door policy to parents and the wider community. Volunteer help with reading in the classroom was often a logical extension of this new outlook. However, a willingness to accept help from *anyone* implied a willingness to accept help from volunteers who might be regarded as unsuitable, for example, in their inability to work well with pupils and/or staff, or to be reliable in their commitment to help, or to respect the confidentiality of information about pupils to which they became privy. Help from such volunteers was often difficult to refuse or to redirect, due to helpers' sensitivities or teachers' scruples.

Elitism

Even if schools succeed in recruiting volunteers who approach their work in schools tactfully, conscientiously and skilfully, it is probably inevitable that only a minority of parents will take up the school's invitation. Not all parents are willing or able to devote time and effort to such schemes. This can create feelings of resentment on the part of some parents toward school helpers or toward the school for allowing their children to be taught by non-teachers. It can also create anxiety on the part of staff that they are perpetuating an unacceptable kind of élitism by alienating the very parents they were hoping to reach.

Staff Disagreement

Some have taken the decision to involve reading helpers in the classroom unilaterally, or in league with a few colleagues, often in the face of opposition from other members of staff. The dynamics of this lack of collectivity are diverse (enthusiastic headteacher and reluctant staff or vice versa; infant-junior staff split; old-young staff split), but in very many cases they impede the development of a lively and secure scheme. Teachers who appeared to be the most confident about their use of reading helpers were those in schools which had adopted the practice collectively as a school-wide pro-gramme.

There are no easy solutions to these practical difficulties, some of which are beyond the control of schools. Nevertheless, the final stage of the research project investigated a number of relatively novel approaches to the involvement of reading helpers in the classroom. These appeared to resolve not only some of the practical problems described above, but also some of the more conceptual dilemmas mentioned earlier in the chapter, which are faced by schools operating more conventional approaches. Four of the more structured schemes studied during this stage are described below.

The 'Reading Workshop' Approach

This is an approach to parental involvement in which parents come to school in groups to work with their own children under the supervision of the classroom teachers. The objective for most teachers operating a workshop approach is to organize a regular weekly session in the classroom when all children work alongside their own parent, carrying out a range of reading-related work which has been set out by the teacher. This approach has in some cases been extremely effective in harnessing parental interest and enthusiasm, in avoiding some of the élitism and lack of confidentiality associated with more selective approaches and in promoting lively parent-child interaction at home. On the other hand, reading workshops generally depend for their success on high levels of (female) unemployment, and the work content of workshop sessions tends to be dominated by rather trivial reading games rather than, for example, sharing real books. The best documented example of a reading workshop approach is the one developed at Fox Hill First School in Sheffield (cf. Weinberger, 1983; Smith and March, n.d.).

Mounting Courses for Parents/Helpers

Some schools have found that many of the practical and principle dilemmas associated with volunteer reading helpers were comprehensively resolved by mounting courses for parents and other prospective helpers which aim to acquaint outsiders with the theories and methods informing the work children carry out at school. The most ambitious of these courses have been well planned and have covered the full spectrum of the school's curricular and non-curricular life, some running for as many as eight or ten sessions (e.g., the same afternoon or evening each week). Not many schools have the resources to achieve such extremes, but schools which have attempted some form of briefing/induction/training have found that the quality of help they received subsequently from helpers has been of a very high standard, and that the unexpected benefits have included improved communication and understanding between home and school as well as increased parental confidence in their role as educators at home.

Surrogate Parents for a Home-Help Reading Programme

Space constraints in this report prohibit elaboration of the conceptual and practical links between volunteer reading help at school and the increasingly common practice of promoting parental help with reading at home.[6] However, one particularly interesting approach to the deployment of volunteer help at school, which was observed in several schools during the project, was the use of helpers as surrogate parents for those children whose parents were unable or unwilling to participate in the school's home-help scheme. No hard evidence yet exists to demonstrate that the reading competence of children helped in this way at school by someone other than their own parent improves as dramatically as that of children who are helped at home by their own parent. Nevertheless, the use of volunteers as surrogate parents at school for such children at least achieves the psychological advantage of ensuring that no children are left out of schemes which usually aim for 100 per cent take-up.

Training Teachers for Work with Parents/Helpers

The practices and attitudes investiaged during the project pointed forcefully toward the need for greater attention, in initial and in-service teacher training, to teachers' liaison with parents and other outsiders. Teachers are increasingly including within their professional responsibilities the task of communicating their aims and methods to the community, and of fostering and supervising a greater educational role on the part of parents and others. Although, as a recent survey shows,[7] a small number of teacher-training institutions have devised a component addressing home-school liaison issues, most do not provide adequate preparation for these professional tasks. Serving teachers repeatedly expressed the need for short courses which could give them the skills and confidence to perform liaison work.[8] In this respect the project revealed the shortsightedness inherent in the view of volunteer reading help as a cheap option.

Notes

1 Space constraints prohibit discussion of the *general* argument in favour of a home-school partnership in education; for such a discussion see Tizard *et al.* (1981) and Wolfendale (1983).
2 However, a number of teachers objected to the implied arrogance in the notion of 'parent education', and indicated their wish to *learn from parents*, who were in an important respect educational experts in their own right.
3 Although many teachers expressed this aim of opening up school reading, not all agreed that inviting volunteers to help with reading at school was necessarily the most effective means to achieving it. Often schemes which encourage parents to help their children with reading at home are informed by this same objective.
4 These views apply with nearly equal force to home reading schemes for parents, although the idea of a parent helping his or her own child at home is usually less challenging to teachers than is the prospect of lay persons helping large numbers of children at school, not necessarily including their own child.

5   Teachers point out the opportunities for reading and language learning inherent in all school activities, such as the speaking and listening associated with practical tasks, the reading demands of following a recipe and the skills involved in selecting appropriate library books.

6   Such schemes are typified by those mounted in Haringey (cf. Tizard *et al.*, 1982), Rochdale (cf. Jackson and Hannon, 1981) and Hackney (cf. PACT, 1984).

7   Cf. Atkin and Bastiani (1984).

8   Useful blueprints for setting up and running courses to develop teachers' skills and confidence in their work with parents and other helpers are set out in Topping and Wolfendale (1985) and Wolfendale and Gregory (1985).

13   Reading with Mother: A Dockland Story

Evelyn Gregory

As Barry Stierer has shown, the encouragement given to parents to help with reading forces us to consider a range of conceptual questions about pedagogy, the curriculum and the management of schools. The glimpse of parent participation we are now given would rarely, if ever, surface as evidence in official reports and research questionnaires. It introduces a necessary dissonance into harmonious pronouncements from official sources.

Here the teachers base their expectations of the children on assumptions about the history of their families and where they live. The parents' efforts to help their children to read are stultified by their feelings of inadequacy, feelings bequeathed by their own experience of school in the same area. Evelyn Gregory faces the pessimism and the paradoxes that confront children growing up where she first learned to read, and refuses simple solutions to complex problems.

This is the story of a group of 11-year-old children living in old London docklands and of their mothers who came to school with them. I ask why these children were having such great difficulty in learning to read when some of their contemporaries in schools a short distance away were experiencing greater success, although most of them spoke English as their second language.

West Ham and its neighbour, East Ham, together form the London borough of Newham which lies just to the east of Bow, Whitechapel and Stepney, the traditional East End of London. The area is bounded by the Thames on the south, the river Lea on the west and the Roding on the east. The northern border is Wanstead Flats, a stretch of common land. The north of the borough has Victorian houses of varying sizes and status; they are mostly owner-occupied. There is a hubbub of bustling corner shops. The streets overflow with traffic and pedestrians, the people of the New Commonwealth who show off the variety of colour and attire. Despite appearances, however, their condition is reported in a local study to be one of 'extreme deprivation' (Tunley, *et al.*, 1979).

A huge dual carriageway slices the northern part of the borough from the south. Here the bustle changes to empty wide roads framed by the contours of corrugated fences, boarded up old shops and stretches of wasteland. Tucked in just off the road, new red brick houses and low flats are being built. The skyscape is dotted with tower blocks. This is the socially superior and 'advantaged' area of the south. But the docks are now dead. Most of the children who live in this area know them only from their grandparents' stories and memories of ships and shipping — the triumphs and disasters of a bygone age in the long fight for permanency in dock work. Again, only casual work is available. Yet, surprisingly, the London Docklands Corporation has recently announced a huge investment is to be made to restore a former tobacco warehouse. Dynamic plans, possibly in line with privatization further up-river, are afoot to revitalize the area. Expensive private housing is being built and a new secondary school is scheduled. Beyond the incidence of increased uncertainty, what the changes will mean for the present population remains unknown.

The School

Our focus is on a primary school in the south of the borough. Built in the 1880s it once housed over 1000 children between the ages of 4 and 15. The log books record the evidence of continual poverty and ill-luck. This view of life is woven into the texture of present-day living, the inheritance of casual labour. As the head of the school explains, people who have always been at the mercy of others, who have felt themselves to be 'ill-used' in the controlling circumstances of their lives, are unwilling to adopt easily a new mode of interpreting their condition and outlook. Most of them have never seen education as a way out, as a means of changing the dominant features of their conditions of existence. Their loophole is the kind of behaviour which more conventional citizens see as crime or villainy. A 'deep' poverty still prevails, although in the area served by the school no one is now living in overcrowded or bad housing conditions.

The school has moved to a new building on a spacious plot in the centre of old docklands. The classrooms look onto a field ringed with new development housing. A motley selection of horses inhabit the field and, chased by local dogs, regularly stampede into the playground. Their presence gives a welcome diversion from work for some of the children.

A combination of austerity and comfort lends the school a hospital-like atmosphere. Modern policy and design have provided the carpeted 'quiet' area and TV rooms, two 'family rooms' and a planted central courtyard. At the same time financial stringency has meant trimming ideals to the austerity of tiny, open-plan classrooms, barely large enough to house the furniture, let along the occupants, and where any raised voice is immediately on show to neighbours. Narrow corridors glisten with shiny new paintwork; the colours are loud and garish. Name plaques are on all the doors: 'family rooms', 'staff room', 'medical room' inform the new residents of their fixed functions. Joy Nolan (whose class we shall study) and the head teacher have taken pains to capitalize upon the potential comfort of the school. Large exotic plants exude warmth in every corner, and the new school has a generous supply of resources. Bookshelves in the quiet rooms and a purpose-built library are laden with new story and information books. Pouffés and armchairs placed strategically create a paradise for the avid reader. It seems a paradox that these things should be beyond the reach of so many of Mrs Nolan's class.

The staffroom is small and cramped. Only by lining the walls with armchairs can everyone be seated so that the effect is of a waiting-room. Much of the time spent here is watch-checking and waiting. There is nowhere to go for lunch and the time is long. Most teachers have travelled far and are tired. Few live in the area. Housing difficulties in West Ham, ample transport communications in the metropolis and a strict adherence to social conventions have turned West Ham teachers into a largely immigrant community. They travel into the area each morning from their homes in all parts of the conurbation and even from the rural areas well outside' (Peschek, 1966). This perhaps understates the fact that few would want to live in the area anyway; '... for the primary school teaching profession has a considerable upper working-class and lower middle-class recruitment. As a group they may be escaping, rejecting or leaving behind the working-class and certainly do not find themselves in the confident position where they can interpret and possibly share the values of that world through the school system' (Jackson, 1979).

Entrance at 1.00 pm: most teachers have already eaten and are enjoying the last few minutes before returning to work. Apart from talk of new posts advertised, there is little conversation. Ironically, perhaps, every week one teacher has her head immersed in *Asterix*. From time to time another teacher crumples a piece of paper and flicks it at her, but she does not look up. One or two 'light' newspapers usually lie on the table and are often glanced at before afternoon lessons begin. The teachers here are caring. They spend long hours managing sports on Saturdays and evenings organizing Parent Staff Association meetings to which few people come. Yet a resignation prevails.

I have come to be with Joy Nolan's class to see if, together, we can work with these children to improve their reading before they go to secondary school in September, for after that their chances of individualised attention decline. We have decided to involve the mothers of the children in what we are trying to do. Here is what happened. At this point it is important to remember that this is a subjective account, and, as such, 'it says as much about the observer as about the subject itself'. (Willes, 1983)

The Children
Scene 1: Enter Paul, David, George, Tina, Tracey, Lucy and Ian. One by one they open the door to the family room which squeaks with newness. They come curiously, without fear. As yet, there has been no failure in this room. We talk about their thoughts on reading and whether they would like to invite their mothers to work once a week with them in school. Nervous questioning on my part: should I speak openly on their difficulties with reading? Would 11-year-olds really want their mothers to come to school and reveal their weaknesses to them with all the complications this might entail? Would they feel 'singled out'?

'Do you like reading?' My question in retrospect seems naive and foolish. Yet Paul, David and Ian search my face and say 'yes'. Ian reads from his chosen book, *Stampede in the Valley*:

Printed text	*Ian's version*
'It takes a herd of cows to make a cloud like that' said Dan.	'It took a hard of cows to make a crash let that' said Dan.
'That dust cloud is too big for wild horses to make. They do not go in herds as big as that,'	'Then dust crashed is too big for wild horses to make that to not go in hard as big as that.'

He reads jerkily, ignoring full-stops.

Tina and Tracey are bolder. Tina is an outsider in the class. Cared for by an elderly nan, her dress is old-fashioned and she suffers from gross overweight. She looks at me warily. Her book is *Goldilocks and the Three Bears* (Cliff Moon). Before starting to read, she warns that she 'can't read a lot of the words. I hate reading. I get the words wrong. I don't like my nan listening to me because my voice is stupid.' She reads all the words and is obviously relieved. Tracey is very different. A sophisticated black girl, whose speech is eloquent in both enunciation and logic, she is defiantly secretive. Renowned in the school for her stock-phrases, 'I'm bored', 'this is so boring', she says, 'I can't do anything. I'm not interested in anything. I hate reading and writing. I can't even copy the words.' She dislikes her book, *Through the Rainbow* intensely.

> *Look at the golliwog. Do you like it?*
> *Would you like to have the golliwog?*
> *Would you like to take the golliwog to bed?*

As with all the children, her voice changes as she reads. Hers becomes a whisper. George, who suffers from irritating asthma and eczema which become more acute as he attempts to read, almost sobs the words out. Different reactions from different children. To our surprise there is a unity in wanting their mothers in school and feeling sure they would come. Why, we wondered ...?

Scene 2: The letters of invitation have been sent. Perhaps the first major mistake is made. Needing both the apparent 'efficiency' and 'reassurance' of factual evidence, the school decides to administer a test to the children before starting. After consideration The Primary Reading Test is chosen as the only one the children are likely to score on. It is carefully photocopied to conceal any sign of its real function.

The venue is the family room the week before the mothers are due to come for the first time. The children rush into the room together, the comfy armchairs still a novelty. Tracey glimpses the paper and suddenly rips open the window, although the room is cool. 'Phew! It stinks in here!' she says. At last she sits down and starts the test. Every few seconds panic takes her and she repeatedly says in her best diction, 'But I don't understand. I can't do it.' Her final words are, 'This is boring. I hate this. I'm not doing any more.' She throws the test on one side and stares straight ahead. The others glance surreptitiously at her but obediently continue. The results of the test were, of course, known before the start. All the children scored a 'reading age' of under 6. The whole exercise had been yet one more indicator of failure to the children — an exercise with 'irrelevant objectives' (Gurney, 1976, p. 82). But the room survived.

The Mothers Appear

Scene 1: Only the mothers of Paul and David appear after the first invitation. Both their children are renowned for 'doing runners' (escaping from school) and rudeness. Both stand nervously huddled in a corner. As we walk down the narrow corridor, they say, 'We don't know if we can do this. Nothing involving reading. Nothing with your brain. We're all right for a bit of cleaning, polishing.' When we sit down, Joan speaks quickly, jerkily, 'There's something wrong with me brain, see. No, it doesn't function properly. Me Son's the same. He's been under Bart's for dyslexia. He's much better now. But they told him that, too. I'm all right with me hands, bit of knitting, cooking, cleaning. I won't have to use me brain, will I?' Torrance and Olson (1985) link children's use of cognitive verbs 'I think, believe, etc.' with attainment of literacy. How can Joan have the self-confidence to 'think' or 'believe' anything if she has such a low estimation of her own 'school knowledge'?

We decide to spend at least our first few afternoons talking together about reading. By that time others may have joined us. Although we really want to read narrative and stories together, it seems that initially this will be too intimidating. Why not use the skills which are so obviously apparent? We decide to make 'reading games' reflecting their children's interests. We shall draw in the children to help us and then talk together without them. Why had the others not come? Kay: 'I don't think they'd come in. They all live in a little world of their own. All do their own thing.' She asks Joan why she doesn't come to the Parent Staff Association. 'I couldn't come to anything like that!' says Joan. 'I might have to read something. ... You see, that's why I never really want to come up the school for anything. I always think I might have to read something. Then my stomach turns over and I go all nervous and cold. I think that's why I could never listen to him read when he brought his reading book home. Me stomach started heaving and I thought, "I can't do it. ..." You know, that's why I took him up the hospital. I thought, "I don't want him growing up like me."' How many 'roles' has Joan avoided in life because she cannot manage the written word? Whether or not she and her son suffer from 'dyslexia', her conviction that they are both being 'cured' by 'specialists' is important. I make the mistake of passing around articles on the good results of parents helping their children with reading. 'Innit funny,' says Kay, 'Them educated people always read *The Times*.' Am I widening the gap between us, strengthening what Hoggart refers to as the 'Them' and 'Us' feeling? We talk about 'our family room'. 'I think it should be cosy and comfortable. You know, like home,' says Kay. 'We'd better not do too much. Sir'll think we're taking over', replies Kay. 'Sir' perhaps typifies their relationship with the school. Volosinov speaks of how 'expression organizes experience' (1973, p. 85) and to the foreigner disguised as an East Londoner at the beginning of the century it was very obvious, 'The man in corduroy and dirty neckerchief no longer addressed me as "sir". ... It was "mate" now — a fine and hearty word with a tingle to it that the other term does not possess. Governor! It smacks of mastery and power and high authority — the tribute to the man who is under to the man who is on top. ...' (London, 1977, p. 15). At 3.30 p.m. Kay slips into an overall and starts to clean — an occasional job she is pleased to have when one of the permanent cleaners is away. Her role as cleaner almost inevitably organizes her expression and language towards those she sees as her bosses: a vicious circle where language and experience intertwine — in the centre are her children 'in trouble'.

All afternoon we have worked, 'copying' reading games, practical work which may later form the basis for talk. Both take their work home to finish. But will they return, I wonder?

Scene 2: They return, Joan under the condition that she will not have to read or write anything. We are joined by Shirley (George's mother) who mirrors Joan's anxiety: 'How can I help him when I can't read properly myself. Every time there's something to be read on TV and they ask me, I always pretend I'm too busy.' She is reassured that she will only have to copy, not write herself. All decide, to Joy Nolan's concern, that they would rather work with someone else's child. The 'beautifying' of the games is becoming prolonged. What will happen when we move from the product itself to its use?

Scene 3: It happens very soon. Mrs Nolan wants more mothers to come and sends out a second invitation which brings Tracey's mother. Elegant, outwardly sophisticated but nervous, she says, 'I don't think I can do it, but I'll try.' Ian's mother comes too. 'It's a bit late now. This should have been done three years ago. But I'll try anything once.' Joan is absent. I wonder if she thought she might have to read something? I ring her. 'I'll try to come later but I have a dental appointment.' I hear panic rising in her voice. Suddenly she admits, 'I can't do it ... I can't read ... I've got dyslexia ... I go to Bart's ... I don't mind making games but I can't read with the children. I don't know the words. ... Just think, if I didn't know the words with the children there, I'd feel such a dibby ... and the children'd say to my kid, "Your mum can't read".' After promises that we need her, if only to type the stories and make games, she promises to return — and she does.

Our work spanned two terms until the children left the school and is, as most stories, marked by pain and pleasure. Only significant moments can find room here. Pleasure and pain for Tracey and her mother, Tracey saying, 'But I don't think I'll be able to remember the words', as she goes off with her mother, but returning at 3.30 smiling and saying, 'I like working with my mum. She's really patient with me. I told her she ought to become a reading teacher.' Tracey's mother, with evident relief, saying, 'I didn't think I would be able to do it before I started but I see now it's quite easy ... it's very interesting.' Then, after a few weeks of success, Tracey says just once, 'I'm bored', and her mother disappears and never returns. Pleasure for Kay who works with her son Paul and returns saying guiltily, 'I've kept him all afternoon.' They joke about their story of throwing Dad downstairs as they completed a booklet from Coventry on *Myself*. And Joan? Mrs Nolan bans the quiet room to the rest of the class and tells Joan that her son David wants some help in choosing a new book from there. Joan enters the quiet room and re-emerges at 3.30 saying, 'He wanted to read to me and I couldn't say "No".' For Shirley, too, there is pain and pleasure. She returns depressed with her son George saying, 'It's no good. He won't do anything. I'm going to end up walloping him if I have to stay with him alone.' Both Shirley's experience and a general sympathy for those whose 'mums won't come' bring us to the decision to work together as a group. Tina (whose reading is perhaps poorest of the group) is one such child. Her nan was not asked — supposedly because she would have to bring the dog which wasn't allowed, but in fact because 'no one else would come if she came.'

We develop a pattern of work. We meet at 1.30 p.m. and talk without the children. Our starting point is reading, but we include everything else: Kay's victory over the council to be rehoused after showing the permanent burn-mark on her daughter's chest where she has to eat in such cramped conditions; the constant illnesses with which their families are beset; Shirley's christening for 100 guests; Kay and Shirley's fish-stalls and where to purchase for them the freshest shell-fish. The women appear so independent in financial matters yet so dependent and helpless whenever 'specialists', be they the doctor or the school, are involved. The teaching of reading, too, is a 'specialism', to be taught by 'specialists' or learned through 'specialist equipment'. Joan has bought David a computer which 'must help him with his reading'. Barthes writes of just this consumerism attached to toys in our present society, 'il veut faire des enfants usagers ...' (Barthes, 1957, p. 64). The myth that money can buy 'specialisms' is strong.

At 2 o'clock the children join us. At first any pre-packaged materials, like those produced by Coventry, are most popular. Having a definite task which can be 'finished off' and 'taken away' seems to give confidence. Gradually the pattern changes. I start by reading or telling a story to the whole group of mothers and children. The mothers wait at first for the 'magic formula' and only much later admit there is none. Then we work in pairs or in small groups in the same room writing and reading our own stories which are then read to the whole group. The atmosphere is relaxed and no one minds admitting that they cannot spell a word. We try to send the children back by 3.00 p.m. to talk again, but they often manage to stay.

Scollon and Scollon (1981) and Foucault (1977) speak of the 'fictionalization' of the Self' essential to becoming literate. The author of a text becomes a third person in relationship to the character of the text and the text itself. Through our stories both mothers and children may be coming to an understanding of the distance of the author from the text and the existence of a decontextualized author, and in so doing may be getting closer to the school's view on literacy. This movement from 'packaged' materials to producing their 'own' knowledge took courage and did not occur suddenly.

Let the final scene in our story be one of pleasure. Mrs Nolan decided to invite all the parents of the school to watch a video of parents reading with children. To explain why only three appeared would need another story. Kay, our spokeswoman, 'the brainy one', was at home looking after sick children. Shirley, almost word-for-word, but with utter conviction, took over her role and explained to them, just as Kay had explained to her, the pleasure in reading with a child.

Evelyn Gregory

Finale: What Have We Learned?

This study tentatively suggests reasons why some indigenous children in one part of a borough, in spite of a home language and culture which superficially appear close to that of the school, may be struggling more with reading than bilingual children just a few miles away. The story of the indigenous group's relationship with the school and the language and literacy represented there throws some light on the question: what importance have social aspirations and how might language and literacy reflect these? Whatever social and economic conditions they are presently living in, for many newcomers to Britain Newham is seen as a 'stepping-off point'; there is an optimism that literacy and education will open doors in life which would otherwise remain closed. For some of the indigenous population in the south there is the pessimism that these doors will remain bolted — where, if anything, only money, not literacy can crack the lock. A fuller study of the language socialization patterns of each group and their link with social aspirations and 'optimism' would prove interesting.

14 'They Changed the Picture in the Middle of the Fight ...': New Kinds of Literacy?

Cary Bazalgette

Cary Bazalgette discusses the competences that children acquire from pictures and from televisual images, often before their formal schooling begins. Drawing upon collaborative research carried out with teachers, she looks at some ways in which children can be encouraged to 'adopt a critical stance towards media texts, including the ones they have produced themselves.' She puts new modes of talking about stories and reading on the agenda and many of her concepts (e.g., 'construction') may be of use in our discussion of more traditional 'texts' — picture books, the first stories that children write themselves.

I start with two stories, both showing young children confidently using literacy competences that are rarely taken into account in school. The first involves a 6-year-old talking with his mother:

6-year-old:	On *Blue Peter* they told us what you have to do if you're on television.
38-year-old:	What do you have to do?
6-year-old:	Do you know what's the most important thing ... what you must never never do if you're on television?
38-year-old:	No, I don't. What is it?
6-year-old:	You must never *never* look at the camera!
38-year-old:	Oh! Why not?
6-year-old:	Er ... well [*long pause*] I think it's because they want us to think we've just *burst* through the wall and found them making the programme.

The next story is borrowed from Ben Moore (1986): 'My own five-year-old came to me when he was watching *The Empire Strikes Back* and announced "They're fighting on Earth at the same time as they're fighting in space." When I asked him how he knew it was at the same time, he said, "They changed the picture in the middle of the fight." this kind of understanding is commonplace among young children.'

Like most contemporary children these two are gaining their first powerful experiences of 'reading' texts for entertainment, information and cultural knowledge from media other than print. Yet, when they come to school, the ways in which they are taught to read will probably devote much attention to print while dealing with other media only erratically, if at all. In this chapter I will uncover some of the processes and concepts that help us look at children looking at televisual pictures, and suggest some ways in which those ideas could help us in redefining literacy.

Schools versus The Media: 'Institutional Jealousies'

The relationship between schooling and the visual media is interesting historically and culturally. When mass schooling was established in the late nineteenth century, it did not take up much of the public school classics tradition that preceded it, but it did as a matter of course acknowledge the only mass medium that was developed by then, which was, of course, print. Schooling made a predictable accommodation with the institutions of book, newspaper and magazine publishing. The new elementary schools undertook to teach working-class children to read. Educators had debated the wisdom of even that move — the skills that unlocked the Bible would also unlock the radical pamphlet — but the market potential of millions of new readers could not be denied. The possibility that working-class children might learn to produce print as well as consume it was never on the agenda.

Instead, the corollary of learning to read print was learning to write by hand. The notion that print and handwriting are *both* media, which differ in terms of their status, their necessary technologies, the audiences they can reach and who has access to them, was not considered important, and on the whole it still isn't. The 'competent consumer' became the taken-for-granted baseline of print literacy.

It is interesting to ask why it was not seen as the task of schools to produce 'competent consumers' of the new media technologies that developed in the ensuing years: photography, film, radio, television. But it is more interesting to ask why that question seems an odd one, even today. We don't need to teach them that kind of competence, would be the response of most teachers down the years: they're too competent by half. The new media are still seen as radically different from the safe, established book-learning which schooling had claimed for its own; they were *rivals* for the attention of the masses. The new media taught their own competences: close-up and fade-out, stars and personalities, soap opera and sit-com. They taught them well, and apparently painlessly, so schools, whose reputation for teaching badly and painfully was ruthlessly reinforced by the media through such products as *Our Gang* and the *Bash Street Kids*, could hardly be blamed for condemning these competences as not worthwhile or even downright dangerous. A hostility has thus grown up between the rival institutions of schooling and media. Teachers bewail the fact that children spend less time with them than they do with television, and 'educational' is synonymous with 'boring' for any self-respecting editor or producer.

This institutional jealousy seems natural to us now, and disguises the extent to which media and schooling can be seen as analogous in the ways that they define and transmit knowledge about the world (Wollen, 1985). It also has two effects that need considering in any discussion of literacy and the media. Firstly, schools ignore aspects of children's experience and knowledge that could be useful in literacy teaching, and could also be developed in their own right. Five-year-olds may not have done much reading — they may well not even have been read to — but they have almost certainly watched a good deal of television. They have watched films, probably on video, but possibly in the cinema as well. They have looked at comics, they have heard radio, records and tapes, and they have experienced a wealth of visual images: not only photographs, as in newspapers, magazines, family albums and street hoardings, but also a huge variety of graphic styles from cornflake packets to computers. They have developed a limited competence in making sense of media products which schools rarely use: indeed, it is usually dismissed as being not worthwhile 'school knowledge'.

Secondly, media producers are for the most part resolutely wedded to the notion that their products are naturally accessible to everyone: nobody should have to learn how to make sense of media products unless they come into such special categories as 'artistic' or 'cult status'. Indeed, most twentieth century media were initially promoted as being amazingly true to life, and realism continues to be a dominant ideal.

These two sets of assumptions underpin professional practice in the institutions of media and schooling. Against them we must set the insights that new theories about language and literacy can offer us. Linguists and semioticians have shown us that the whole universe of signs, from toilet door symbols to Renaissance frescoes, is organized into systems of codes and conventions that we have *learned*, just as we learned verbal language. In other words, it makes sense to say that we 'read' a photograph or a TV programme in a way analogous to that in which we read a written text (Barthes, 1972).

'Reading' Television

Enquiries into the process of reading itself have suggested that reading is more than an accretion of competences in decoding marks on a page: the reader is an active, knowledgeable person who brings understandings to texts and *makes* sense of them, rather than just consuming them. It thus makes less sense to differentiate between 'readers' of books and 'viewers' of audio-visual texts on the grounds that the latter are passive consumers of easy or obvious meanings. The cinema audience of 1895 would make as little sense of *Eastenders* as an 8-year-old would of *Pride and Prejudice*. Film, television, photographs, radio all have their own languages which are constructed, have developed over time, use agreed conventions and are learned by their audiences.

All the same, reading a written text is clearly different from 'reading' an audio-visual text. Writing is a symbolic system whose elements do not resemble the things or ideas they refer to. The 'reader' of, say, *The A Team* has a head start over the reader of *Roger Red Hat* because the images in *The A Team* do resemble real people, cars, landscape, etc. A very young child new to 'reading' *The A Team* will still take a while to learn the codes and conventions of basic TV drama such as close-up, eyeline matching, parallel editing, jump cut, establishing shot and so on; and a little longer to recognize the generic markers of fantasy action drama, but most children will have this pretty clear by the time they are 5 or 6. Comprehending narrative structure may take quite a bit longer, perhaps until 7 or 8. In other words, children's audio-visual media competence remains way ahead of their print media competence for a long time; for some this discrepancy is permanent.

But if this can be learned by the child without adult intervention, why should it be any concern of the schools? 'Because it's pernicious rubbish and they should stop watching it', would be one ready answer (and not a very auspicious one for any educational project). 'Because they can't tell fact from fantasy and it makes them psychologically and morally confused', goes another. But the fact-fiction distinction, contrary to popular opinion, is not an easy one to make, and most children spend much of their time assessing the relative reality status of different cultural products (Hodge and Tripp, 1986). 'Because it makes them violent/racist/sexist', is a third argument, and probably the most nearly pertinent of the three, although the dismal failure of thirty years' media 'effects' research to prove any simple connections between media products and behaviour or beliefs should warn us to tread warily here (Durkin, 1985).

All these responses spring out of schooling's determination to see the new media as somehow intrinsically different from the old literacy. Written texts also contain pernicious rubbish but we do not stop teaching children to read in case they end up reading *The Sun*. Despite disclaimers about the difference between audio-visual and written language systems, it is illuminating to bring our ideas about reading into our consideration of audio-visual media. Do we stop teaching about books and other written texts once children have a basic competence? Do we regard literacy as 'basic competence'? Is learning to write less important than learning to read? If the answer to all these is 'no', then why should we resist the idea of teaching about audio-visual media as well as print? To put it another way, shouldn't the concept of literacy be extended to include all the media of expression and communication?

Our knowledge about reading and writing can offer us assumptions upon which to base our ideas about extending the notion of literacy, but when we come to ask what this would mean in practice the reading-and-writing analogy may be less helpful. Our culture constantly suggests to us that reading a written text requires a learned skill, while audio-visual texts are 'transparent': their meaning is just 'there'. How can we uncover, and understand, the process of reading that does go on when we confront an audio-visual text?

One way of making a start is to look at a single photograph.

Figure 1

What has gone on in the few seconds it takes to glance at this photograph and make assumptions about its meanings? To unravel this process we need to look at it for longer than we normally would, and set aside our inhibitions about stating the obvious. It is a black and white photograph showing a young woman's head and shoulders. Her body and head are half-turned towards the camera and her eyes are turned to look into the lens. She is wearing a light coloured V-neck jumper and a dark shirt. There is clear but not harsh lighting on her face, casting a soft shadow under her chin. The background is a completely plain darkish grey. She has long wavy dark hair which hangs down her back and is brushed back from her face and ears. She has dark eyes and quite distinct dark eyebrows. She is smiling and showing her top teeth which are even and white.

That is a fairly objective account of the formal features of the photograph as I took them in with a glance. You might add others, or dispute the observations I have made. But we would also include in our response some interpretations of the image, which would depend more on the knowledge we bring *to* the photograph from our social and cultural experience, and which are thus likely to differ more. I would say that the young woman is in her teens, is of Asian origin and is having a formal portrait taken, in school or for a passport. You might argue for a different age or ethnic group. I would say she is relatively relaxed and has an attractive open smile; you might say she is stiffly and artificially posed. Adding words to the photograph might narrow down this range of interpretations and also suggest a context. A handwritten caption such as 'Amrit on her 16th birthday' would suggest a different context, and different interpretations, from a headline, 'Arranged Marriages: The Brutal Truth'. Thinking about captions and contexts would then get us into questions about the ways Asians and/or women are represented in, or excluded from, the media.

Looking at another photograph in the same way would yield a similar amount of detail, and enables us to make comparisons.

Figure 2

Like the previous photograph, this one was also most probably taken for private use such as the family album: the furnishings of the room suggest it is not a fashion photograph and its indoor location indicates it is probably not a news photograph. We can also link it to the previous one as an image of a young woman. But other features suggest differences: it is an old photograph; it is a photograph that marks a major life-event. We can thus distinguish between photographs and categorize them in many different ways: not only by subject matter or style, but also in terms of how they circulate in our culture, the audiences for which they seem to be designated, the groups they represent.

It is equally possible, though unreproducible here, to consider how a more complex text can be read: the title sequence to a television programme, for example, or an advertisement. A sequence of twenty seconds or less will contain many images and a sound track of words, music, noise or all three; we will make meanings out of the relationships between the images, and between sound and image, as well as from the interrelated parts of each separate image. We will also interpret the ways the sequence is edited: the duration of each shot and the way changes from shot to shot are achieved, whether by cuts, fades or mixes.

An alternative or additional way to uncover the complex processes that are at work when we encounter an audio-visual text is to make one ourselves. We will discover that a huge range of choices can be made even in making a single photograph. This will include not only the kinds of detail we can tease out in the analyses described above, but also such elements as shutter speed and aperture, the kind of paper we choose to print on and whether we crop the picture or not. All these choices will affect the way the photograph is 'read'. But even the simple action of looking through a camera viewfinder brings to life for us the primary choice that is made in constructing any visual image: the imposition of a frame. Different decisions about the position of the frame make a difference to the meanings that can be produced from the image.

These activities show that audio-visual texts do contain codes and conventions that we read actively, drawing upon our own knowledge. But these activities can also be used in the classroom to demonstrate the same things to children. Teaching about the media at any age has to start by working against beliefs that the media themselves have already taught us, casually but inexorably, even by the age of 5.

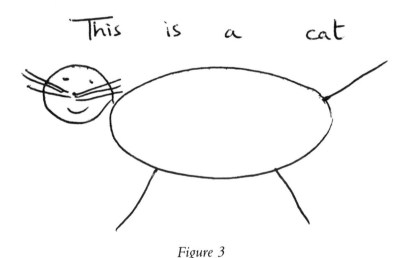

Figure 3

When a child writes such a caption and then draws such a picture the caption lies, of course: this is *a picture of* a cat. There is, as we have seen, a difference. Unusually though, shifting this belief in the transparency of the media is not destructive. It is a liberating process that acknowledges the children's own language mastery and develops it. Such a process not only extends children's capacity to enjoy the media but also begins to offer them language and methods to make critical judgments — a more important goal than offering them the critical judgments ready-made. It also begins to alter the power relation between children and the media: particularly through making their own meanings, children can become alerted to the possibilities of alternatives and change.

'Teaching' the Media?

So far I have written about the rationale for teaching about audio-visual media, and possible methods of starting, as though they just developed in a commonsense way out of other practices. Of course, they have not. Media education has a history. In fact, like all hybrids it has several histories, and several contradictory definitions but there is no room to recount them all here.

Some media education comes out of a sociological tradition, that is interested in how the media help to socialize us and construct our ideas about the world. It tends to be interested in non-fictional material such as news, documentary and advertizing, and in how the media deal with ethnicity, gender and class. Another strand comes out of a literary tradition that seeks to establish certain texts that are 'worth studying'. Another comes out of cultural studies and is interested in the pleasures of popular texts in particular, such as soap opera, light entertainment, cinema stars or the family album. Yet another, and very different, input comes from educational technology and the teaching of media production skills as analogous to professional media practice. Different tendencies in media education will depend upon different understandings of what the media are and what they do: there is the Left conspiratorial view; there is Leavisite disdain and so on.

Most teaching about the media developed, at least until the mid-1980s, in secondary, further and higher education. It developed in ways characteristic of those institutions: specialist and mainly academic courses on film in universities and at O- and A-level for example; units of work on specific media or on concepts (such as representation) spanning several media, within English or social studies courses for the 14–16 age range; practical work on video or film animation in colleges of art. These reflect the need to carve out timetable space and to gain credibility and status, usually through an examinable course. Such a context inevitably perpetuated the professional boundaries that separate literature and art from other media and from each other, though it was mainly English teachers who found their concerns naturally extending into audio-visual media.

In primary schools the situation was, and is, different. Because of the ways media education had developed for older age groups, it was often thought to be too difficult even for 11–13-year-olds, let alone younger children. Most of the work with older children tended to be critical analyses of media texts: looking at photographs, television programmes, newspapers and films and discussing or writing about them; this was perceived as antipathetic to the primary tradition of 'learning by doing' (even though the older children *were* learning critical methods by 'doing' them). Because of the integrated nature of the primary curriculum much media work was incorporated invisibly: as a theme or project or as an adjunct to other work, for example, making a video of a class play or outing. Thus many teachers felt they could assert that any work involving audio-visual media 'counted' as media education.

Some Key Concepts

But to return to my recurrent analogy: would any work involving books 'count' as literacy teaching? To some extent, and in a broad sense, it does. But we also have goals for literacy: we have a sense of what a literate person can do, and ways of measuring their competence. We need to develop goals for 'literacy' in audio-visual media too, and to develop its key concepts. Many efforts have been made in this direction, mostly outside Britain (Bryant and Anderson, 1983), but many of these betray a 'hidden curriculum' of resistance to audio-visual media in which it goes without saying that they are intrinsically different from print media because they threaten children's moral or intellectual development. A British group with which I am involved is attempting to identify a small number of very basic but separately definable conceptual areas which characterize media education, even though they may at this stage be very abstract and imply for each area a vast range of potential content and approaches.

> We are asking children to adopt a critical stance towards all media texts, including ones they have produced themselves, as opposed to just using or making texts. On this basis, we are seeking to develop awareness of the following concepts. But it should be noted that these areas are not ultimately separable and cannot be organized into a linear form or a

hierarchy. Aspects of each would be the main emphases in any media education, even with very young children. For example, reception class infants can consider *what difference it makes* to use a pencil, a chalk or a felt tip pen for their drawings.

1. CONSTRUCTION

   The fact that all media texts are constructed, using codes which have developed historically, and which we learn. What these codes or 'media languages' are and how they can be used. The technologies upon which they are based. Who produces texts and why.

2. CIRCULATION

   The fact that media texts are directed to audiences, that audiences can be constituted in many different ways, and that there are different ways of reaching them. That audiences bring meanings to texts and read them actively and therefore, different readings of any text are usually possible.

3. NARRATION

   Events or states of affairs are organized in particular ways in all media texts — these ways will differ according to the kind of text. The difference between 'story' and 'plot'; the manipulation of time; the role of character; selection and editing; narrative voices; point of view and identification.

4. CATEGORIZATION

   Media texts can be grouped in various ways: by technology, genre, intended audience, etc. What groupings can be made, and why. It makes a difference to the interpretation of a text, to see it in terms of a particular category.

5. REPRESENTATION

   The fact that there are differences between social groups, events etc. in the world and the ways they are represented and questioned in media texts. That some events and groups may be systematically excluded from media texts, and why. How these relationships can be explored. That there are different levels of realism. Caricature and stereotyping. (BFI/DES, 1986)

However, identifying key concepts at such a basic level provokes a further question. By what argument would one assert that these concepts are applicable only to audio-visual media? Couldn't they apply to print media as well? I have suggested that our conventional understandings of literacy can help us to develop a rationale for teaching about other media. I now want to turn this proposition on its head, and suggest that the ways in which media education has developed may have implications for our understandings of literacy. Do we ask children to adopt a critical stance towards the books and posters we use in the classroom, towards educational TV, towards their own writing? Is it better, for example, to eliminate racist and sexist material from our stock cupboards, or to find ways of criticizing both them and the conditions that enable them to exist? Do we discuss who gets into print, and how, and why — and who doesn't?

There is no real rationale for separating media into different categories and teaching them differently, except insofar as their technologies demand it. To establish 'media education' or 'media literacy' as new buzz-words for primary schools in the 1990s would be a good way of achieving limited change. To redefine literacy might be a real change.

Acknowledgements

Figures 1 and 2 are taken from *Picture Stories: Starting Points for Media Education in Primary Schools*. British Film Institute, 1986; photographs by courtesy of Doris Staples, Jim Adams and the Inner London Education Authority.

Part 5: Current Concerns

In her study of bilingualism called *Many Voices* Jane Miller (1983) shows how difficult it has always been for monolingual teachers to take full cognisance of the linguistic competences of bilingual pupils. They represent a challenge to the straightforward teaching of traditional curriculum subjects and seem to distort the organization of a school. The children are seen as, plainly, different.

We have still a great deal to learn about this subject, with its contradictions and social tensions, and so we are grateful to the writers of the next two essays for letting us see them at work in classrooms where bilingualism is a resource rather than a problem. Valerie Emblen has made a special study of the inter-language needed to help Asian pupils as they progress in mathematics in their primary school in London's East End. Mary Maguire's study comes from Canada where bilingualism is the official language policy. She works in Quebec, the heartland of French Canada, where identities are constructed in terms of the history and culture of the speakers, and where the educational policy of 'immersion' is now well advanced.

At this time we need individual testimonies to see how bilingual students regard themselves in their personal, social and political situations, and a deeper understanding of how bilingual speakers enrich and refresh the study of language by children in school. This would make possible more sensitive and positive moves, by teachers and children working together, towards the ending of racial prejudice.

15   Other Mathematical Puzzles: Entering the Discourse

Valerie Emblen

'The crucial moment of understanding lies in a specific relationship of the signified to signifier' (Walkerdine, 1982). Nowhere is the relation of language and learning more explicitly crucial than in mathematics. Following Walkerine's (and Vygotsky's) view, that word meanings are socially learned from the start, Valerie Emblen traces the discoveries made by her bilingual Asian pupils as they use their social perceptions and growing language competences to help them to behave like mathematicians. This is an exciting example of tutorship in the 'zone of proximal development' (Vygotsky, 1978), where the teacher's understandings are enhanced by encountering those of the children. The episode also shows, across the curriculum, the predicting and hypothesizing which are characteristic of advances in language thought if the pedagogy makes these things possible. The teacher also brings into sharp focus the relation of theories of deficit which surround the schooling of some of these children to issues of racism and intolerance.

This chapter describes some attempts to rethink the teaching and learning of mathematics in an infant school where most of the children do not speak English as their mother tongue. It is argued that, as the children experiment with language, so they can be encouraged and helped to experiment in mathematics in ways which lead to conceptual understanding.

We are in Spitalfields, that area of East London which has been the refuge of successive waves of immigrants, the silk weavers, the Huguenots and others whose talents have enriched our culture. About 95 per cent of the families of children who currently attend Thomas Barton infant school have come from the rural district of Sylhet in Bangladesh. Some have arrived recently. Their mother tongue is Sylheti, so in their early days in school they speak very little English, although their understanding outruns their speech.

There are other Asian children in the school. They will all become bilingual, but in the early days of their school learning they need vital support for their mother tongue if they are to perceive themselves as successful learners. So the authority has seen to it that Bengali, Sylheti, Urdu and Gujerati-speaking teachers work with the children so that they understand what is expected of them. In this way they feel supported as they begin to learn English and to become London school children. The language policy of the school assumes that the children are all active learners who make sense of the sounds and symbols that they hear and see, and who express in meaningful ways their thoughts, needs and ideas. Their approach to both language and learning is experimental at all times.

Here is Shamima, a 6-year-old Sylheti speaker, enjoying the traditional question and answer rhyme. Our version goes like this:

Where's the mouse?
In her house.
Where's her house?
In the wood.
Where's the wood?
The fire burned it.
Where's the fire?
The water quenched it ...

About three weeks after we had read the poem it was Jahed's birthday. He blew out his birthday candles in morning assembly. Shamima leaned over to me and whispered confidentially: 'He quench it, Miss'

The openness of this process is very exciting. Teachers can see the help that is needed and the most effective ways to offer it. It allows conversation and exchange of ideas long before the child is fluent in English. The children use all their language resources, constantly striving for clarity and, over time, moving closer to the English of their English-speaking peers. This seems the best way to learn a language. It is also joining utterance to the roots of thought.

Traditional Mathematics Teaching

Sooner or later the children are involved in the early stages of mathematics. They don't come to this as a novelty, any immigrant family learns quickly the economic facts of life and counts the currency carefully.

Traditional mathematics teaching is the careful grading of structures which are chosen to build up in the child's understanding a clear and conceptual pattern. The teacher has to understand why she has chosen a particular exercise, what its purpose is and be clear about its timing in the experience of the learner. The child is not involved in this, she is to accept the teacher's initiating moves and to learn to perform the exercise in the teacher's terms. Thus, the very skills which mathematics encourages: questioning, predicting, hypothesizing, are excluded. Consequently, the way the children are encouraged to learn their new language becomes at odds with the way they are to learn mathematics. Ironically, the rationale for the formal teaching of mathematics is that the children have 'too little language to do mathematics in English'.

The traditional teaching of mathematics in English can be either formal or informal, but the classroom discourse of both sets of practices can exclude some children from learning because there are forms of the teacher's language which are alien to the children's understandings. I had to create in my classroom a learning situation which began with the children's linguistic and learning skills and to proceed from these to the mathematical idea I wanted to introduce. That is, I don't believe that by learning the language of the teacher the children would directly learn the mathematics. This would simply create a gap between us.

Taking Advice

Here was my problem and a challenge. How was I able to create a coherent language and learning policy for my class as a social unit? How could my pupils confidently enter the discourse of mathematics in a meaningful way, in the way that they plainly showed related language and thinking in their learning of English?

I sought advice; it fell into two categories. The first went something like this:

> because of the nature of mathematics learning in young children, if you provide a rich stimulating environment, the children can do a lot of useful learning without the need for interaction in English between teacher and child.

My worry about this advice as the basis of a pedagogy was that it seemed to offer two versions of mathematics learning in my classroom, one for fluent speakers of English, the other for beginners. The distinction would be made not by my children's need for or ability in mathematics learning but solely by their performance in English. The second went something like this:

> give the children some mathematical games and activities to be going on with until they have learned enough English to join in properly

This piece of advice suggests that mathematics has no place in the learning of English.

Behind both of these solutions is a theory of language and learning with implicit views of deficit; the children are not ready to learn; they have not had enough of the right kind of play; their homes do not give them the right kind of experience; they need something before they can begin. When we think of the survival skills that many children and their families need and use, we realize how ethnocentric is our thinking, how ignorant of the richness of other cultures. Mathematics are, quite simply, made from children with sharp understandings, who ask the right questions and who can take much less for granted than their peers. I believe that the best way for bilingual children to learn the English they need for their mathematics is to learn that mathematics.

The Children's Responses

I know children are fascinated by numbers. From the earliest years they incorporate numbers into their drawings. Figure 1 is the picture by a five year old girl. When telling me about it she said: 'Girl seeing numbers look, she counting, English counting'. I know they look for patterns and regularities: they look for rules and can generate them if they have had enough examples from which to extrapolate. This is from a tape of three 6-year-old girls counting to 100 in English. All are Sylheti speakers. They had remembered up to thirty-nine:

All	Thirty-eight, thirty-nine
Ramina	Thirty-ten
Nomtaz	(In Sylheti), Nah, nah, it doesn't go like that (in English) twenty-eight, twenty-nine et.. thirty er

Shilpi	Forty, forty-one
All	Forty-two, forty-three, forty-four, forty-five, forty-six, forty-seven, forty-eight, forty-nine
Shilpi	Er sixty er
Nomtaz	Nah, nah, thirty, forty, fifty
Ramina	Fifty, Fifty-one

In this way, sharing knowledge and drawing on the regularities of the system they counted to one hundred at which point Shilpi said to me:

Shilpi	Miss, we better an you, miss.
Teacher	Oh, why's that?
Shilpi	We do English and Bengali, you do English

Children need to ask their own questions. These may not be the same ones as the teacher asks. This was brought home to me when I was working with Cindy, an English-speaking child. We were using one of the Checkpoint cards which have been designed by the ILEA inspectorate in mathematics so that teachers can test the development of a child's conceptual structures. This particular card is to test the understanding of tens and units. I put some bricks on the table and used the recommended wording on the card: 'Tell me as quickly as you can how many bricks there are on the table.' Cindy jumped up and rushed along the school into her classroom. A moment later she ran back, flopped into her chair and gasped: 'Sixty-five.' Somewhat taken aback, I asked her: 'How did you know?' 'You just asked my friend', was the prompt reply.

When the teacher keeps to herself entire control of the situation and does not discuss its purposes and implications with the children or offer them any explanation, then they are left to guess what sort of response is required and their replies may seem quite arbitrary. Bilingual children are especially disadvantaged in situations of the question-and-answer kind as they may find it difficult to ask for clarification or to explain why they made that particular mistake. By asking their own questions and testing the answers they begin to build up a knowledge of mathematics as a rule-governed system. Here are examples of how it happens.

We had been collecting number symbols from many parts of the world. Parents and families had come to school to write the number systems they knew or to speak their counting into a tape recorder. There were many interesting outcomes, both mathematical and social, especially for Aziz who, as the only Arabic speaker in the school, took responsibility for the Arabic numerals. If you wanted to know about them, you had to ask Aziz — a historical situation if ever there was one.

One day I was aware of three 6-year-old boys talking about the numbers which were displayed on the wall. The discussion was in Sylheti, obviously serious. Eventually, Abul Shahid articulated what they had in mind: 'Look, Miss, this one, one, one. This two.' They were wondering why many of the systems used two symbols to write the number 'ten'. This led us to an investigation of how a decimal system works. The children who had asked the question were joined in discussion by others. It was then possible to ask and answer questions in English, for by this time we had a shared frame of reference; we all knew what had to be discovered so we used our common language. There are many English classrooms in which this kind of discussion about mathematics never takes place at all. The children simply follow 'the rules'. Once the children are engaged in the investigation of mathematical ideas, they also become involved in the discourse and so start to learn the appropriate language.

Mathematics is learned from someone who behaves like a mathematician. We all need 'the opportunity to communicate with someone who knows more than oneself.' (Skemp, 1971) The opportunity 'enables us to test our ideas against another's greater understanding and so to gain immediate and explicit confirmation or disconfirmation of particularities' (Salmon, 1980).

This makes great demands on communication and on the resources of both the expert and the beginner. I have often had to consider if this works against the children who do not share a first language with their teacher. But I have become very aware that the sharing of meanings is not wholly dependent on the amount of English the child knows. A shared frame of reference, someone who will listen and, above all, the need to say something, these things allow ideas to be explored. When they have something they really want to say children can go to great lengths to transmit their meaning. One day in my classroom I felt an urgent tugging and someone was saying, 'Miss, Miss'. Five year old Tipu pulled me over to the sand tray and pointed to his three sandpies lined up in order of size. 'Father Bear, Mother Bear, Baby Bear' he proudly announced.

I was working towards mathematics learning that depends a great deal on the sharing, by teacher and child, of a common task. To make this possible I had to relax some of my authority over the ordering and timing of the curriculum and to hand over some of the responsibility for initiation to the children. This took me a long time to learn as I found it difficult to break away from a structured, teacher-controlled model of mathematics learning. It took me some time to come to terms with the need to work out what kinds of strategies I needed to become a collaborator. My perceptions have been influenced by the language and metaphors which have always been widely used in the teaching of mathematics: the discourse used in the reports of the Mathematical Association (see the Report for 1965 paras v vi) and Dienes (1969). Teachers are so constrained by this professional discourse which contains an inherent threat that failure by pupils to master any one of the early concepts as terms in language could lead to the complete collapse of their mathematics learning at a later date. But I am convinced that, in order to allow the children to enter the learning process and to be at home inside it, I must allow them to bring to mathematics the skills and learning techniques which they already know. At home, young children initiate talk and adults respond to them and are at pains to understand their meanings (Wells, 1985). At school, this process is reversed and children are asked to respond to the teacher's moves.

Perhaps because of the educators' interpretation of the thinking of Piaget on the pedagogy of mathematics teaching, especially his notions of egocentrism, the learning of mathematics has generally been seen as a matter of individual development. Children are considered, singly, to be 'good' or 'not good' at mathematics. Yet mathematics is a socially constructed system. It is socially used. Its main function is communication (Cockcroft, 1983). There seems good reason to suppose it can be learned socially, (Choat, 1978). We know that the social context in which a child works influences her thinking (Donaldson, 1978). But that social context does not lie entirely outside the child (Walkerdine, 1982). Part of this social context is the way the child has come to perceive it.

In the following extract Buzler a six-year-old boy and his two friends are creating a strategy for finding the heaviest of three things. They start by discussing which they think is heaviest and Syeduz and Buzler disagree:

Syeduz: That one big, that one little, that one nothing.
Buzler: (shaking his head) That one too heavy.
Syeduz: That one one, that one second one, that one third one.
Buzler: That one too heavy.
Syeduz: That one heavy, that one little little heavy.
Buzler: That and that is heavy. That not so heavy.

The children are using English because the teacher is there, although there is no pressure on them to do this. As yet they have no standard ways of expressing comparisons in English but their meanings are clear. It seems valuable for their mathematics learning that they are able to explore ideas in English even before they know the correct forms. It must also help them to learn English. Buzler is eventually proved wrong in his prediction. This hurt him, but not too much, so he would try again. The teacher cannot ignore the feelings, hopes and fears children bring with them to their learning. Through social interaction children support each other's learning, but they also bring all of themselves to the learning task. Social skills, such as holding a point of view, are important. So too is arguing a conviction, whether in mathematics, English or any other subject. It is also crucial to learning how to argue to see the point of view of the other person, notably in the area of the subject to be learned.

I am not arguing for a pedagogy that is less rigorous or less demanding for young children. It seems likely that interactive social classroom practices lead to the relational understandings that Skemp (1971) sees as the aim of school mathematics, where children are searching to make meanings. At the same time they are seeking out the grammar that governs both the system of language and the system of mathematics. Learning in this area is not easy. I feel that some of the attempts I have made to simplify it for children have only increased their difficulties by separating them from what they already know how to do. Children who are learning a second language know what helps them to learn it. This does not mean that teachers opt out of teaching. Instead, they gear their teaching to supporting the children's efforts. I am more and more convinced that children know how to do the things that will help them to do mathematics and that as a teacher I should allow the children to use all their own skills to support their learning.

16 How Do They Tell?
Ecrire c'est Choisir

Mary Maguire

One of the most significant, politically upheld experiments in bilingualism in first schools is being carried out in Canada where French is the official second language. Children of parents who opt for 'immersion' programmes are taught in French in their early school years. The evidence of second language learning from this nation-wide experiment will influence, in one way or another, subsequent language policies in schools.

In Quebec, where Mary Maguire is closely involved in these special programmes, French is the cultural first language, but Christopher speaks English at home and so is learning French in school. In this essay we see Christopher choosing a language to write in. He believes he is equally at home in both. Detailed linguistic analysis would, we believe, reveal something different, but we can see here a competent narrator offering his teacher and a researcher new material for speculation. We have printed Christopher's texts as they came to us.

Recently, as part of a larger research project which is concerned with how a selected group of 10 and 11-year-old children in a 'French immersion school' in suburban Montreal approach and perceive the writing of stories in English and French, I have been observing how the titles of their texts signal their intentions, topics and meanings. I offer two arguments: first that writing stories in school in any language foregrounds certain aspects of choosing undertaken by the writer. Then, for a researcher to uncover the raison d'être of the kinds of selection which are characteristic of bilingual children's story-making means perceiving pathways to both the literary texts in which the children 'live' in a secondary sense, and the pathways within the social situations, construed as texts, in which they actually dwell.

The Canadian constitutional debate of 1981 affirms that the Canadian nation, its people and its literature exist in a dialectic of regional, ethnic and linguistic tensions and self-consciousness. The Canadian preference for a mosaic culture, in which all the regions retain their distinctiveness, situates the problematique of differences in children's narrative texts. Since the initiation of children into literacy occurs in this dialectic of regional, ethnic and linguistic tensions, two questions are posed. First, what do the children and their tales tell us about their view of written language? Then, what do the stories tell us about the cultures children are creating in this particular sociolinguistic context in Quebec, and what can we learn about the contextual configuration of the environments, the worlds, they are creating and perceiving?

That Quebec is 'different', is written into many texts on Quebec politics, history, culture, language, schooling. It appeared recently in the debate on school board reform and Quebec curriculum, *La Régime Pédagogique*. Thus, to document children's narrative choices within these sociolinguistic and educational areas is to understand *difference* in the general sense, of elements, features or factors that distinguish codes, genres and situations, and also in the sense of Jacques Derrida's variant of the word, 'difference', terms of art, which implies choice and selection (Derrida, 1967).

In 1984–5 I set out to observe thirty children, one day a week, in two multigrade 5–6 classrooms in a West Island, mainstream community. The parents, teachers and school administrators are school oriented and consciously concerned about children's language proficiency in English and in French. This community has been perceived traditionally as a homogeneous speech community, the last garrison of 'Anglo-culture' within the province. It has also experienced considerable demographic shifts since the 1976 language legislation bill declared French the dominant language and its purpose to immerse children in the French language and culture of Quebec. Many anglophone families have since moved out of the community and the province, and many francophone and 'allophone' (other ethnic and linguistic groups) families have moved into the community. I spent the mornings (8.30–11.30 am) in the French immersion classroom when the children were taught by Marie Josée, a francophone teacher, and the early afternoons (1.10–2.00 pm) when Mrs G., a second generation Greek teacher, was in charge.

With the help of Mrs G. and Marie Josée I selected six children whose stories would be the centre of my study. However, in this chapter I focus on Christopher. Christopher views himself as a competent and willing story-writer in both classes. In describing how he goes about arranging events in his stories, he says:

> Well usually when I write a story ... I just think up in my head as it comes ... I don't uh ... use ... some ... uh ... I don't know some sort of a design or graph to ... to do the steps of a story and figure it out beforehand ... like ... uh ... some other writers might do. I ... I just take it off the top of my head ... and ... write it down and ... hope that I don't write myself into a corner. (Interview 15.7.85)

His teachers alternate between constraining the children to write within the conventions, the generic handrails, of a particular type of story such as a mystery, 'un roman policier', or a 'pourquoi' story, and liberating the children to create their own stories. Christopher says, he 'usually tries to keep *sujet libre*', when given the opportunity to write in either language on his own topics, which more often than not included, 'moi même et mes deux partenaires de la police secrète' (myself and my two partners of the secret police') and within his preferred genre of adventure, which generated 'des missions à la station d'espace des Martians' ('missions to the Martians' space station'). He knows he can write other types as well, 'well only if I have to write ... it ... I try to write as many adventures as I can ... if I can't, I just can't.'

Christopher's Rememberings Retold

In talking about his story-making experiences, Christopher's commentaries become retellings in themselves and provide insight into the genesis of his playing with time and space. He recalls his best English story-writing experience was in grade 4. After a field trip to the *Montreal Gazette*, which included visiting a darkroom, Christopher wrote a twenty-six page story.

> C. So I wrote about me and two other friends of mine and we went into a dark room and we fell through a trap door and ... there was like a zoo ... and it had ... all kinds of animals.

   I.   Uh, uh.

   C.   And as we were going we found out that ... uh, we were going past all the cages to our own cage ... we found that they're was two other of our friends who ... gone through another door, through the dark room and gotten captured ... and we escaped ... and we had to write down on our shirts and hands where we were ... where the passage ways lead so we could get home ... and back through the trap door and then we escaped.

It is this experience which provides insight into the reasons for his frequent choice of such lexical items 'as passageways, corridors, tunnels'. He recalls his best story-writing experience in French in the year of the study.

   C.   Well ... that was this year ... that was a twelve page story that I wrote in French. ... It's about me and Klaus and another boy in my class and ah ... two of our friends who are space cadets ... who are fighters in ... in the Marines ... in air in the space marines and who had been captured by Martians so we stole this huge space ... space ... huge space station was being made and that was like (...) millions (...) and so we stole it and rescued them and brought it back and nobody knew it was us who stole it ... because ... we just snuk in and took it and went back ... but they knew but the ... the ... like the police knew it was stolen but they didn't know it was us ... and we just transported it back to our room and ... nobody knew it was us ... our friends.

     Christopher's stories and retellings involve an interplay between the monologic and dialogic modes. His journeys have a social function; they are written for his classmates. There is an individual aspect to his journeying as he says, 'Je suis engagé dans mes histoires, c'est moi qui parle à terre.' There is an artistic aspect to the worlds he creates; as he plays within the genre of adventure, he mixes the modern world of *L'Etoile du Guerre* with the mythical figures of both English and French story traditions. The Loup-Garou, a trickster figure from French folklore, enters his class and disrupts the genre of 'dictée' writing, a thing regularly done at 9.00 a.m.

La Loup-Garou

'Et maintenant, classe, on va faire la dictée', Marie-Josée a dit. Soudainement, 'Rowr', et un loup-garou a sauter dans la classe.

'Eh Claus, Keith, c'est la loup-garou qui a terrorisé tout la fille,' j'ai dit à mes deux partenaires de la police secrète. Oui, je sais que nous sommes jeunes, mais il-y-avait un déficit des agents, donc ils nous laissaient entre la force.

'Je vais alerté la general par la téléphone remote,' Keith a dit, 'Allo, géneral, c'est nous les agents double-zéro, un, deux, et trois. On été en traine de faire la dictée, quand la loup-garou a sauté dans la classe. Que ce qu' on peut bien faire?'

'Utilise tes projectiles du sommeil pour le capturer,' la general a dit.

'Eh, Keith, Claus a murmurer. 'Tout le monde a partir, et le loup-garou veins ici.'

'Au revoir, general,' Keith a dit.

Tous nous trois ont pris les compases de mathematiques, et ont lanée a la loup-garou.

'Eeeeyei'!' la loup-garou a crié, et il a couru vers la porte.

'Vite, suive le,' Keith a crié.

Nous l'avons chassé jusqu'au les bureau d'administration. Il a couru a la machine de couper les papier, et a dechirer le lame de la planche.

'Ou est tout le monde?' j'ai demander.

'Ils ont évacué,' Keith a repondé.

'Rrrooowwwrrr' a grogner, et il a nous attaké avec sa lame.

'Vite, on doit retraite pour preparé les projectiles.' Nous avons couru vers les classes des petits, et on a desendu les escalier.

'Est-ce que ta fusée est preparé Keith?' Claus a demander.

'Oui, et toi?'

'Oui. Est-ce que tu est prè Christ?'

'Oui,' j'ai repondu, Keith, dit au general de envoié un hélicoptèr avec un cage.

Pendant que Keith a parlé au general, Claus et moi ont tirée sur la loup-garou. La loup-garou a été touché, mais avant qu'il a tombé, il a lancé la lame, et a il coupé mon fusé en deux.

L'hélicopter est arrivé, et la loup-garou a été capturer. Soudainement, la loup-garou a changeé en forme humaine. C'était Lex Luthor, l'ennemi du Superman. Il était apporté a un laboratoire pour été étudié.

The English 'Glooskap Character' lives within one of his French 'pourquoi' stories, *Comment L'été Arrivée au Canada*. Christopher explains he can live 'dans cette monde aussi.'

Dans le reigne du Glooskap il faisait froid. Ce froid était causer par le géant Hiver, et ses assistantes, Mort et Famine.

Toute la terre a été couverte de neige et de glace. Il n'y avait pas un arbre vivant. Les feux n'étaient pas assez chauds. Toute la nourriture a été mangée, et il ne pourait plus pousser de fruits ou de légumes, parce-ce que la terre était trop dure.

Glooskap a esseyé toute sa magie, mais rien a passé. Si rien n'était fait, tout la région mourrait!

Glooskap est allé chez Hiver pour essayer de persuader le géant d'arreter. Mair quand il a vu le royaume d'Hiver, il a été hypotise par sa beauté. C'était comme dehors, mais avec la beauté. Il y avait des arbres, pas des arbre morts, mais des arbre vivants.

Un jour, un oiseau est venu chercher Glooskep. Il a parlé a Glooskap des régions au sud, ou la Reine reigne.

Glooskap a décidé d'aller au sud pour chercher la Reine, la seule personne plus forte qu'Hiver, et la seule personne qui effraye Hiver.

Glooskap a traversé l'océan sur Blob la baleine. A la fin de la traversée, Glooskap va sur terre. Il a suivi un chemin jusqu'a ce qu'il voit un cercle sans arbre. Dans ce cercle it voit des femmes en cercle, avec une dame au milieu.

'Ca doit etre la Reine' pense Glooskap.

Avec sa magie, il souleve la Reine. La, il l'attrape.

Il emmene la Reine dans sa région. Il ne trouve personne. La géant a utilisé sa magie pour les mettre en sommeil. Glooskap dit a la Reine ce qu'il veut, puis les deux vont chez Hiver. Hiver leur souhaite la beinvenue, parce-ce qu'elle veut les mettre en sommeil. Les trois ont parlé, et Hiver a éssayé a donner le sommeil, mais ca n'a pas marché. Hiver pensait que son pouvoir était nul, et elle a commencé a pleuver. La Reine dit: 'J'ai prouvé que je suis plus forte que toi. Je te donne toute la terre au Nord. Tu peux revenir a la région de Glooskap six

mois par l'année, mais moins durement. Les autres six mois,
je vais régner ici.''

Hiver n'a pu rien faire mais qu'accepter.

Et maintenant Hiver et la Reine partagent la région de
Glooskap.

The concept of the north is well known to the Canadian literary
imagination as the region of challenge and adventure. Christopher's
spontaneous stories are all centred in action; his titles in English —
'Alien Attack, Mission: Base Destruction', 'Ben', 'The Burglar' — or
in French — 'La Rayon de Reduction', 'Ghostbusters et Fils',
'L'Etoile de Guerre' — signal his favourite topic and focus. Sometimes his focus is on the adventure itself or on a particular character
or characters who function as 'actants' in his stories, usually the
mates of his writing group. His open-ended commentaries about his
stories become stories about stories and reflect his personal living in
his stories. Consider the following excerpt from an interview:

> well, most of my stories are about me and my friend Claude
> going on special missions ... to stop the Martians from
> invading earth and destroying it and taking it over ... as we're
> being special agents, whoo ... whose job it is to do this ... and
> our leader or boss is someone named the general ... whose
> first name isn't mentioned in the story and ... all usually stop
> off at his office ... to receive the mission and to tell us about
> them ... before we actually start them.

Here is the beginning of Christopher's preferred ('best') story from
the year of the study.

Mission Vanthium

A half hour later, we were in the underwater base, Triton
dome, named that, because it is a dome shape. We were
getting our radar-proof, heavily armed, lightening-class
medium cruiser ready for blast-off.
Claude, do you think we'll need space suits? I asked.
'No, the Martian probably created an artificial atmosphere on
the planet.'
'Well, let's blast off,' I said.
Ten minutes later, we were flying towards the asteroid belt.

What is Christopher doing? What is he learning? In *Mission Vanthium* and his commentary about this story, I see Christopher playing out the game of adventure within the rules of narration. He describes why *Mission Vanthium* is the best English story he wrote during the school year:

C.   I think it was my best story because it was the longest ...
     and most of it wasn't just pow, pow you're dead tell the
     Martians and it was ... I think the funniest cause it wasn't
     all frightening like I said before ... and it was mostly us,
     me, Claude and I — trying to figure out ways to get the
     Vanthium, Vanthium, a chunck of Vanthium which is a
     radioactive stone in my mind, to back ... back to earth ...
     so it usually ... we go it ... we stole the Vanthium from
     the Martians not by using brute force but more by
     strategy and our minds ... so I think that was probably
     my best one.

J.   What did you learn from writing that story?

C.   Well — I learned that adventure stories aren't *all pow,
     pow* you're dead and that sometimes ... your people do
     use strategies and their minds to get by the bad guys and
     — a lot of my other stories, we use brute force to get by
     the Martians which isn't that bad because sometimes
     brute force can be funny and humorous, but, but ... this
     but this time I learned that it's not always funny and that
     sometime strategy is a good thing to use.

J.   Who is telling this story?

C.   Well ... I tell it ... but it and it's in the past tense, so ... it's
     not actually happening then ... I'm telling what hap-
     pened.

J.   What were you trying to do when you wrote this story?

C.   Well — I was trying to write a humorous, a humorous
     com- ... adventure story ... which would be long ... I try
     to make all my stories long ... and uh — it would involve
     strategy, using strategy and adventure, and brute force ...
     and I was just trying to write a good story that everyone
     in my class would like.

J.   How did you decide about the tense of this story. How
     did you know what time to use when writing this story?

C.   Well — the first part how did I decide about tense of the
     story is pretty easy ... because almost all of my stories, I
     use the past tense because I'm telling the story — cause ...

because it's an adventure about me and the second part
how did I know what time to use when writing this
story — is well — you can, it's easy to figure out what
time you're going to be using if someone is telling the
story because it's going to be past tense if someone is
telling it to you after it happened ...

The speed with which Christopher moves his characters in his
stories (as in *L'Etoile du Guerre*, 'une heure apres on était dans le
corridor', or in *Mission Vanthium*, 'We blasted off and went into hyper
space. Twenty minutes later, we docked in our underwater base. We
gave the Vanthium to the general, he put it in lead, and it joined the
other chunk at the bottom of the sea') shows a child narrator building
an image of a future oriented world as he interprets the world around
him. This raises an interesting question: to what degree are the salient
features which emerge in the stories of bilingual children contingent
upon the degree to which they become, as Greimas says, 'actants' in
their own stories?

Differences

Christopher's French teacher perceived story writing and the reading
of stories in French to be 'difficult'. Although she read to the children
I rarely observed her reading stories from the Quebec literary
tradition. In fact, Christopher recalls only one French story, *L'ecole
du Rêve*, being read to him during the school year. He chose to read
Tintin, *Asterix* and *Iz No Goud* for most of the year. While in English
story writing he uses literary models and connects them to his
personal goals, his story writing in French contains only subtle
features of the French story tradition derived from the *bande dessinée*,
the art form which the English call comics.

While Christopher does not perceive story making experiences
to be very different in his two classrooms, he does notice that
differences in gender and tense, (both of which are fixed and variable
marked features of the French language) can make story writing
harder in a second language. His use of gender is both motivated and
unmotivated in his stories; for example, it can be motivated by
morphological analogy 'une après-midi' or by semantic analogy,
"une nouvelle" or by metonymic use of nouns, like 'une puce à
protuberance (a silicon chip)'. Other words tend to be masculine

when there is nothing to indicate otherwise such as 'un radar, un laser'.

His French stories raise an interesting question: are there forms which children could use in storymaking but which do not actually appear? For example, the passé simple is a feature specific to the French story telling tradition but it did not occur frequently in the assigned or spontaneous stories of Christopher and his mates. Christopher perceives differences in language at a micro level, such as gender or tense. In interviews he mentions such features as un/une; le/la. He knows the French verb system can affect story writing but not necessarily *his* story-writing.

> J.   How does it affect your story writing?
> C.   Well, no, not really unless I mix up un or une, well that doesn't really change anything unless it's a play on words ... then it might change ... if it's 'le' or 'la' or 'un' or 'une', it might be one but it might be the other you're supposed to use.

He offers the following commentary on the French verb system:

> C.   But in French it's a little more complicated because you have to like ... the ... use passé ... because you see ... the first one you learn is passé ... um ... I forgot what it is ... I shouldn't have forgotten.
> J.   You've forgotten the names?
> C.   Yeah, like there's futures and indica ... they're indica ... india ... indica .... I forgot how to pronounce that indicative or something like that and there's different groups, like first group, second group and third group or ...
> J.   Why don't you use that same example and don't worry about the name so much just the use like he is running, he ran.
> C.   il cour, there is no ... like he ... like there's so ... it's just il cour ... il a couru I think, il corrait (...). Ah, well it's like that ... there's endings ... passé — what is it ... passé anyway. In one of the groups it's j'ai mangé or j'ai couru so you gotta, you got to make it with another verb je or tu a ... there's sixteen that go with je suis ... there's 16 verbs that go with je suis or tu es.

He goes on to say that certain verbs may be used for certain types of stories.

> C.   ... it would probably depend on what kind of story ... they wanted to write because ... there are different topics and they use different words ... like comedy ... usually uses funny words or stuttering or sometimes ... people stutter to make it funny ... or like actions or adventures ... there ... there's usually ... there's running, shooting, punching, that's different words for that and mysteries ... there's like ... run ... like creeping around spying and it all really depends on what kind of story you want.
>
> J.   Uh, Uh, how about in French?
>
> C.   Well in French ... I think it's probably the same thing except it's in another language and the words would be translated into French ... so its mostly the same thing except for the language.

At the global level of topic and interplay between time and space dimensions, he appears to differentiate not so much on the level of a particular linguistic code but more on a level of the language of narration, of a particular type or story. The further I probe into Christopher's stories, his world and space, the more I see that a child's stories are not sufficient evidence to assess a child's narrative competence. There is no doubt in Christopher's mind that story making is a natural activity in both languages. He did not perceive much difference between the story writing situation in either class although he did perceive differences in realizing stories in French to be harder than in English, a universal perception held by all thirty children in this study and their French teacher as well.

Conclusions

Carol Fox (1983) talks about the 'diversity of ways in which young children can transform their literary experience into their own narrative purposes'. If by the time as Fox argues that they come to literacy learning in school they have the seeds of future literary competences', interesting questions arise: What do children do when they take up the role of narrator for themselves within the genre of schooling? Scholes says that, 'a written text is a record of transaction between a writer and the language in which the text is composed. It is always the production of a situation.'

To situate children's stories in an educational context means discovering pathways to their texts, their worlds and their lives. Since Christopher shows us that the plots of his stories or histories can be differentiated from the experience or history which provides its raw materials, and that understanding the genesis of children's story making cannot be uncovered by focusing only on the text, or only on the social context.

Are their stories structured around certain events and then remembered as a story which is told and retold? Or are the events structured at some deeper level from which narratives are constructed according to the dictates of a specific performance situation? What is the teacher's role in nurturing the active role or voice of the child as narrator, the child as natural symbolist? Discovering the answers to these questions means searching for new pathways in understanding how the social text in itself disables or enhances a child's narrative competence, performance and the literary texts the child prefers to create.

A single performance is only a skewed sample of available skills, and an imperfect measure of narrative competence. Children know more about narrative structure and story-making than their stories sometimes display. Their decisions to include information and specific features are derived from a complex interplay between their own conceptualizations of the functions of story-making and their teacher's conceptualizations. The patterns I see evolving in the children's perceptions of narrative and narrating in English and in French suggest that the differences are not necessarily language-specific but are influenced more by what the child narrator feels licensed to create and what resources he feels he can draw upon in the story-making process. Rosen (1972) argues that we cannot avoid the questions of what our pupils are doing when they take up the role of narrators for themselves? Are the differences uncovered perceived or preferred differences within the language or the story or the language of a particular type of story? How do these perceived differences arise? Are they more a consequence of the interplay between the ways in which children decide to create a story and their perceptions of for whom the narrative text serves and what it can accomplish in a particular story-telling and story-writing situation?

I challenge the predisposition among literary scholars to look at narrative, as a genre having a pre-existing form into which one pours aesthetic experience, as well as the strong propensity among theorists, educators and researchers to conceptualize a Procrustean bed for narrative in general and children's narratives in particular, within which individual narratives may or may not lie.

Part 6: Who are the Experts?

At the banquet of learning teachers have always found themselves seated slightly below the salt. Their claims to expert professional status have never been fully recognized. They have had to stretch out their hands farther than most for the knowledge they need, and have often been slighted as pretentious when making claims for the importance of their discipline, education. A particular kind of disregard falls on those who are thought not to know their place in the order of things.

Lately, things have changed a little. No research in classrooms can be carried out without the help of teachers. Many classroom practitioners have complained when their resources and results have been raided; some have even declared themselves less than impressed by the understanding shown by the raiders. Certainly, when teachers now say that in some areas they are their own experts, they are listened to with respect (Eyers and Richmond, 1982). What we cannot deny is that, in the matter of research in classrooms, they are where the evidence is.

What, then, of those committed to the continuing education of the educators? The findings of psychologists, sociologists, anthropologists, linguists and historians are all pertinent. Every page in this book bears this out. But, as we have all discovered, the application of theory to practice is not straightforward; it is more a matter for patient exploration. Valerie Walkerdine, whose work is esteemed highly by all the contributors to this volume, says, 'Neither the teacher nor the children can change without the production of new discourses in which to read their actions and to produce different actions and different subjectivities' (Walkerdine, 1982).

Children's identities and teachers' identities are part of what is made in every classroom. Those responsible for helping teachers to establish themselves in this demanding profession — called 'trainers' if the military model is in force, or 'tutors' if the relationship is gentle

— have often taken the course of professional development to be a kind of top-dressing on an already existing qualification in an academic discipline. But, for beginners and tutors, a preparation year is as active a period of change as one is likely to experience at any other time. The same is true for courses taken later after years of classroom hardening.

Teachers and tutors of teachers know the value of 'recent and relevant' experience of classrooms. The problem is not to acquire it, but to resist developing a set of behaviours which stand in for both teaching and learning. As a result, a deeper collaboration between those who work in classrooms and those who only visit them is urgently called for. We offer the following two essays as a pair, the teacher and the tutor are in roles which can be exchanged the better to see what they are doing. The writers are too sensitive to the complexities of the situations they describe to prescribe modes of conduct for each other. Their work together has taught them both the successes and the pitfalls of collaborative learning. Their analyses indicate that work of this kind must always be in progress.

17 Conversation One-to-One: Knowing Jason

June McConaghy

If the perspectives of our authors have sharpened those of our readers, these conversations of Jason and his teacher, a selection-to-make-a-record, are open for inspection as classroom text in terms of the preceding essays. The sub-text of the dialogue is clear: a perceptive, acutely observant, lonely child spends most of his day in institutions, coping with their social demands and discovering his own longings, moods and struggles. His teacher, following the age-old injunction to 'get to know the children', finds herself entrusted with confidences which weigh heavily as concern, but which have also to be turned into frames of reference for reading, writing and reasoning in the context of the work of a whole class and of her research enquiries. Jason enjoys the authorized favouritism of only this essay. A specific response to this account is given in the next chapter by June McConaghy's teacher-collaborator.

When I first met Jason, one of my 6-year-old students, I had no idea that he would play such an important part in helping me to understand more clearly some of the things in his world. Through his stories he shared with me some of the ways that he viewed and tried to make sense of the things that influenced his learning and growth as a person. He displayed the kind of meaning that he gives to his curriculum through his actions, his writing and in our conversations.

It was the first day of school in September when I first saw Jason standing near the door of the classroom hugging his orange plastic lunch pail. Unlike most of the other new children Jason had not come to school with his parents but he had been dropped off by a teacher from the Happiness Factory Daycare Center where he spent long hours before school in the morning and after school until his parents picked him up on their way home. I found a seat for Jason and I could not help but notice how pale and rather unhappy he looked in his torn jean jacket and crumpled baseball cap. It was only later as I came to know him that I began to understand why he often felt so sad.

In one of our early conversations we talked about that first day of school, and Jason remarked: 'I remember I was too scared to even think, cause I didn't know what you would have to do in here or what you would be allowed to use or anything. Like I thought you would read those books but I thought only the teacher would get to use those felt pens at the writing centre.' Many children worry about meeting the expectations of the teacher. They come to school already busy trying to 'read' the teacher even before they can read print. It is often difficult for them to interpret a new situation clearly, including the things teachers say and do. Jason encountered this kind of situation soon after the school year began.

It was early in the afternoon when we were getting organized for centre time when Jason called out from the back of the room in a voice filled with panic, 'I can't write a story. I can't spell and anyway I've got no imagination.' Jason was responding to a request I had made that he go to the writing centre with a small group of children to begin writing a story. He had not had any school experience before entering grade 1, but even if he had, it may not have helped him to understand that drawing a picture was writing a story in my classroom. It would seem that Jason had not understood my intentions and he had interpreted writing a story to mean literally that. However, I too had not understood something even more important. I had failed to realize just how my request might appear to him, from his point of view. Paulo Freire reminds us that 'our tendency as teachers is to start from the point at which we are and not from the point at which the students are' (Freire, 1985, p. 15).

Jason, like most of the children we meet in their early years of schooling, was still spontaneous and eager to show the point at which he was, if allowed to initiate his own learning. We can build on the experiences of children as natural learners by observing what they are trying to do and by responding to these things in a way that will help and encourage them to learn even more.

Sometimes Jason and I would talk when he came in early to help tidy up the room or prepare materials. We were at the painting centre mixing up jars of fresh paint. I asked Jason if he would like to put on a paint shirt so he would not get paint on his clothes.

'These olds things,' he said, 'they are practically rags now.'
[He held up his leg to show me the huge holes in the knees of his pants.]

'Maybe Mom could mend those,' I said.
'No, she would never have the time. Look at my shoes,' he went on.
[I saw that his toes were almost out, but I made no further suggestions about his clothes.]
'What do you think of the painting centrc Jason?' I asked.
'It's good, not as good as the writing centre, but if you want to paint and learn to mix colours it's good. For me, I think painting pictures is a waste of time, I'd rather write stories and only make pictures to go with the story if the picture fits. I'd rather make words.'

Jason did not spend much time at the painting centre but he did make a lot of words at the writing centre in his scribbler called *My Stories*, and in his journal. I knew that he was very aware that print conveyed meaning and that he was beginning to use it purposefully to communicate his ideas to others. When he did paint a picture he usually 'made' words somewhere on the painting the way he did on the one that was hanging to dry above the easel. It was a simple painting, several strong stokes going in different directions in blue and brown. Jason had entitled the picture 'The Storm' and under-neath he had printed with the brush:

'This is an awful storm and I think nature can feel.'
'Do you know where you got the idea for this painting?' I asked.
'I got thinking about it when you were reading that book about *Wonder and the Storm*,' he replied.

Jason was referring to Robert McCloskey's book, *A Time of Wonder*, that I had read to the class a few days before. I was surprised that Jason had been inspired by this particular book as it was a very different kind of story from the ones that he had shown an interest in before. It is a story that takes the reader to coastal islands during the summer where nature is experienced in all its force and gentleness. The children who are visiting the islands leave at the end of summer to return to school 'a little bit sad. ... It is a time of quiet wonder.' Not all children experience literature in the same way. *A Time of Wonder* spoke personally to Jason's need and desire for quietude in his life. As we continued to talk about the story he told me about other kinds of books that he would not read to children if he were the teacher. 'If I were a teacher I would never read books that got everyone all excited and noisy. I would read calm beautiful stories that made me feel quiet.'

I looked forward to talking to Jason again about some of the times when he does feel quiet and calm. We had the opportunity a few days later in the school library. We began to look at a book together.

> 'I thought we could read *Emily's Bunch* again,' he said.
> [Jason chuckled as he looked at the picture of Emily dressed up in a pillow case with a face of a monster crayoned on the front.]
> 'She was smart at the end when she fooled her brother. Anyway you have to trick people sometimes especially if they are bigger than you. Hey, hey, I never noticed all these things in this book when I read it before. That always happens to me.'
> 'What happens?' I asked.
> 'Well, when I read a book for the first time I read it too fast and then I miss a lot of things, or if there are a lot of people and noise around I don't see things. Like here we are in the library and no one else is here and I'm just seeing those globes on top of the bookcase. I never knew they were there before.'

Jason knew that he could see things more clearly when he was quiet and given time. He often expressed his frustration at being rushed from one place to another. He wrote about his feelings in his journal: 'My mom gets mad at me cause I'm slow and I can't hurry up and rush out so she's late for work.'

It is not only working parents who are guilty of rushing children about. Sometimes in our effort to cover the curriculum or produce readers and writers, teachers try to hurry children through the stages of language development by teaching them about language in stories and books rather than allowing them to grow through living and using it. I wondered where Jason did find quiet places to perhaps sit and think and figure things out.

> 'Well, not at school, at least not in the lunch room,' he said. 'It's really loud in there. There's screaming and everything going on. And it sure isn't quiet at Daycare, especially in the van when you are driving there. But I always get in first so I can sit next to the window cause I don't like to be squished in

the middle. Oh, I know one place I feel quiet and that's in bed. I sleep a lot because I'm tired all the time.'
'Didn't you write about that this morning?' I asked.
'Want me to get it and read it to you?'

Jason returned to the library with his writing book. He read his story: 'I have been feeling sad today and I had no one to play with at recess. It's boring at home when Mom and Dad watch TV. I sleep a lot but I don't like to sleep sometimes.' When he finished reading he said, 'Did you notice how I wrote about how I was feeling sad at the beginning of the story? Well, that's because one time when I didn't know what to write in my journal, you said, why don't you write about how you feel?' Then he asked about my own writing.

'Do you write a lot at home?'
'Yes, a lot,' I said.
'Oh, and you probably write a lot about how you feel too.'

Jason was developing as a writer who understood that writing involved talking and sharing not only the content of the 'story' but sharing the process of writing with another writer. He was writing about his personal experience with loneliness, an issue in his life that he was trying to sort out.

'What do you mean when you say it's boring at home when Mom and Dad watch TV?' I asked.
'Well, you see, I sit at the table to eat while they eat in front of the TV, and that's boring.'
'Why don't you sit with them to eat?'
'I do on special vacations but we just got a new couch a few weeks ago, and I might spill something on it. And if they sat at the table, they couldn't see their shows, could they?'

Jason was using his own narrative to organize his feelings and thoughts about a situation that was creating conflict. On the one hand he had a sense that it was a logical explanation but he seemed to be confused because it just did not 'feel' right. It did not seem to 'fit' his idea of what he thought a family should be like.

As Jason and I continued to talk he revealed his fantasy about family life and about himself if he were a father.

'Well, if I were a Dad,' he began, 'I would like us to sit and just talk about things like you and me are doing right now and I'd ask them lots of things.'
'What kinds of things?'
'I'd ask them what they did at school, like did you finish any puzzles lately, because I would probably be into puzzles myself. Then I'd ask them what they liked best at school and they would probably say writing because I'm into writing myself.'

While Jason's story tells us the way he imagines things might be and the way he would like them to be, he also reminds us of the importance of talking with each other in order to construct our own meaning of things in our lives. His narrative also reveals his understanding of knowing another person by imaginatively placing oneself in their place.

Just as Jason found it difficult to understand the way his family organized their lives, he experienced similar difficulties in accepting many of the rules within the school system. One of our conversations focused on his recent snowball fights in the school yard, which was against the rules. 'Kids are such babies,' he said. 'They cry when they are hit by a snowball or if they get pushed down. When I get pushed, I just push back harder ever if he is bigger than me.' Sometimes Jason thought up his own ways of getting around the rules. On one occasion in winter when the children were reminded that they could not stay in for recess unless they brought a note from home, Jason produced his own note written on a crumpled piece of paper, the size of a gum wrapper. 'This is all that is left,' he said, 'the other part fell in the snow.' Jason often told me that he did not think that rules were necessary at school but they were important at other places such as summer camp. 'You've got to have rules there, because a person could get drowned or lost in the woods, but that could never happen at school.'

I wondered if Jason saw the Daycare Center as another rulebound institution, within which he was expected to function.

'Do you find Daycare like school Jason, or is it more like home?' I asked him.
'Daycare is different from school,' he said. 'They don't have any water fountains or desks and you don't have to listen there because it's not a place you go to learn anything.'
'Why do children go to daycare then?' I asked.

'Well I think they put you there for someone to take care of you and they want you to have fun too. But I mostly rest there and think about other things.'

'Do you ever think about school when you are resting?'

'Sometimes I do. I think about what we are going to do the next day, like what I'll write about. Sometimes I'm right and sometimes I'm wrong. But mostly I think about all the time I have to stay at school and then how I'm too tired to play when I get home.'

As Jason was describing his 'resting and thinking' at the Daycare, it was easy for me to imagine a scene where he was stretched out on the floor in the middle of a group of active children running back and forth, stepping over him as he lay staring into space. This was a familiar scene in our classroom when Jason was present, for it seemed that he had found his own way of closing out the noise and confusion around him when he entered his own world of dreams. Sometimes these dreams were shaped and illuminated by Jason's literary experience with stories and books. I remember reading Bernard Waber's *Lyle and the Birthday Party* to the class one day. It was not long after the story ended that Jason told me his own story about his sixth birthday party:

> I turned six for my birthday party on Saturday. We celebrated, me and three other friends. We all went skating, counting my Mom and Dad it would be four adults. Chip and Elsie were their names. Mom and Dad mostly wanted grownups, I mostly wanted kids. I never said anything about Chip and Elsie cause they just wanted them to come.

At first this personal narrative seemed to have little connection with the story by Waber. Some teachers might find this kind of response irrelevant and a distraction from the story. But Jason was reading literature well, for he was transcending the text in a way that raised his awareness of his own experience. Many children who become personally involved in the story have often been able to read or have been introduced to books at home. However, Jason told me that his parents rarely read books with him, at least not in the way we read at school.

'They don't know about authors and stuff,' he said. 'It's only the books at school that have authors. The ones at home are different. Anyway, I don't get read to much, but it would always be Mom if I did. Sometimes she makes me read out loud too, because she says it's good for your brain and helps your brain to think more and you'll get smarter.'

'You mean that reading is good for your brain, like drinking milk helps you to grow?'

[Jason laughed at my absurd analogy. He continued,]

'And she makes me sound out words I don't know.'

'Does that help?' I asked.

'No,' Jason stated very emphatically, 'and I just keep telling her that I can figure it out by what makes sense, but she won't believe me, so I just mostly read by myself.'

Jason was getting two different views of reading. The view at home was providing him with the idea that reading was something that he must learn to do, which is difficult but necessary, and yet he is not seeing anyone around him doing it for enjoyment. He is being told *how* to read as though by telling he is going to learn. However, Jason has learned to compromise between what he knows works for him and what his parents want him to do and so he 'just mostly reads by himself'. At school he is learning that reading can be fun, and that it can provide him with stories in real books by real authors. Jason's early introduction to authors and the whole concept of authorship seemed to fascinate him to the point that he identified with authors very quickly when he began to engage in his own writing. I asked him where he got his ideas for his own stories: 'Usually from my head, but sometimes from books we read like that one I wrote about *The Mouse and the Boy*. I got that idea from the story of the *Mouse and Tim*.

Once upon a time there was a little mouse. He was as small as a bee and he was as furry as a poodle. It was a mouse. A boy had him as a pet. One day he ran away. He came back in a week, the boy was happy. They lived happily ever after. The end.

Jason was aware that many of his ideas for writing were rooted in the literature that he read independently and that we read together. He was writing every day, and I began to notice that his writing book was always out on his desk and that he used every spare minute to work on another story. Sometimes he took his book home, and showed me the next morning how much writing he had done. We often talked about his views on writing at the writing centre. I tape recorded the following conversation.

J. This writing centre is getting too crowded.

T. I agree, I wonder why it's so popular?

J. Cause everybody wants to write and draw and stuff.

T. Why do you like writing so much?

J. Cause you learn the most of any of the other centres.

T. What kinds of things?

J. Well, you learn to make up stories, like at the puppet centre you make up stories, but here you write them down. You learn how to spell words and you write them and you learn how to illustrate.

T. Illustrate?

J. Of course, you know on the front of books you always say the author and who it is and the illustrator, the guy who makes the pictures.

T. What do you find the hardest thing about writing?

J. Mostly the spelling, but sometimes what to write about. Then I remember sometimes when I'm writing and you ask me questions like 'What happens next?' and so I just ask myself the same kind of questions and then write it down.

Although Jason was crediting me with demonstrating a strategy for getting kids to go on with their story and to write 'more,' I was also demonstrating one of the secrets of a real author in capturing his reader by creating the desire to know what happens next. It was becoming obvious that as Jason was becoming a writer he was also becoming a reader.

Jason was beginning to love stories and books and he was reading independently many of the books that I was reading to the class. We chatted about the books we had read and often read a book to each other when we met. Our most recent conversation began with our sharing our reactions to a book read that day entitled *Rotten Ralph*. While our conversation began about the content of the story it ended with Jason trying to figure out the complex process of reading.

'Now this is what I call a really funny story. What a cat! Want me to read it?' [I turned on the tape recorder.]

J. Ralph ruined Sarah's pardy ... party. ... Is that the right way to spell party?

T. Yes.

J. Oh I thought there was a 'd' there. Who took the 'd' out of party? I want to start all over again because I stopped … through his best pipe. … My Dad doesn't smoke a pipe, in fact, he doesn't smoke at all cause I taught him not to.

T. How did you do that?

J. Whenever I saw him smoking a cigarette then I told him not to. He knew it was bad but it was just hard for him to stop. Hey, look at this cat in the Dad's chair. My Dad's favourite chair would be the rocking chair. There are some hard words in this book like 'afternoon'.

T. You didn't seem to have any trouble reading 'afternoon'.

J. No it just felt natural. It just sort of feels like I'm saying what I want to write and then you are writing it in the book that you're reading.

T. Did you think learning to read would be hard?

J. Yeah, cause I never read hardly anything before. Sometimes I did read some words that I knew. But I never knew 'is' or 'the' or 'and' or anything like that. I just knew words like cat and dog, but I didn't know how to spell them. I guess sometimes you know how to read things but you don't know how to spell it. Like I can read afternoon, but I couldn't spell it. The secret is that you know how to read most things you know how to write.

T. Do you think you can write most words that you can say?

J. Yes, that's just what I was going to explain. Like when you are little you know how to say almost every word but you don't know how to spell. Hey, if anyone knows about this I would like to know who it is and then I could know too.

Jason told me on another occasion that 'he thought he had books in his head' because 'when I go to write a story I just close my eyes and read what I want to write.'

Jason did not understand the mystery of *how* he was learning to read but he saw himself as a reader who wanted to know what was happening. He was also unaware that just how children learn to read remains somewhat a mystery even to the experts. However, there are many things that teachers need to know about reading other than the intricacies of the reading process. We need to be reminded that reading is learned best by reading, by sharing and by being immersed in the fullness of language. Reading is wanting to know the story, or as Jason said asking 'what happens next?' As Jason talked about his emerging knowledge of language, he was creating his own under-standing and meaning for himself. He was learning about language by using it.

Jason shared many more stories with me throughout the year, a whole collection of personal narratives about the things of his world. His story-telling about his experiences reveals not only his perspec-tive but opened up a window on his world through which the adults in his life might better understand how to respond more sensitively to the kinds of things this child was trying to do.

It was home time on the last day of school before spring break when Jason and I last talked.

'Are you planning anything special for the holidays?' I asked him.
'No, I have to go to Daycare while Mom and Dad are at work. Could I take my writing book with me and I could write some more stories while I'm there?'
[He tucked his scribbler into his knapsack.]
'Could we talk more after school starts again?' he asked.
'Yes, I'll want to hear your stories.'
[Jason was heading towards the door.]
'I'd better go, the Daycare van will be here and I don't want to sit in the middle and get squished.' 'Bye,' he called, 'have a good break.'
I waved, 'Thanks Jason, bye.'

18 The Inservicer Inserviced:
Is Your Theory Your Practice?

David Dillon

Whenever educational policies seem to demand new directions in teaching and learning, the text of the classroom is the site for negotiation between teachers, whose province it rightly is, and those in other institutions who are deemed to have some expertise in the business of education. Here David Dillon, whose editorship of Language Arts has had a marked influence on teachers' interpretation of the nature of their knowing, examines the collaborative work he did with June McConaghy. As teacher educator, he lays out the process of his thinking about the social and political implications of partnership between professional peers, and ponders the reversal of interactional roles in ways that relate equally to inservice seminars and to lessons in classrooms.

The work reported by June McConaghy in this volume (see Chapter 17) originated in a research project on young children's literary experiences and their emergent literacy which we began jointly several years ago in her primary classroom, but which eventually became entirely her own project. During those few years our learning relationship moved through several stages. These stages reflected, but also helped to cause, shifts and clarifications in my understanding of the notion of primary teachers making sense of their experience in their classrooms, (i.e., learning), especially of my role as a teacher educator in that process. The project itself was a touchstone, a lens through which I came to problematize inservice education generally.

Two recent incidents stand out clearly for me as measures of where my understanding has come to. A year ago I was to lead a roundtable discussion at a national conference of English teachers on the topic of 'Teachers as Learners and Researchers'. Even though I had proposed the topic myself some time before, by the time the conference occurred I wondered what, if anything, I could say to teachers who wished to make more, or different, sense of their experience in their classrooms. Apart from the question of saying anything or not, I felt even more uncomfortable simply assuming — and being given by primary teachers — a position of alleged expertise on their understanding. These teachers had just come from daily encounters with lots of energetic, different and challenging youngsters, a situation I struggled to encounter once a week and then only as a visitor. What was I doing there? Why were they looking at me for advice? Couldn't they see the emperor had no clothes on?

The second incident occurred more recently at the 1986 'Language in Inner City Schools Conference' held at the University of London Institute of Education. In his opening address John Richmond excoriated the shameful connotations of 'inservice training', pointedly referring to the lack of respect for teachers, their disenfranchisement and the behaviouristic notions of 'shaping' their learning contained in that term. Richmond was the first school-based educator I had heard speak so plainly and so strongly on this topic I had been struggling with myself. Yet I remember the incident so well, not because of the clarity or strength of Richmond's message, but because I was finally ready to *hear* what Richmond was saying, without any knee-jerk defensiveness, and to agree with him.

These incidents are instances of the imbalances I experienced and the problem I had to clarify for myself.

Demystifying the Status Quo

I slowly became aware that the issues I was identifying in my project with June, and in my role generally as an educator of primary teachers, were largely political, that is, the attempt by one person to exert influence, even unawares, over the thinking and behaviour of another person. June and I shared and discussed background readings (which I had introduced) on the subject of her enquiry; I spent approximately one day per week in her classroom to observe, but mostly to participate in her teaching and interaction with her pupils; and, most importantly, we discussed and tried to interpret what we (but mostly June) saw each week in her class. In the early stages of the project when I found myself theorizing about integrating the experiences June had had during the week with her pupils, I began to question my behaviour. It seemed arrogant for me to theorize about June's experiences, without providing equal and reciprocal opportunities to June to do the same. It seemed too easy to co-opt June's learning, to seize the initiative and use it for my *own* learning, not June's. I realized that I wasn't fostering June's reflection on her own experiences, that is, her own construction of her own knowledge. Apart from the shaping of my learning, mainly leeched from June's experiences, there was the danger of imposing that shaping on her understanding. This kind of behaviour on my part, and in an assenting way on June's part too, accepted that the teacher educator (the knower) has the job of shaping and validating the learning of the teacher (the doer), often by fitting it into the conventional public body of knowledge as a given topic which, it is assumed, is shared by the profession at large. Such behaviour reflects highly differentiated, imbalanced, and to a large extent mutually exclusive roles. She was the teacher as experiencer in the trenches, the teacher as worker, I was the teacher educator as theorizer of that experience, aloof from and above the fray, the teacher educator as intellectual. I knew that June and I were falling into general and widespread patterns of professional behaviour.

I wondered what might be the effect of these roles and their associated behaviours on teachers and teacher educators generally. There seemed to be several possibilities. First, it could lead to a sense of diminishment on the part of the teacher, more specifically to feelings of incompetence and inadequacy (the 'I'm only a teacher' syndrome). I came to understand more deeply the potential danger of people relating to each other in this way as the result of a recent experience I had with a friend. Through a series of circumstances and through my own reflection, I came to a clear understanding of my behaviour and motives. Feeling excited, even liberated, by my discovery, I wanted to share it with my friend and began to do so. I had barely started when my friend broke in and, with exasperation, said, 'That's what I've been trying to tell you for months! You see, when things happen like that, you've got to realize that you can't. ...' And she launched into *her* explanation of my discovery. As I was left frozen in mid-sentence, I felt my understanding was taken from me, being validated by someone else who 'knew' and could expand quickly on my still-stumbling explanation, 'packaging' it in a way I wouldn't and hadn't yet had a chance to. Worst of all, I felt diminished, transformed instantaneously from 'excited discoverer' to 'slow learner'.

I could have left the situation at that and simply thought and felt less of myself, as I'm sure is the case for many learners in analogous roles. However, I began to *resist* this top-down effort to shape my beliefs and understanding. I'm sure this is also the case for large numbers of teachers in relation to teacher educators (the 'what do the eggheads at the university know about the daily realities of being in classrooms with children?' syndrome). The efforts of teacher educators to influence the understanding and behaviour of teachers may well be resisted by many teachers who continue operating on their own understanding of things, forming a sub-culture unknown to those with prestige and influence in the education field, those whose voices have outlets, those who do much of the shaping and caretaking of the public knowledge. If this does happen, the 'culture' of many teachers in the schools becomes characterized by the academics as a sort of working-class culture, largely unknown to and misunderstood by the intellectually upper-middle-class culture of teacher supervisors or educators whose values, perspectives and ideas have been validated as officially reflecting a society. This minority culture thrives, paradoxically, through resistance to efforts at assimilation. I am reminded of Gramsci's analysis of political and ideological revolution in society at large. He warned of the dangers of Marxist intellectuals trying to play the role of abstract theorizers for the working classes, while remaining cut off from popular ideology and feeling in society. Gramsci (1971) concluded that such a stance would ensure that the intellectuals would not affect popular culture and thinking and, in turn, would remain unaffected by it. The two groups, despite the exchange of much energy and rhetoric, would remain as two solitudes and the revolution would not occur.

> The intellectual's error consists in believing that one can know without understanding and even more without feeling and being impassioned; in other words that the intellectual can be an intellectual if distance and separate from the people-nation, i.e., without feeling the elementary passions of the people. ... One cannot make politics-history without this passion, without this sentimental connection between intellectuals and people-nation.

A third possibility is 'acculturation', a teacher becoming a part of the dominant educational ideology. Individuals, often through schooling, are forced to choose between their minority culture and the dominant one or, even worse, discover too late that they have been accultured and cannot 'go home' again. Glenda Bissex, a former primary teacher and currently a teacher educator in the US, may be a poignant example of such a price. After discussing the recent interest in North America in the notion of 'teacher as researcher', she writes, 'If teacher research had been on the horizon ten years ago, I might still be in a classroom myself rather than having been driven to choose between knowing and doing' (1985). The point Bissex misses is that she always *was* knowing as well as doing when she was in the classroom. Yet her knowledge did not seem to her to be of an acceptable kind and form. It remained invalidated and ignored by others who 'counted' and, it sounds, by herself. No wonder she felt she was not knowing. Sadly, it seems all too true that teachers have been denied satisfaction in learning and in knowing that their learning counted in the larger system of influence, prestige and power. In order to experience that validation and prestige, too often they have had to move out of their classrooms, as Bissex did, and 'up' in the system, thereby cutting themselves off from the major source of their learning — the children they taught every day — and becoming part of the club that had been unwilling to validate their personal classroom knowledge in the first place. I wonder if Bissex was ever aware of what she *knew* when she was teaching before she became aware of what she knew as a teacher educator.

These possible scenarios all stem, it seems, from the traditional roles and relationships of teacher educators and teachers of children, a hierarchical relationship of authority and expertise — and thus of power. There are forces at work today to transform (even to subvert if necessary) these traditional roles and relationships, to replace them with a relationship of shared and reciprocal collaboration, to try to keep teachers' learning integral. Such is one of the major assumptions of this volume. So too is it one of the principles of what in North America is referred to as 'teacher as learner/researcher', 'teachers becoming their own experts', 'teachers answering their own questions', and so on — phrases already in danger of becoming clichés. Before exploring these alternatives, however, I wish to point out how this apparently alternative, even radical, movement can also be subverted to mask the subtle staying power of the status quo, even in the face of pressure to change, so that 'the more things change, the more they remain the same.'

The major prompt for my concern is the tendency in recent years for university researchers, on their own initiative, to explain to teachers how to do 'research' in their own classrooms, usually by applying 'accepted' research techniques. It strikes me as an attempt by the 'official' researchers to maintain their expertise and authority in the face of a growing threat to it ('If we can't transmit knowledge about teaching to teachers we can transmit knowledge about research'), when the pressing need may be to develop a different set of criteria and procedures, especially by those teachers who are engaged in this relatively unexplored and unarticulated process. (See the articles by McConaghy (1986) and Burton (1986) for important first steps toward this goal.)

The use of the term 'research' in this discourse seems to be a key element since many teachers feel mystified and inexperienced in the face of whatever 'research' is supposed to mean and turn willingly for guidance to those who are supposed to know. Sadly, they seem not to link it at all with their continual experience of learning in the classroom. I would worry less about this matter if I saw teacher educators playing this teacher researcher role in their own college and university classrooms and sharing their insights, equally and reciprocally, with primary and secondary teachers. I very rarely encounter such reports. Indeed, some established structures preclude such a possibility and surreptitiously suggest that the word 'teacher' in the phrase 'teacher researcher' refers only to primary and secondary, not to tertiary, teachers. One such structure is the teacher researcher grants of the National Council of Teachers of English in the US. Only primary and secondary teachers are eligible to apply for them (assuming that teacher educators would not want to — or need to — apply for them?) Yet it is a board of university researchers and teacher educators who make decisions about the grants, presumably on the basis of accepted criteria of educational research. This radical movement seems in great danger of being mainstreamed by the powerful and pervasive system in which it is trying to grow and must struggle against.

When I speculate about why these things happen, I think first of the usual expectations of the traditional roles of teacher educator and teacher educatee: knower and doer, leader and follower, change agent and change object. Beyond these roles seems to lie the power of public knowledge over personal knowledge. Public knowledge takes on the aura of being right (in some absolute way) by the sheer weight of numbers who accept it or by association with those who have prestige, such as university professors. Finally, I wonder if the expected roles of teacher educators and teachers of children in regard to public knowledge lead all of us to act out of *fear*.

Teacher educators are expected to be the creators, guardians and purveyors of public knowledge. One of my colleagues commented how tired he was one term because he was trying to stay 'a few steps ahead' of three graduate students he was advising, each of whom was currently writing a thesis. Yes, I thought, it must be very tiring to write three theses in one term, just to keep a leg up on one's students. These expectations are made worse by the system of scoring points in which teacher educators work, whether in the form of articles published, research grants received, projects directed, or talks given. It is a competitive system that can easily lead to competitive grasping, a system based on Newtonian notions that there is only so much meritorious matter in the educational universe. Such a system has made it difficult for me to learn to give teachers' learning back to them freely. I was helped to this realization, uncomfortably, by June in our work together as she became stronger with me, politically. As June took her learning back from me (at that time I had neither the wisdom nor the generosity to give it to her freely), I saw published articles, talks and entries on my annual report slipping away from me and I was afraid not of not being right, but of not scoring points. In such a competitive atmosphere altruistic collaboration can be very difficult.

Teachers of children are also part of an established system and they seem susceptible to their own fears. They are usually engaged in trying to gain access to public knowledge, the knowledge that not only counts but counts as 'right' in education. In their own educational decision-making, they apparently fear that they may be wrong by not coming up with the right (public) answer, rather than trusting their own interpretation of their experience. June is now a primary consultant (advisor) for the Edmonton Public School Board, a teacher educator herself. One of her first and overwhelming impressions of what teachers do in order to learn is that they do not try to make sense of their experiences in the classroom, but rather they try to make sense of someone else's already made sense of his or her own experiences with kids, and then impose that second-hand sense on their own classroom. The persons whose sense-making they seek to interpret for themselves are, of course, the published experts, not fellow teachers. This tactic can cut them off from their experience in their own classrooms more than it can give them a purchase on it.

Khrisnamurti (1975) suggests that the ultimate function of education is freedom from fear. What is it that we fear? Is it fear that keeps the *status quo* in place? Does freedom from fear go hand in hand with demystifying the *status quo*? Where in the system can this cycle of fear first be broken?

Composing a Different Story, Learning New Roles

Coming to this awareness of problems in myself and in the system was far easier than actually changing anything. What I clearly saw was the need for a *collaborative* stance which redefined the roles of teacher educator and teacher educatee. Rather than the teacher educator being farther along the same path as the teacher, and the teacher striving to see things as the teacher educator does, I saw us working side by side, and performing somewhat different, yet complementary, roles.

This starting point may not seem earth-shattering since we all can rattle off the learning theory principles of each teacher ultimately shaping his or her own experience, authoring his or her own knowledge, from the base of personal experience. What makes it a powerful notion for me, however, is putting it into a political context: it means *really* allowing and, actively fostering teachers making sense of *their own* experience, honouring it, validating it and not holding my own, or the current public variety, above it.

So I had to ask myself what my role with teachers would be, what expertise any authority of mine — apart from my university position — rested upon. I discovered that it is not a case of the emperor having no clothes on, as I once thought, but of wearing different clothes. If I have a certain view and understanding of humankind, of the nature of learning, of our lives together on this planet, then, as Freire reminds me, I must live that process and stance myself. Teachers must be able to commission me to demonstrate that process and stance. What I found most surprising was how much this conclusion took my focus from primary teachers and put it largely on myself. Here's some of what I had to do and be in order to be a sense-maker of my own experience.

1 I have learned to be a problematizer for myself, a messer-up as much as a cleaner-up in regard to learning. After two decades of research on creativity Jacob Getzels (1976) concluded that what characterized the small minority of creative people in the general population was their ability, not as good problem-solvers, but as good problem-finders. We all have the ability to be problem-finders but we have often learned not to be. We can learn again to be problem-finders in education, especially through others who live that stance (such as Margaret Spencer who helped me find the problem of this chapter for myself).

2   I find it is an endless but essential job in teaching to move toward praxis, an integration of theory and practice, of reflection and experience. We all value and desire a coherence in which reflection in the head meshes with personal experience, when behaviour matches attitude, when action is consistent across comparable circumstances. Such a move toward coherence usually results in a personal transformation.

3   The goal of this transformation is that it must be continuous. Any kind of stasis works against learning and contains the danger of becoming a rigid orthodoxy. Complete stasis is not the nature of any living organism. We need to be uncertainly certain, as Freire suggests, to be structuring our reality but always in a fluid, continuous revision. In a recent discussion on how we all seek to get things sorted out — with a connotation of finality — Harold Rosen suggested, tongue-in-cheek, that we need the term 'sortescent' to suggest a continuous process. Another way to view it is as the continual storying and restorying of our lives, of the taking on a series of roles in the dramas we create and live.

Just as when reading a novel, or writing one for that matter, we maintain a double consciousness of the characters as both, as it were, real and fictitious, free and determined, and know that however convincing and absorbing we may find it, it is not the only story we will want to read (or, as the case may be, write) but part of an endless sequence of stories by which man has sought and will always seek to make sense of life. And death. (David Lodge, 1979)

4   All human activity is purposeful, but in teaching the key question is *whose* intentions are being operated upon; a teacher's role usually gives us great scope to operate on our own intentions and learning. Too often, unfortunately, student activity also operates upon the teacher's intention. A key focus for me has become to provide opportunities for primary teachers to operate on their own intentions, especially since, as Polanyi (1958) suggests, operating on our own intentions releases tacit energies from within us, leading to our empowerment. Sometimes I feel that I sense well a teacher's 'zone of proximal development' (to use Vygotsky's

(1978) term) from having traversed it myself. Such a situation suggests patience and sensitivity in discovering intentions — our own and others'.

What all these points suggest is an inward-looking, inner-directed focus or thrust for myself. The alternative approach suggests that we can only change ourselves, and so that is where our efforts are best directed, toward fulfilling that responsibility.

In an attempt to better understand this still poorly understood alternative to teaching I find myself turning to metaphors. One is the notion of parents eventually having to let their children become the persons they are going to become. In fact, 'letting' them seems minimal. Wanting it, accepting it, supporting it and rejoicing in it (especially if the child is satisfied and has 'authored' that life) suggests embracing this occurrence rather than merely tolerating it. Gibran (1955) reminds us that our children are not our children. We can be with them but not possess them. We can accompany them to the threshold of the house of tomorrow, but we cannot enter it with them, for it is their house and not ours. Thus it is, I believe, with teacher educators and teachers.

The teaching-learning process tends to create diversity, individuality and uniqueness. If those in authority are insecure, such variations can be a threat. Indeed, many instructional 'movements' in education have tended to seek a degree of uniformity in practice, to convert the heathen who have practised a different religion, to try to reach that seductive goal of getting things sorted out once and for all. These desires are based not only on fear of the different (and thus unknown) but also on a particular and all too common notion of power — that of exerting one's own power over others. Much work has been done in recent years in fields such as therapy, social work and business, (e.g., Peters and Waterman, 1982) to understand, articulate and explore alternative notions of power. While much of the work makes fine distinctions, it basically describes a process in which those with power derived from their place in a social system *give* that power to those subordinate to them and trust them to use it well. By doing this, those in authority ideally do not *lose* power or authority but actually receive it back again. Assumptions underlying such a process are collaborative rather than competitive, based on trust rather than fear. In addition, rather than being based on what I called earlier a Newtonian, fixed-amount notion of power, this process affirms that we are linked to an inexhaustible source of energy, with more than enough for all. But just as we can make it flow, so too can we block it.

Indeed, security and coherence is never a state we finally arrive at, but one we continuously strive for and come to understand and live more fully, as a Christian is always becoming a Christian, a Buddhist a Buddhist, an artist an artist, and so on. Fortunately, to prevent me from ever thinking that I have 'arrived', I experience incidents every now and again to show me the imperfect way that I've come not only to understand these ideas, but also to live them. While working on the draft of this very chapter, I had a conversation with a graduate student who asked me what I had learned at a recent course I had attended. As I tried to summarize my learning, she asked me more and more clarifying and extending questions which prompted me to explain more and more. However, she soon stopped me to tell me how uncomfortable she had become with the traditional professor-student tone which I had imposed on the conversation. She was feeling talked down to, her own background and expertise ignored. She was right. The conversation had shifted in tone, showing me how easy it was for me to take on a role I know so well, but which I like to think I'm beyond. Her awareness, though uncomfortable for me, helped me move toward greater awareness myself.

The attention she drew to this experience made it the exact opposite of the role I had experienced with my friend in the incident related above. The two incidents became like mirror-image bookends for me, bracketing a continuum of roles and models of teaching and learning, as well as relationships among people, which now helps me see situations more clearly. It also reminds me of how difficult it is to eradicate what Raymond Williams calls 'a hegemony of the fibers of the self' and of engaging in what Freire calls 'making Easter every day' — to die to the old oppression and to be continually reborn to the new in order to struggle against the old. It is instructive to hear Williams in more detail as he discusses 'creative practice'.

> Creative practice is thus of many kinds. It is already, and actively, our practical consciousness. When it becomes struggle — the active struggle for new consciousness through new relationships that is the ineradicable emphasis of the Marxist sense of self-creation — it can take many forms. It can be the long and difficult remaking of an inherited (determined) practical consciousness; a process often described as development, but in practice a struggle at the roots of the mind — not casting off an ideology, or learning

phrases about it, but confronting a hegemony in the fibers of the self and in the hard, practical substance of effective and continuing relationships.

I have focused thus far on my own insights, responsibilities and roles as a teacher educator in trying to struggle against a system of beliefs, structures and understandings. Teachers — and in the case of this particular project June — are partners in this process and will affect its outcome. They have, as I do, a choice of the kind of ideology or story they follow in their learning and they may tell one different from mine. However, if they choose to engage in this revolutionary dance with me, they too have certain roles, rights and structures. Epistemologically, they must, as June did, assert and exercise their right as ultimate authors of their knowledge and expertise and be willing to validate their own learning. Politically, they must, as June did, demystify me, destroying myths (which they themselves may have helped me create at times) about what my own expertise and authority really are.

But more than just a change in attitudes, this stance implies a change in the *structures* which reflect and confirm the established system. Gramsci (1971) noted that a revolution does not first occur so that structures in the system might then change, but rather that structures must first change in many small-scale instances to prepare the soil, as it were, and allow a revolution to happen eventually. Many existing structures, while holding out to teachers the seductive image of change, have actually prevented them from learning and changing and, as Garth Boomer (1975) suggests, leave them feeling responsible, even guilty for that lack of change. Some possibilities of structural analysis and change are provided in a teachers' journal entry made during a course taught by James Britton (1985) at New York University.

> I think there is a tendency (plot?) within the educational bureaucracy to
> — keep teachers subordinate, no real authority in any sense of the word is given to the teacher.
> — keep the 'banking' system in operation so as to perpetuate the system
> — keep the investment in such things as special education, curriculum specialists, media centers (that no one uses), professional libraries (that no one uses).

These 'services' (?) are offered in lieu of the real support teachers need in the form of
— released time to reflect
— released time to collaborate, not trade war stories
— dollars and time to attend conferences.

While I can do things which may foster a critical vision in teachers, while I can try not to co-opt these efforts, I have learned that I certainly cannot do it for them. Britton, after quoting from that teacher's journal, concludes: '... the teaching profession, classroom teachers themselves, are the only group both concerned enough to change the system and strong enough to be effective.'

Concluding Comment

I have quoted from a teacher, rather than suggest my own solutions for what I perceive are teachers problems, since any solutions or change and even identification of problems must come from and be effected by teachers themselves. My responsibility is not to subvert that process, but to support it. I am aware of a delicate balance that must be maintained, of a danger of easily falling back into the very stance I have been trying to unlearn, of seeing things in to simplistic, black-and-white, or all-or-none perspective. I am not advocating some kind of anti-intellectual or anti-public knowledge stance. Like Maxine Greene (1986) speaking of young children's education, I want teachers to become part of the established culture in order to be able to engage in the 'conversation', but also to be able to act back upon that culture and contribute actively to it. It is only against the tyranny of public knowledge that I argue.

I am not advocating a passive, *laissez faire* stance toward teacher education. Such an interpretation would be akin to widespread misconceptions about informal education for children. Rather I have suggested that teachers and teacher educators engage openly in heuristic, rather than persuasive, dialogue, with all participants open to being influenced by others, yet committed to staging their own experience.

Finally, I am not advocating withholding my own interpretations and goals (or my own access to public knowledge) from the teachers I work with. Rather I agree with Freire, a teacher educator, who asserts his *responsibility* to share his vision and dream with teachers, but at the same time to *challenge* teachers to create and articulate their own vision and dream.

Annotated Bibliography

When these essays were brought together it became clear that the writers, most of whom did not know each other, were referring to the same books to illuminate their points of view. We have selected some of these titles as particularly useful for those who wish to continue their own investigations into the theory and practice of language and literacy in the primary school.

BRUNER, JEROME (1986) *Actual Minds, Possible Worlds*, Cambridge, Mass., Harvard University Press.

Here is the distillation of a lifetime's involvement with children's thinking and learning, brought up to date and presented with characteristic grace and magnanimity by a humane psychologist of great distinction. It is a book about language and mind, and more. Bruner explores two ways of approaching reality: the scientific and the literary; the one responding to thinking about cause and effect, the other to the telling of stories. Drawing on recent work in literary theory Bruner looks at narrative as the making of 'possible worlds'. In doing so he posits new ways of investigating both imagination and reasoning.

HALLIDAY, M.A.K. (1979) *Language as Social Semiotic: The Social Interpretation of Language and Meaning*, London, Edward Arnold.

Written between 1972 and 1979 by a linguist sympathetic to problems of language in education (He is the godfather of *Breakthrough to Literacy*), these essays bring together ways of looking into 'linguistic processes from the standpoint of the social order'. The core of Halliday's argument is that social reality, or a culture, 'is itself an edifice of meanings which constitute a culture'. The emphasis of the book is on the need to study language in the context of its use. Current research in the language used in classrooms owes much to Halliday. In this volume he also explores language in urban communities, as well as 'anti-language'.

HEATH, SHIRLEY BRICE (1983) *Ways with Words: Language, Life and Work in Communities and Classrooms*, Cambridge, Cambridge University Press.

Most of the contributors to this volume have made reference to this important ethnographic study which reads like an anthropological novel. The researcher uncovers ways in which literacy is learned in contrasting communities in North America. She reveals these processes to be part of the texture of subtle and intricate social patterns, connected with power, religion and cultural imperatives. Her emphasis on literacy as 'ways of taking from a culture' usually through stories told within it and about it, should inhibit neutral, technological and unfeeling studies of reading and writing.

HENRIQUES, JULIAN *et al.* (1984) *Changing the Subject: Psychology, Social Regulation and Subjectivity*, London and New York, Methuen.

This work presents a radical reappraisal of psychology and a critique of the ways in which our theories, though historically conditioned, have pervasive effects on social practice. The stance taken by these writers is consonant with our concerns in that we would wish to change ways of looking at literacy. Walkerdine's chapter on early childhood is most apposite: 'Particular disciplines regimes of truth, bodies of knowledge, make possible both *what can be said* and *what can be done.*'

MILLER, JANE (1983) *Many Voices: Bilingualism, Culture and Education*, London, Routledge and Kegan Paul.

The plurality and diversity of languages spoken by children in cities all over the world is now generally recognized. Teachers who appreciate the skill of bilingual pupils are usually keen to move towards the development of a multicultural curriculum. In this study we can hear the voices of those who explore their experiences of bilingualism, including those aspects of it which the prevalence of racism. There is ample evidence that teachers who can exploit the linguistic resources of children who speak more than one language can enrich their classrooms and the lives of their pupils.

ROSE, JACQUELINE (1984) *The Case of Peter Pan, or the Impossibility of Children's Fiction*, London, Macmillan.

This book is as provocative as its title to those who assume that there is nothing problematic about books for children. Yet, how rarely do we ask ourselves: What is a child's book? Why do skilled artists and writers select children as their audience? Why should we write books for children to read, if not to let them know what counts as being a good child? 'Children's fiction; says Rose, 'sets up the child as an outsider to its own processes and aims, unashamedly, to take the child *in.*' By using this argument as a challenge to read books for children as something other than a miniaturized version of adult literature, we may better understand what they are actually about in a wider context of social meaning-making.

STREET, BRIAN V. (1984) *Literacy in Theory and Practice*, (Cambridge) Cambridge University Press:

This work is a significant example of the way in which insights from the now wide field of literacy studies need to inform our practice in classrooms. Street has read extensively in linguistics, history, cultural studies, psychology and sociology. He has also carried out field studies in varied cultures.

His account of 'maktab' literacy in Koranic schools and its adaptation to the changing economic fortunes of the learners is fascinating. If taken seriously, his view that in talking about literacy we are always talking about 'concrete social forms and institutions that give meaning to any particular practice of reading and writing' could shift the form of research in classrooms.

TIZARD, BARBARA and HUGHES, MARTIN (1984) *Young Children Learning: Talking and Thinking at Home and at School*, London, Fontana.

The core of this study is a collection of recorded conversations of 4-year-old girls and their mothers. The findings challenge the notion that professional teachers know more about how to talk to children in an educative way than their parents. The authors show, in fascinating detail, how the young initiate and sustain conversations and pursue, with purpose and concentration, agendas for their own learning. In contrast, when they are in nursery school they often appear passive and subdued. If children 'reserve their best thinking for outside school', then teachers must be alerted to the consequences.

VYGOTSKY, L.S. (1962) *Thought and Language*, Cambridge, Mass., MIT Press (originally published in Russia in 1934). *Mind in Society: The Development of Higher Psychological Processes*, Ed. by M. Cole *et al.*, Cambridge, Mass. and London, Harvard University Press.

Teachers find in the works of this remarkable scholar (called 'the Mozart of psychology') two strong ideas which illuminate the relation of language and learning. The first is that language — the prime mover in the organization of doing and thinking — is socially learned in interaction with others, and its forms of use reflect the history of its users. The second is the explanation of the now widely recognized Zone of Proximal Development — the space between what learners can actually do and the level they can reach with help from adults or 'more competent peers'. 'Human nature', says Vygotsky, 'presupposes a specific social nature and a process by which children grow into the social life of those around them.' Add to this the idea that, after a skill has been practised, its uses are increased by 'conscious reflection'. Teachers are bound to let children see that what they do today with help they will do by themselves tomorrow. It is helpful to link this with Tizard's claim that when parents give good answers to their children's questions, the children go on to ask even better questions.

After having a fairly strong but restricted following, of which James Britton was in the vanguard, Vygotsky has reappeared as a teacher with remarkable insights and theories which are now generating powerful studies.

WERTSCH, JAMES V. (Ed) (1985) *Culture, Communication and Cognition: Vygotskian Perspectives*, Cambridge, Cambridge University Press.

Using Vygotsky's socio-historical approach to thought and speech, the contributors to this volume, who include Jerome Bruner, Courtney Cazden, Michael Cole and Sylvia Scribner, whose writings appear in the general bibliography, show the power of his ideas even at this distance in time from their conception. The editor has divided the volume into sections: the first is devoted to explications of Vygotsky's writings, the second to the application of his ideas, especially the Zone of Proximal Development, to avoid 'the dead-ends of contemporary psychology'. In the context of our arguments we recommend especially Chapter 13, in which Karsten Hundeide examines the ways in which an adult and a child 'with quite different interpretations of a situation can interact', and Chapter 14, in which Ellice A. Forman and Courtney Cazden explore 'Vygotskian perspectives in education: the cognitive value of peer interaction.'

GENERAL BIBLIOGRAPHY

AHLBERG, J. and AHLBERG, A. (1977) *Burglar Bill*, London, Heinemann.

AHLBERG, J. and AHLBERG, A. (1978) *Cops and Robbers*, London, Heinemann.

AHLBERG, J. and AHLBERG, A. (1986) *The Jolly Postman*, London, Heinemann.

AMES, L.B. (1966) 'Children's stories', *Genetic Psychology Monographs* 73, pp. 337–96.

ANDERSEN, H. (1974) *The Complete Fariy Tales and Stories* (trans. E. Haugaard) London, Gollancz.

ANDERSON, R.C., MASON, J. and SHIREY, L. (1984) 'The reading group: An experimental investigation of a labyrinth', *Reading Research Quarterly*, XX, 1, pp. 6–38.

ARISTOTLE. (1940) *Poetics* (trans. I. Bywater, editor W. Hamilton Fyfe), Oxford, Oxford University Press.

ARNOLD, H. (1982) *Listening to Children Reading*, London, Hodder and Stoughton.

ASHTON-WARNER, S. (1980). *Teacher*, London, Virago.

ASSESSMENT OF PERFORMANCE UNIT. (1981) and (1982) *Language Performance in Schools: Primary Survey Reports, Nos. 1 & 2*, London, HMSO.

ATKIN, J. and BASTIANI, J. (1984) *Preparing Teachers to Work with Parents*, Nottingham, University of Nottingham School of Education.

AWDRY, W. (1949) *Thomas the Tank Engine*, London, Kaye and Ward.

BACKMAN, J. (1983) 'The role of psycholinguistic skills in reading acquisition: A look at early readers', *Reading Research Quarterly* XVIII, 4, pp. 466–79.

BAKER, A. (1984) 'Dawn reads to her teacher' in NATE PRIMARY COMMITTEE *Children Reading to their Teachers*, London. National Association for the Teaching of English.

BAKER, A. (1985) 'Developing reading with juniors' in MOON, C. (Ed.) *Practical Ways to Teach Reading*, London, Ward Lock.

BARNES, D. (1976) *From Communication to Curriculum*, Harmondsworth, Penguin.

BARTHES, R. (1957) *Mythologies* (English text 1972), London, Jonathan Cape.

BARTHES, R. (1972) *Mythologies*, London, Cape.

BARTHES, R. (1975a) 'Introduction to the structured origins of narrative', *New Literary History*, 6, pp. 257–72.

BARTHES, R. (1975b.) *S/Z*, London, Cape.

BARTLETT, F.C. (1932) *Remembering*, Cambridge, Cambridge University Press.

BELL, A. (1982) 'A case of commitment', *Signal*, 38, pp. 73–81.

BENNETT, J. (1979) *Learning to Read with Picture Books*, South Woodchester, Thimble Press.

BENNETT, J. (1980) *Reading out*, South Woodchester, Thimble Press.

BENVENISTE, E. (1971) *Problems in General Linguistics* (trans M.E. Meek) Florida, University of Miami Press.

BERNHEIMER, C, and KAHANE, C. (1985) *In Dora's Case*, London, Virago.

BETTELHEIM, B. (1976) *The Uses of Enchantment*, London, Thames & Hudson.

BELSEY, C. (1980) *Critical Practice*, London, Methuen.

BISSEX, G. (1980) *Gnys at Work*, New York, Harvard University Press.

BISSEX, G. (1985), 'On becoming teacher experts: What's a teacher-researcher?', *Language Arts*, 63, pp. 482–4.

BRETHERTON, I. (1984) *Symbolic Play*, New York, Academic Press.

BRITTON, J. (1985) 'Teachers, learners and learning' in CHORNY, M. (Ed.) *Teacher as Learner*, Calgary, Language in the Classroom Project.

BRITTON, J., BURGESS, T., MARTIN, N., MCLEOD, A. and ROSEN, H. (1976). *The Development of Writing Abilities 11–18*, London, Macmillan.

British Film Institute/Department of Education and Science (1986) *Working Party on Primary Media Education*, unpublished seminar report, London, BFI.

BROWN, R. (1971) 'Talking to children: Language input and acquisition' in SNOW, C.E. and FERGUSON, C.A. (Eds.) *Talking to Children*, Cambridge, Cambridge University Press.

BROWNE, A. (1981). *Hansel and Gretel*, London, Julia MacRae.

BRUNER, J.S. (1975) 'The ontogenesis of speech acts', *Journal of Child Language*, 2, pp. 1–19.

BRUNER, J.S. (1984) 'Language, mind and reading' in GOELMAN, H. *et al*, (Eds) *Awakening to Literacy*, London, Heinemann.

BRUNER, J.S. (1986) *Actual Minds, Possible Worlds*, Cambridge, MA, Harvard University Press.

BRYANT, J. and ANDERSON, D.R. (Eds.). (1983) *Children's Understanding of Television: Research on Attention and Comprehension* London and New York, Academic Press.

BURGESS, T. (1984a) 'The question of English' in MEEK, M. and MILLER, J. (eds) *Changing English: Essays for Harold Rosen*, London, Heinemann Educational.

BURGESS, T. (1984b) 'Diverse melodies' in MILLER, J. (Ed.) *Eccentric Propositions*, London, Routledge & Kegan Paul.

BURTON, F. (1986) 'Research currents: A teacher's conception of the action research process', *Language Arts*, 69, pp. 718–3.

CAMERON, P. (1973) *The Cat who Thought he was a Tiger*, Harmondsworth. Penguin.

CASSIRER, E. (1944) *An Essay on Man*, New York, Yale University Press.

CHOMSKY, N. (1957) *Syntactic Structures*, Cambridge, MA, Institute of Technology Press.

CHOMSKY, N. (1965) *Aspects of the Theory of Syntax*, Cambridge MA, Institute of Technology Press.

CLAY, M. (1972) *Reading: The Patterning of Complex Behaviour*, London, Heinemann

COHEN, R. (1985) 'Early reading; The state of the problem', *Prospects 53*, XV, 1.

COHN, P. (1980) 'Sub-cultural conflict and working class community in HALL, S *et al* (Eds.) *Culture, Media and Language*, London, Hutchinson.

COOK-GUMPERTZ, J. (Ed.) (1986) *The Social Construction of Literacy*, Cambridge, Cambridge University Press.

COOK-GUMPERTZ, J. and J. (1981); 'From oral to written culture; The transition to literacy' in WHITEMAN, M.F. (Ed.) *Writing Vol. 1*.

CRAGO, M. and H. (1983) *Prelude to Literacy: A Pre-school Child's Encounter with Picture and Story*, Carbondale and Edwardsville, IL, Southern Illinois University Press.

CULLER, J. (1975) *Structuralist Poetics*, London, Routledge & Kegan Paul

CURWEN, J.S. (1981) *Old Plaistow*, London, J. Curwen & Sons.

DANNEQUIN, C. (1977) *Les Enfants Baillonnés*, Paris, CEDIC, Diffusion Nathan.

DAVIES, B. (1982) *Life in the Classroom and Playground; the Accounts of Primary School Children*, London, Routledge and Kegan Paul.

DES (1982) *Mathematics Counts: The Cockcroft Report*, London, HMSO.

DERRIDA, J. (1967) *L'ecriture et la Différence*, Paris, Sevil.

DE SAUSSURE, F. (1959) *Course in General Linguistics*, London, Peter Owen.

DE VILLIERS, J.G. and DE VILLIERS, P.A. (1978) *Early Language*, London. Fontana/Open Books.

DOMBEY, H. (1983) 'Learning the language of books' in MEEK, M. (Ed.) *Opening Moves: Work in Progress in the Study of Children's Language Development: Bedford Way Papers No. 17* London, University of London Institute of Education.

DOMBEY, H. (1986) 'Aural experience of the language of written narrative in some pre-school children and its relevance in learning to read. Unpublished Ph.D thesis. University of London.

DONALDSON, M. (1978) *Children's Minds*. London, Fontana.

DONALDSON, M. and REID, J. (1982) 'Language skills and reading; A developmental perspective in HENDRY, A. (Ed.) *Teaching Reading: The Key Issues*, London, Heinemann.

DURKIN, K. (1985) *Television, Sex Roles and Children*, Milton Keynes, Open University Press.

EYERS, S. and RICHMOND, J. (Eds.) (1982) *Becoming Our Own Experts*, Talk Workshop Group, London, ILEA, English Centre.

FERGUSON, C.A. (1977) 'Baby talk as a simplified register' in SNOW, C.E. and FERGUSON, C.A. (Eds.) *Talking to Children* Cambridge, Cambridge University Press.

FERREIRO, E. (1984) 'The underlying logic of literacy development' in GOELMAN, H. *et al* (Ed.) *Awakening to Literacy*, London, Heinemann.

FERREIRO, E. and TEBEROSKY, A. (1983) *Literacy Before Schooling*, London, Heinemann.

FISKE, J. and HARTLEY, J. (1978) *Reading Television*, London, Methuen.

FOUCAULT, M. (1972) *The Archaeology of Knowledge*, London, Tavistock.

FOUCAULT, M. (1977) *Language, Counter-memory, Practice*, Ithaca, Cornell University Press.

FOX, C. (1983) 'Talking like a book; Young children's oral monologues' in MEEK, M. (Ed) *Opening Moves: Work in Progress in the Study of Children's Language Development: Bedford Way Papers, No. 17*. London, University of London Institute of Education.

FOX, C. (1984) 'Learning from children learning from home', *Language Matters 2*, London, Centre for Language in Primary Education, ILEA.

FOX, P. (1984) *One-eyed Cat*, Scarsdale, NY, Bradbury Press.

FREIRE, P. (1975) *Pedagogy of the Oppressed*, Harmondsworth, Penguin.

FREIRE, P. (1985) 'Reading the word and reading the world: An interview with Paulo Freire', *Language Arts*, 62, pp. 15–21.

FREUD, S. (1900) *The Interpretation of Dreams*, Harmondsworth, Penguin (this edition 1976).

FREUD, S. (1920) *Beyond the Pleasure Principle*, Harmondsworth, Pelican.

GARDNER, H. (1975) 'Children's metaphoric productions and preferences'. *Journal of Child Language*, 2, pp. 125–41.

GARDNER, H. *et al* (1978) 'The development of figurative languages' in NELSON, K. (Ed.) *Children's Language: Volume 1*, New York, Gardner Press.

GARDNER, H. (1984) *Frames of Mind*, London, Heinemann.

GARDNER, H. (1984) *Art, Mind and Brain*, New York, Basic Books.

GARNICA, O. (1977), Some prosodic and paralinguistic features of speech in young children in SNOW, C.E. and FERGUSON, C.A. (Eds.) *Talking to Children*, London, Cambridge University Press.

GARVEY, C. (1977) *Play*, London, Fontana.

GARVIE, E. (1981) *Break Through to Fluency*, Oxford, Basil Blackwell.

GENETTE, G. (1980) *Narrative Discourse*, Oxford, Basil Blackwell.

GETZELS. J. (1976) *The Creative Vision*, New York, Wiley.

GIBRAN, K. (1955) *The Prophet*, New York, Knopf.

GOELMAN, H, OBERG, A. and SMITH, F. (1984) *Awakening to Literacy*, London, Heinemann.

GOODMAN, K.S. (1973a) 'Miscues: Windows on the reading process' in GOODMAN, K.S. (Ed) *Miscue Analysis, Applications to Reading Instruction*, Urbana, IL. ERIC.

GOODMAN, K.S. (1973b) 'Reading: A psycholinguistic guessing game' in KARLIN, R. (Ed.) *Perspectives on Elementary Education* New York, Harcourt Brace.

GOODMAN, Y and ALTWERGER, B (1981) *Print Awareness in Pre-School Children, Program in Language and Literacy: Occasional Paper 4*, Tucson, AZ, University of Arizona.

GRAFF, H.J. (1979) *The Literacy Myth: Literacy and Social Structure in the Nineteenth Century*, New York and London, Academic Press.

GRAMSCI, A. (1971) *Selections from the Prison Notebooks*, New York, International Publishers.

GREENE, M. (1986) 'Landscapes and meanings', *Language Arts*, 63, pp. 776–84.

GREGORY, R.L. (1977) 'Psychology: Towards a science of fiction' in MEEK, M. *et al* (Eds.) *The Cool Web*, London, Bodley Head.

GUMPERZ, J.J. (1981) 'Conversational inference and classroom learning' in GREEN, J. and WALLAT, C. (Eds.) *Ethnography of Language in Educational Settings*, Narwood, N.J, Ablex.

GURNEY, R. (1976) *Language, Learning and Remedial Teaching*, London, Edward Arnold.

HALL, M.A. (1985) 'Focus on language experience learning and teaching', *Reading*, 19, 1, pp. 5–12.

HALLIDAY, M.A.K. (1975) *Learning How to Mean: Explorations in the Development of Language*, London, Edward Arnold

HALLIDAY, M.A.K. (1976) *System and Function in Language*, Oxford, Oxford University Press.

HALLIDAY, M.A.K. (1978) *Language as Social Semiotic: the Social Interpretation of Language and Meaning*, London, Edward Arnold.

HALLIDAY, M.A.K. and HASAN, K. (1976) *Cohesion in English: English Language Series*, London, Longman.

HARDCASTLE, J. (1985) 'Classrooms as sites for culture making', *English in Education*, 3, pp. 8–22.

HARDY, B. (1968) 'Towards a poetics of fiction: an approach through narrative' in *Novel: A Forum on Fiction*, Brown University.

HARSTE, W.V. and BURKE, C. (1984) *Language, Stories and Literacy Lessons*, London, Heinemann

HASAN, R. (1971) 'Rime and reason in literature' in CHATMAN, S. (Ed.) *Literary Style: A Symposium*, Oxford, Oxford University Press.

HASAN, R. (1986) 'The ontogenesis of ideology' in HALLIDAY, M.A.K. *et al* (Eds.) *Semiotics, Language, Ideology*, Sydney, Sydney Association for Studies in Society and Culture.

HAUSSLER, M. (1984) *Transitions into literacy: Program in Language and Literacy: Occasional paper 10*, Tucson, Az, University of Arizona.

HEATH, S.B. (1978) *Teacher Talk: Language in the Classroom*, Washington, D.C., Centre for Applied Linguistics.

HEATH, S.B. (1980) 'Questioning at home and at school; A comparative study' in SPINDLER, G. (Ed.) *Doing Ethnography; Educational Anthropology in Action*, New York, Holt Rinehart & Winston.

HEATH, S.B. (1982) 'What no bedtime story means; Narrative skills at home and at school', *Language and Society*, 6, pp. 49–76.

HEATH, S.B. (1983). *Ways with Words: Language, Life and Work in Communities and Classrooms*, Cambridge, Cambridge University Press.

HENRIQUES, J., HOLLOWAY, W., URWIN, C., VENN, C., and WALKERDINE, V. (1984) *Changing the Subject: Psychology, Social Regulation and Subjectivity*, London and New York, Methuen.

HER MAJESTY's INSPECTORATE. (1982) *Bullock Revisited*, London, HMSO.

HER MAJESTY's INSPECTORATE. (1983) *Effects of Local Authority Expenditure Policies on the Education Service in England in 1982*, London, HMSO.

HODGE, B. and TRIPP, D. (1986) *Children and Television*, London, Polity Press.

HODGSON, J. and PRYKE, D. (1983) *Reading Competence at 6 and 10* Shropshire, Shropshire County Council.

HOGGART, R. (1957) *The Uses of Literacy*, Harmondsworth, Penguin

HOLDAWAY, D. (1975) *The Foundations of Literacy*, Sydney, Ashton Scholastic

HOLT, J. (1965) *How Children Fail*, Harmondsworth, Penguin.

HONG-KINGSTON, M. (1977) *The Woman Warrior*, London, Picador.

HUEY, E.B. (1908) (reprinted 1968) Cambridge, MA, MIT Press

HUNDEIDE, K. (1985) MA, 'The tacit background of children's judgements' in WERTSCH, J.V. (Ed.) *Culture Communication and Cognition: Vygotskian Perspectives*, Cambridge, Cambridge University Press.

HYMES, D. (1964) *Language in Culture and Society*. New York, Harper and Row.

HYMES, D. (1970) 'On communicative competence' in PRICE, J.B. and HOLMES, J. (Eds.) *Sociolinguistics*, Harmondsworth, Penguin.

HYMES, D. (1971) 'Sociolinguistics and the ethnography of speaking' in ARDENER, E. (Ed.) *Social Anthropology and Language*, London, Tavistock.

JACKSON, B. (1979) *Starting School*, London, Croom Helm.

JAKOBSON, R. (1960) 'Linguistics and poetics' in SEBEOK, T.A. (Ed.) *Style in Language*, New York, Wiley.

JAKOBSON, R. (1971) 'Two aspects of language and two types of aphasia' *Selected Writings 12*.

JOSIPOVICI, G. (Ed.) (1976) *The Modern English Novel: The Reader, the Writer and the Work*, London, Open Books.

KERMODE, F. (1979) *The Genesis of Secrecy: on the Interpretation of Narrative*, Cambridge, MA, Harvard University Press.

KNAPP, M. and KNAPP, H (1976) *One Potato, Two Potato: The Folklore of American Children*, New York, Norton.

KRISHNAMURTI, J. and BOOMER, G. (1975) *Beginnings of Learning*, London, Gollancz.

KRESS, G. (1982) *Learning to Write*, London, Routledge & Kegan Paul.

KUNDERA, M. (1984) *The Unbearable Lightness of Being*, (trans. M. H. Herin) London, Faber.

LABOV, W. (1972) *Language in the Inner City*, Oxford, Blackwell.

LACAN, J. (1973) *The Four Fundamental Concepts of Psycho-analysis*, Harmondsworth, Penguin.

LACAN, J. (1977) *Ecrits: A selection*, London, Tavistock Publications.

LANGER, S. (1942) *Philosophy in a New Key*, New York, Harvard University Press.

LEAVIS, F.R. (1948) *The Great Tradition*, London, Chatto and Windus.

LEESON, R. (1985) *Reading and Righting*, London, Collins.

LEVINE, K. (1986) *The Social Context of Literacy*, London, Routledge & Kegan Paul.

LIONNI, L. (1970) *Fish is Fish*, London. Abelard Schumann.

LODGE, D. (1979) *How Far Can You Go?*, Harmondsworth, Penguin.

LOMAX, C. (1977) 'Interest in books and stories at nursery school', *Educational Research*, 19, 2, pp. 100–4.

LOMAX, C. (1979) 'Effects of story-telling on a vocabulary' in CLARK, M.

and CHEYNE, W. (Eds.) *Studies in Pre-School Education*, London, Hodder and Stoughton for the Scottish Council for Research in Education.

LONDON, J. (1977) *The People of the Abyss*. London, Journeyman Press.

LURIA, A.R. (1976) *Cognitive Development; Its Cultural and Social Foundations* (Ed. M. Cole, Trans. M. LOPEZ-MORILLAS and L. SOLOTAROFF, Cambridge, MA., Harvard University Press.

McCONAGHY, J. (1986) 'On becoming teacher experts: Research as a way of knowing', *Language Arts*, 63, pp. 724–8.

MACKAY, D. *et al* (1978) *Breakthrough to Literacy*: *Teacher's Manual* 2nd ed London, Longman.

McKEE, D. (1980) *Now Now, Bernard*, London, Andersen.

MACNAMARA, J.L. (1972) 'Cognitive basis of language learning in infants', *Psychological Review*, 79, pp. 1–13.

McNEILL, D. (1966) 'Developmental linguistics' in SMITH, F. and MILLER, G.A. *The Genesis of Language*: *A Psycholinguistic Approach* Cambridge, MA, MIT Press.

McTEAR, M. (1985) *Children's Conversations*, Oxford, Blackwell.

MAIR, M. (1976) *Metaphors for Living,* Nebraska Symposium on Motivation Nebraska, Nebraska University Press.

MALINOWSKI, B. (1935) *Coral Gardens and their Magic*, London, Allen and Unwin.

MARK, J. (1983) *Handles*, Harmondsworth, Kestrel.

MEDWAY, P. (1980) *Finding a Language*, London, Writers and Readers Cooperative.

MEEK, M. (1982) *Learning to Read*, London, Bodley Head.

MEEK, M. (1983) *Achieving Literacy*, London, Routledge & Kegan Paul.

MEEK, M. (1988) *How Texts Teach*: *What Readers Learn*, South Woodchester, Thimble Press.

MEYER, L.A. (1982) 'The relative effects of word-analysis and word supply correction procedures with poor readers during word attack training', *Reading Research Quarterly* XVII, 4, pp. 544–5.

MICHAELS, S. (1981) 'Sharing time: 'children's narrative styles and differential access to literacy', *Language in Society* 10, pp. 423–43.

MILLER, J. (1983) *Many voices*: *Bilingualism, Culture and Education*, London, Routledge & Kegan Paul.

MILLER, J. (1984) *Eccentric Propositions*: *Essays on Literature in the Curriculum*, London, Routledge & Keegan Paul.

MOON, C. (Ed.) (1985) *Practical Ways to Teach Reading*, London, Ward Lock.

MOORE, B. (1986) 'Positive programming', *Child Education*, 63, 11, November.

NATE PRIMARY COMMITTEE. (1984) *Children Reading to their Teachers* Sheffield, National Association for the Teaching of English.

NELSON, K. and SEIDMAN S. (1984) 'Playing with scripts' in BROTHERTON, I. (Ed.) *Symbolic Play*.

NEMKO, B. (1984). 'Context versus isolation; Another look at beginning readers', *Reading Research Quarterly*, XIX, 4, pp. 461–7.

OLSEN, D. (1977) 'From utterance to text', *Harvard Educational Review*, 47, 3, pp. 257–81.

ONG, W.J. (1983) *Orality and Literacy; The Technologizing of the Word*, London. Methuen.

OPIE, I. and OPIE, P. (1959) *The Lore and Language of School Children*, Oxford, Oxford University Press.

OPIE, I and OPIE, P. (1985) *The Singing Game*, Oxford, Oxford University Press.

P.A.C.T. (1984) *Home-school Reading Partnerships in Hackney: A Handbook for Teachers*, London, Hackney Teachers' Centre.

PALEY, V.G. (1986) 'Listening to the children', *Harvard Educational Review*, 56, 2, pp. 122–32.

PATERSON, K. (1978) *Bridge to Terabithia*, London, Gollancz.

PATERSON, K. (1981) *Gates of Excellence; on Reading and Writing Books for Children*, New York, Elsevier/Nelson Books.

PESCHEK, D. (1966) *Policies and Politics in Secondary Education: Case studies in West Ham, Greater London Papers No. 11*, London, London School of Economics and Social Sciences.

PETERS, T. and WATERMAN, R. (1982) *In Search of Excellence*, New York, Warner Books.

PIAGET, J. (1951) *Play, Dreams and Imitation in Childhood*, London, Routledge & Kegan Paul.

PITCHER, E.G. and PRELINGER, E. (1963) *Children Tell Stories*, New York, International Universities Press.

POLANYI, M. (1958) *Personal Knowledge*, Chicago, University of Chicago Press.

POLLARD, A. (1985) *The Social World of the Primary School*, London, Holt.

POTTER, J. *et al* (1984) *Social Texts and Contexts*, London, Routledge & Kegan Paul.

RABAN, B. (1986) *Children Learning to Read and to Write: Language at Home and at School Vol. 13* Cambridge, Cambridge University Press.

RICOEUR, P. (1970) *Freud and Philosophy: An Essay on Interpretation*, New York, Yale University Press.

RODRIGUEZ, R. (1982) *Hunger of Memory*, New York, Bantam.

ROGERS, D. (1976) 'Information about word meanings in the speech of parents to young children' in CAMPBELL, R. and SMITH, P. (Eds.) *Recent Advances in the Psychology of Language*, New York, Plenum Press.

ROMAINE, S. (1984) *The Language of Children and Adolescents*, Oxford, Basil Blackwell.

ROSE, J. (1984) *The Case of Peter Pan, or The Impossibility of Children's Fiction*, London, Macmillan.

ROSEN, H. (1972) *Language and Class: A Critical Look at the Theories of Basil Bernstein*, Bristol, Falling Wall Press.

ROSEN, H. (1984) 'Making it tell', in *Report of the 17th Conference: Language in Inner City Schools: A Telling Exchange*, University of London, Institute of Education.

RUMELHART, D. E. (1979) 'Some problems with the notion of literal reading' in ORTONY, A. (Ed.) *Metaphor and Thought*, London, Cambridge University Press.

SALMON, P. (Ed.) (1980) *Coming to know*. London, Routledge & Kegan Paul.

SANCHES, M. and KIRSCHENBLATT-GIMBLETT, B. (1976) 'Children's traditional speech play and child language' in KIRSCHENBLATT-GIMBLETT, B. (Ed.) *Speech Play: Research and Resources for the Study of Linguistic Creativity.* Philadelphia, PA, University of Pennsylvania Press.

SCOLLON, R. and SCOLLON, S.B.K. (1981) *Narrative, Literacy and Face in Interethnic Communication: Vol. VII: in Discourse Processes* (Ed. R.O., Freedle) Norwood, NJ, Ablex Publishing Corporation.

SCOTT, J. (1982) 'It's not what you expect: Teaching irony to third graders', *Children's Literature in Education*, 47, pp. 153–63.

SENDAK, M. (1967) *Where the Wild Things Are*, London, Bodley Head.

SINCLAIR, J. and COULTHARD, M. (1975) *Towards an Analysis of Discourse*, London, Oxford University Press.

SKEMP, R. (1971) *The Psychology of Learning Mathematics*, Harmondsworth, Penguin.

SMITH, F. (1971) *Understanding Reading*, New York, Holt, Rinehart and Winston.

SMITH, H. and MARSH, M. (n.d.) *Have you a minute? The Fox Hill Reading Project*, Sheffield, Fox Hill First School, Keats Road, Sheffield, S6 1AZ.

SNOW, C. (1977). 'Mother's speech research: From input to interaction' in SNOW, C.E. and FERGUSON, C.A. (Eds.) *Talking to Children*, Cambridge, Cambridge University Press.

SOMERFIELD, D.M., TORBE, M. and WARD, C. (1983) *A Framework for Reading*, London, Heinemann.

SOUTHGATE, V., ARNOLD, H. and JOHNSON, S. (1981) *Extending Beginning Reading*, London, Heinemann.

SPENCER, M. (1976) 'Stories are for telling', *English in Education* 10, 1, pp. 16–23.

STEBBING, J. and RABAN, B. (1982) 'Reading for meaning: An investigation of the effect of narrative in two reading books for seven year olds', *Reading*, 16, 3, pp. 153–61.

STEEDMAN, C, 1982. *The Tidy House*, London, Virago.

STEEDMAN, C, URWIN, C. and WALKERDINE, V. (Eds.) (1985) *Language Gender and Childhood*, London, Routledge & Kegan Paul.

STEIN, N.L. and GLENN C.G. (1979) 'An analysis of story comprehension in elementary school children', in FREEDLE, R.O. (Ed.), *New Directions in Discourse Processing Vol. 12*, NJ, Ablex.

STEWART, S. (1978, 1979) *Nonsense: Aspects of Intertextuality in Folklore and Literature*, Baltimore, John Hopkins University Press.

STEWART, S. (1984) *On Longing: Narratives of the Miniature, the Gigantic, the Souvenir and the Collection.* Baltimore, John Hopkins University Press.

STIERER, B.M. (1985) 'School reading volunteers: Results of a postal survey of primary school head teachers in England', *Journal of Research in Reading*, 8, 1, pp. 21–31.

STREET, B.V. (1984) *Literacy in Theory and Practice*, Cambridge, Cambridge University Press.

STUBBS, M. (1983) *Discourse Analysis*, Oxford, Blackwell.

SUTTON-SMITH, B. (1959) *The Games of New Zealand Children*, Texas, American Folklore Society, University of Texas Press.

SUTTON-SMITH, B. (1984) 'The realization of play' in SMITH P.C. (Ed.) *Play in Animals and Humans*, Oxford, Basil Blackwell.

TEMPLE, C., NATHAN, R. and BURRIS, N. (1982) *The Beginnings of Writing*, Boston, Allyn & Bacon.

TIZARD, B. and HUGHES, M. (1984) *Young Children Learning: Talking and Thinking at Home and at School*, London, Fontana.

TIZARD, B., MORTIMORE, J. and BURCHELL, B. (1981). *Involving Parents in Nursery and Infant Schools: a Source Book for Teachers*, London, Grant McIntyre.

TIZARD, J., SCHOFIELD, W.N. and HEWISON, J. (1982) 'Collaboration between teachers and parents in assisting children's reading', *British Journal of Educational Psychology*, 52, pp. 1–15.

TOPPING, K. and WOLFENDALE, S. (1985). *Parental Involvement in Children's Reading*, Beckenham, Croom Helm.

TORRANCE, N. and OLSON, D.R. (1985) 'Oral and literate competencies in the early school years' in OLSON D.R., TORRANCE, N. and HILDYARD, A. (Eds.) *Language Literacy and Learning*, Cambridge, Cambridge University Press.

TREVARTHEN, C. (1974) 'Conversations with a two-month-old', *New Scientist*, 2 May, p. 230.

TUNLEY, P., TRAVERS, T. and PRATT, J. (1979) *Depriving the Deprived*, London, Kogan Page.

TURNER, I. (Ed.) (1978) *Cinderella dressed in Yella*, Sydney, Heinemann.

URWIN, C. (1984) 'Power relations and the emergence of language' in HENRIQUES, J. *et al* (Eds) *Changing the Subject: Psychology Social Regulation and Subjectivity*, London, Methuen.

VOLOSINOV, V.N. (1973) *Marxism and the Philosophy of Language*, London and New York, Academic Press.

VYGOTSKY, L.S. (1978) *Mind in Society: The Development of Higher Psychological Processes*, Cambridge, MA. Harvard University Press.

VYGOTSKY, L. S. (1962). *Thought and Language*, Cambridge, MA., MIT Press.

WADE, B. (1982) 'Reading rickets and the uses of story'. *English in Education*, 16, 3, pp. 28–37.

WALKERDINE, V. (1981) 'From context to text: A psychosemiotic approach to abstract thought' in BEVERDIGE, B. (Ed.) *Children Thinking Through Language*, London, Edward Arnold.

WALKERDINE, V. (1982) 'Sex, power and pedagogy', *Screen Education*, p. 38.

WEBB, Father D. (1985) *Photographs to illustrate 'The Singing Game'* by I. & P. Opie, Oxford University Press.

WEINBERGER, J. (1983) *Fox Hill Reading Workshop: A Project Involving Parents in Children Reading in the Primary School*, London, Family Service Units.

WEIR, R. (1962) *Language in the Crib*, The Hague, Monton.

WELLS, C.G. (1981) 'Describing children's linguistic development at home and at school' in ADELMAN, L. (Ed.) *Uttering Muttering*, London, Grant McIntyre.

WELLS, C.G. (1985) *Language Development in the Pre-School Years, Language at Home and at School*. Vol. 2, London, Cambridge University Press.

WELLS, C.G. *et al.* (1981) *Learning Through Interaction: Language at Home at School. Vol. 1*, London, Cambridge University Press.

WELLS, C.G. and FRENCH, P. (1980) *Language in the Transition from Home to*

School: Final Report to the Nuffield Foundation, Bristol, Centre for the Study of Language and Communication, University of Bristol.

WELLS, G. (1987) *The Meaning Makers*, London, Hodder & Stoughton.

WELLS, G. and NICHOLLS, J. (Eds.) (1985) *Language and Learning: An Interactional Perspective*, Lewes, The Falmer Press.

WENDON, L. (1978) *Pictogram*, London, Wheaton.

WERTSCH, J.V. (Ed.) (1985) *Culture Communication and Cognition: Vygotskian Perspectives*, Cambridge, Cambridge University Press.

WHALEY, J. (1981) 'Readers' expectations for story structures', *Reading Research Quarterly*, XVII, 1, pp. 90–114.

WILLES, M. (1983) *Children into Pupils*, London, Routledge & Kegan Paul.

WILLIAMS, R. (1977) *Marxism and Literature*, Oxford, Oxford University Press.

WILLIAMS, R. (1981) *Culture*, London, Fontana.

WILLIS, P. (1980) Notes on method, in HALL, S., HOBSON, D., LOWE, A., WILLIS, P. (eds.) *Culture, Media and Language*, London, Hutchinson.

WOLFENDALE, S. (1983) *Parental Participation in Children's Development and Education*, London, Gordon and Breach.

WOLFENDALE, S. and GREGORY, E. (1985) *Involving Parents in Reading: a Guide for In-service Training*, Northampton, Reading and Language Development Centre, Nene College.

WOLLEN, T. (1985) 'Television, media studies and schooling', *Television and Schooling*.

Notes on Contributors

MYRA BARRS is the Director/Warden of the Centre for Language in Primary Education of the Inner London Education Authority. She has worked as a teacher, educational publisher and advisor. Her articles have appeared in *Changing English* (Heinemann, 1984), *Language Arts* (NCTE) and *English in Education* (NATE).

CARY BAZALGETTE has worked as a teacher adviser in the Education Department of the British Film Institute for the past seven years. She has also worked as a teacher of English and film-making in London secondary schools and as a full-time parent. She has edited teaching packs on the media for secondary and primary schools, and is currently working with primary teachers to develop a media education curriculum for the primary school.

GILLIAN BEARDSLEY is Senior Lecturer in Teaching Studies at Worcester College of Higher Education where she works with students and teachers on pre-service and in-service BEd Hons programmes, and on a Diploma in Children's Literature. She has taught in primary schools in the UK, Canada and the USA. Her particular interests are in language and literacy in early childhood education.

JAMES BRITTON is Emeritus Professor of Education in the University of London. His publications include *Language and Learning* (Pelican, 1972), *Prospect and Retrospect* (Ed. Gordon Pradel, Boynton/Cook, 1982). He also edited (on behalf of the International Federation for the Teaching of English) *English Teaching: An International Exchange* (Heinemann Educational, 1984).

DAVID DILLON is Professor in the Department of Elementary Education at the University of Alberta, Edmonton, Canada. Much of his time is spent in courses with pre-service and in-service teachers. He also edits *Language Arts*, a journal of the National Council of Teachers of English, concerned with teaching and learning in the primary school.

HENRIETTA DOMBEY is Principal Lecturer at Brighton Polytechnic where she teaches in the Primary Department. Her particular interest is early reading and the part played in this by the experience of listening to stories read aloud. She is currently Chair of the National Association of the Teaching of English.

VALERIE EMBLEN teaches at Thomas Buxton infant school in the East End of London. Her particular concern is to make the curriculum available to young bilingual learners.

CAROL FOX is Senior Lecturer at Brighton Polytechnic. Most of her research into the narrative and literary competences of young children was carried out at Newcastle upon Tyne Polytechnic as part of a Language in Schools project directed by the late Dr K. Yerrill. She is interested in the rich possibilities offered by children's oral story-telling for their personal, social, cognitive and linguistic development.

EVELYN GREGORY is Senior Lecturer in Education at Goldsmiths' College, London where she is primarily concerned with initial teacher education. Prior to this she spent a number of years working in primary schools in East London. Her current research is in the field of bilingualism and early literacy development.

ELIZABETH GRUGEON is a research assistant in primary education in the School of Education at the Open University. She has worked in secondary and primary schools for many years, as well as preparing and teaching courses for distance students of the Open University.

DAVID HUTCHINSON a sociologist, works in primary teacher education at Goldsmiths' College in London. His main research interest is in children's writing.

JUNE MCCONAGHY is a primary teacher who works as a language arts consultant with the Public Schools in Edmonton, Alberta, Canada. She edits and writes for language arts publications. Her research at the university of Alberta is in literature and the literacy of young children.

MARY MAGUIRE teaches graduate and in-service courses in the Faculty of Education of McGill University, Montreal. Her current interests lie in the socio-cultural aspects of literature and literacy in bilingual and multilingual contexts.

MARGARET MEEK (SPENCER) is Reader in Education in the University of London Institute of Education where her work in teacher education includes research into literacy, literature (especially writing for children) and the relation of educational theory to classroom interactions.

COLIN MILLS is Senior Lecturer at Worcester College of Higher Education where he teaches language and literacy on initial training and in-service courses. His research interests are in the social and cultural aspects of children's reading.

CLIFF MOON is Senior Lecturer in the teaching of reading at Bulmershe College of Higher Education, Reading. He was a primary school teacher for seventeen years during which he developed a framework for a wide range of reading resources published as *Individualized Reading*, published and updated annually by the Reading and Language Information Centre. He is the author of a number of books for learner readers.

BARRY STIERER is a Research Associate in the University of Bristol School of Education where he is a member of the team evaluating DES pilot records of achievement in schools. He was previously a researcher at the University of London Institute of Education where he studied the social organisation of classroom literacy activities and the validity of reading tests.

GEOFFREY WILLIAMS teaches language in education in the School of Teaching and Curriculum Studies at the University of Sydney. He is currently working on a research project to analyze the construction of ideology in children's fiction, using systemic functional linguistics.

ROB WITHERS is Lecturer in Education in the Department of Education at Bristol Polytechnic. He previously taught in primary schools in inner London. His particular interest, in addition to primary education, is the reconstruction of a philosophy of education.

Index